BERND KORTMANN

English Linguistics: Essentials

Anglistik · Amerikanistik

studium
kompakt

English
Edition

D1726696

system use

Cornelsen

studium kompakt Anglistik • Amerikanistik

Linguistics: Essentials

Die Hochschulreihe studium kompakt Anglistik • Amerikanistik wurde von den Verfasserinnen und Verfassern in Zusammenarbeit mit der Verlagsredaktion entwickelt.

Verfasser: Professor Dr. Bernd Kortmann
Verlagsredaktion: Dr. Blanca-Maria Rudhart
Layout: Gisela Hoffmann
Technische Umsetzung: Ingo Ostermaier
Umschlagsgestaltung: Bauer + Möhring grafikdesign, Berlin

Die Deutsche Bibliothek – CIP-Einheitsaufnahme:
Kortmann, Bernd:
studium kompakt Anglistik • Amerikanistik:
Linguistics: Essentials/Bernd Kortmann. –
     1. Aufl. – Berlin: Cornelsen, 2005
     ISBN 978-3-464-31162-2

www.cornelsen.de

1. Auflage, 2. Druck 2007/06

Druck: CS-Druck CornelsenStürtz, Berlin

ISBN 978-3-464-31162-2

 Inhalt gedruckt auf säurefreiem Papier aus nachhaltiger Forstwirtschaft.

Table of contents

This is the revised, updated and enlarged English edition of **Linguistik: Essentials**, a very successful (and most positively reviewed) textbook used in many English language and linguistics departments in Germany since its first publication in 1999. Its primary aim is to introduce university students to the central branches, core concepts, and current trends in the study of English language and linguistics, giving them guidance in a constantly growing and fragmented discipline. The individual chapters are designed to serve a dual purpose: on the one hand, as an introduction to a given branch of linguistics and a point of departure for more detailed studies on the basis of, for example, specialized textbooks or handbook articles; and, on the other hand, as a point of reference to return to in order to check the wealth of knowledge acquired in the meantime against the information given in the book.

English Linguistics: Essentials has grown out of 15 years of teaching experience with students of English linguistics at all levels. Ultimately, it goes back to a class for advanced undergraduates which the author jointly developed with Ekkehard König at the Free University of Berlin in 1991. The German edition has proved to be a useful companion for university students all through their academic studies as it combines the essentials of the core branches of linguistics with an account of the state of the art at the turn of the 21st century. In many English departments in Germany it is used as a standard textbook in introductory classes to linguistics. Advanced undergraduates, too, especially those approaching their exams in linguistics, and graduates enrolled in Masters programmes in linguistics as well as student tutors and teaching assistants have found (and will surely continue to find) this book equally helpful. Primarily addressed to a student audience, the German edition has also found many readers among school teachers of English seeking to (re-)connect with the essentials and latest developments in linguistics in general, and the study of the English language in particular.

Part of the reason why this book has appealed to so many readers is the reader-friendly layout with many mnemonic devices in the text, the large number of survey figures and tables summarizing and putting in perspective the most important points of the previous discussions, and, for each chapter, checklists with the key terms, exercises for revision and questions for further study (with an answer key for the former). The exercises and study questions in particular are extremely useful for self-study. The book uses standard terminology familiar from internationally widely-used textbooks in individual linguistic sub-disciplines.

Given the extremely positive feedback from many colleagues and student readers on the German edition, there was no reason to change anything substantial as regards the overall approach (largely theory-neutral, but functionalist in spirit), the selection of topics addressed in the book, its overall structure, the structure of the individual chapters, the style, or the layout. In six chapters the (or, for those who would like to cast the net wider, seven of the) core branches of linguistics are addressed: phonetics and phonology (chapter II), morphology (chapter III), grammar (chapter IV), semantics (chapter VI), pragmatics (chapter VII), and sociolinguistics (chapter VIII). Chapter V is specifically concerned with the structure of English from a contrastive (English-German) and typological perspective. This chapter can be profitably read even by readers whose knowledge of German is rudimentary or non-existent since it places contrastive linguistics within the other branches of comparative linguistics, adopting a specifically typological perspective, and discusses bundles of distinctive structural properties of English not addressed elsewhere in the book. The only chapter which has undergone a major change in the English edition is the much expanded chapter I. It introduces the reader to the major dichotomies and research traditions of 20th century linguistics (structuralism, formalism, functionalism), recent developments in the field, i.e. corpus linguistics and the renewed interest in (including innovative approaches to) historical linguistics, and a brief evaluation of the state of (English) linguistics at the turn of the 21st century. This chapter is designed as a kind of mastermap for a better understanding of the basic assumptions underlying linguistic research in the past and present and for helping the reader to judge, for example, which research tradition informs a given study, the work of a given author, or the work in a given branch of linguistics.

How to read this book: In principle the individual chapters can be read independently of each other. Also, it does not matter whether in a given class a bottom-up approach is chosen (from sounds and sound structure to discourse and language variation) or a top-down approach. However, for the individual structural levels of English it will be most useful to follow the order chosen here (and in almost all established international textbooks), i.e. phonetics (II.1) preceding phonology (II.2), morphology (III) preceding grammar (IV), English grammar (IV) preceding English structure from a comparative perspective (V), semantics (VI) preceding pragmatics (VII), and the structural accounts of the sound structure and grammar of English (II and IV) preceding accounts of (especially non-standard) varieties of English in the chapter on sociolinguistics (VIII). As regards chapter I, absolute beginners may be well advised to read no further than section I.2.1 (covering central dichotomies and structuralism as the oldest and most deeply entrenched research tradition in modern linguistics), and to leave the other parts until they have worked through (most of) the other chapters.

Acknowledgements: In general, the author would like to thank all those many colleagues, student readers and participants of his own classes for their feedback on the individual formulations, exercises, and solutions in the German edition. Most of their comments have found their way into this book; moreover, it was their unanimously positive feedback which, in the first place, encouraged the author to suggest an English edition to the publishers. This edition would not have come about without the support of many people. Thanks are due to Cornelsen publishers for having financed a draft translation and to Dr. Blanca-Maria Rudhart who has been a most careful, reliable, and encouraging editor all through the writing and production stage. The author would also like to thank all those colleagues working in or (for a short while) affiliated with the English department of the University of Freiburg who took a critical look at individual chapters and commented on them, often extensively: Ulrike Gut, Brigitte Halford, Christian Mair, and Hubert Cuyckens (Catholic University of Leuven, Humboldt Fellow in spring 2005). It is simply a pleasure and privilege to be part of such a vibrant and stimulating research environment. Above all, the author would like to thank all the members of his editorial team. Without the help of this dedicated and highly competent team it would have been impossible to keep the deadline for the submission of the manuscript. It is immensely reassuring to have such knowledgeable, critical, perceptive, and efficient readers right next door. A thousand thanks to Lieselotte Anderwald, Verena Haser, Nuria Hernandez, Susanne Radtke, Benedikt Szmrecsanyi, Susanne Wagner, and Veronika Westhoff! Every single one of the many people mentioned here has contributed to making this a better book. For any remaining shortcomings the author alone takes full responsibility. At the same time, all readers are invited to contact the author if they have questions, critical comments, or suggestions.

Dedication: In the writing and production stage of this book (and others before), I have been extremely privileged to have had the support of a wonderful team consisting of assistant professors, postdoctoral, doctoral and graduate students – topped by the best secretary of all, Melitta Cocan! Looking back on the 10 years that I have now held a chair in English language and linguistics at the University of Freiburg, I can say that I have been truly blessed in this respect. It is to the current and former members of this marvellous team that I would like to dedicate this book – they are the real essentials in my professional life!

Notational conventions in the checklists

/ alternative terms	e.g. heteronymy/incompatibility
↔ (pairs of) opposite terms	e.g. sense ↔ reference
( ) subcategories of a superordinate term	e.g. homonymy (total ↔ partial)
; terms separated by a semicolon are subcategories of a superordinate term on the same hierarchical level	e.g. phonetics (articulatory; acoustic; auditory)

I Linguistics at the turn of the 21st century: An overview

Linguistics is the scientific discipline concerned with the study of language. Central aspects of how to go about the scientific study of language and languages can be made clear with the help of various pairs of oppositions (or: dichotomies). Anyone planning to investigate language or individual linguistic phenomena first needs to take a clear decision on which perspective to adopt, on the ultimate goal(s) of the investigation, and on the amount and nature of the data to be analysed for this purpose. These questions lead to some of the most important dichotomies (cf. section I.1) and theoretical frameworks (or: research traditions) in the discipline (cf. sections I.2 and I.3).

I.1 Central dichotomies

- **synchronic – diachronic**, synchrony – diachrony: Do we want to describe the state of a language at a particular point or period in time (i.e. take a snapshot of a language), or do we want to document linguistic change 'through time' (Greek *dia* = through, *chronos* = time) by comparing successive (synchronic) language states with one another and exploring especially the transitions from one language state to the next?

- **descriptive – prescriptive:** In a synchronic approach, do we want to give a neutral description of the actual language use, or do we want to adopt a normative approach and formulate rules for 'correct' language use?
- **form – function, language system – language use:** In a descriptive approach, do we want to investigate purely formal aspects, thus the structure (or: the system) of a language on its different levels (sound, word, sentence structure) in abstraction from language use, or do we want to investigate which functions linguistic structures fulfil and, dependent on the speaker and the speech situation, for which communicative purposes they can be used?
- **language-specific – comparative:** In a descriptive synchronic approach, do we want to investigate merely one language, contrast two languages with each other (e.g. for pedagogical reasons in foreign-language teaching; contrastive linguistics), or compare a multitude of languages with one another, with the aim of determining the patterns and limits of language variation and maybe even language universals (language typology)?
- **applied – not applied:** Do we want to apply the results of our study in, for example, foreign-language teaching, translation, the compilation of dictionaries (lexicography), or police investigations and the law court (forensic linguistics)? Or are our research results supposed to be of purely academic relevance? In the latter case, what we want to find out can be either of descriptive interest (i.e. we want to learn more about a particular language – either looked at in isolation or in comparison with other languages), or of theoretical or general interest. If it is general linguistics we are interested in, we want to learn more about language as such, as the most important medium of communication among human beings, about general principles of language structure, language use, language acquisition, language change, etc., and about the most appropriate theories or theoretical frameworks within which general (especially grammatical) properties of language can be modelled.
- **empirical – introspective:** What should form the basis of our linguistic analysis? Should it be based on authentic data as they are compiled, for example, in large machine-readable corpora of the English language (the largest corpus available at present being the British National Corpus with altogether 100 million words)? Should linguistic research thus increasingly work quan-

titatively and with statistical methods (corpus linguistics)? Or should it be based on introspection, that is on the intuitions of linguists concerning what is and what is not possible in (a) language?

Depending on the answers to these questions, we are engaged in synchronic or diachronic linguistics, descriptive or prescriptive linguistics, formal or functional linguistics, contrastive linguistics or language typology, applied, theoretical or general linguistics. Whichever of these approaches (and others not mentioned here) is or are chosen, it is important to be aware of the fact that the different approaches often come with particular theories and models of language and linguistics and, as a consequence, with different viewpoints, methods and terminology. For this reason, it is frequently the case that different terms co-exist for one and the same phenomenon, and that this phenomenon is judged and interpreted in different ways by different people.

different approaches

In accordance with the dominant orientation of modern linguistics, in general, and English linguistics, in particular, this book has a strictly synchronic, descriptive, and empirical orientation, focussing for the most part on the English language system (chapters II-IV and VI: phonetics, phonology, morphology, grammar, semantics). This includes a comparison of the most important structures of English and German (chapter V: contrastive linguistics). Language use, especially the use of English, as dependent on different speakers or groups of speakers and their communicative goals in varying communicative situations takes centre stage in chapters VII (pragmatics) and VIII (sociolinguistics).

orientation of this book

The two central dichotomies that capture best the fundamental changes of direction in the development of 20th century linguistics as opposed to linguistics in the 19th century are synchrony – diachrony and language system – language use. The 19th century was the century of historical linguistics. Linguistic research was characterized by the search for regularities and laws in language change, the search for genetic links between languages (key words: family trees, Indo-European), and the reconstruction of older language periods and languages in historical-comparative linguistics (or: comparative philology) by means of comparing with each other younger language periods and languages for which written data material was available.

I.2
Three major research traditions in 20th century linguistics

19th and 20th century in comparison

historical-comparative linguistics

The 20th century, on the other hand, is the century of synchrony. This is certainly the most important aspect of the paradigm shift which affected linguistics in the decades after 1900, a paradigm shift which is inseparably linked to the name of Ferdinand de Saussure, the famous Swiss linguist who taught at the University of Geneva a century ago.

2.1 Structuralism

Ferdinand de Saussure

Cours de linguistique générale (1916)

Saussure is generally considered to be the founder of modern linguistics, more precisely the founder of structuralism, the 'bible' of which is the *Cours de linguistique générale* (1916). The *Cours* offers an introduction to general linguistics based on Saussure's lecture materials and the lecture notes taken by his disciples and was not published until after his death (in 1913). In this book the reader will find thorough discussions of numerous ideas concerning a new approach to the study of language only some of which are found in the works of linguists at the end of the 19th century (e.g. in the writings of the German Georg von der Gabelentz and, above all, those of William Dwight Whitney, the eminent American linguist of the late 19th century). Besides the all-important separation of synchrony and diachrony, and the call for the primacy of synchrony, this set of ideas includes, above all, the call for a kind of linguistics which solely concentrates on language as a closed system in which all elements are linked to one another, and in which the value (*valeur*) of every single element is defined by its place in the system alone. For example, the Simple Past in English (*she worked*) has a different status than its counterpart in German, the preterite (*Präteritum*), because it contrasts both with the Past Progressive (*she was working*) and the Present Perfect (*she has worked*). German grammar does not only lack a counterpart of the English progressive form; *Präteritum* (*sie arbeitete*) and *Perfekt* (*sie hat gearbeitet*) are in most contexts interchangeable without a difference in meaning. The different status of Simple Past and *Präteritum* within the grammars of English and German, respectively, thus partly results from the value of the Present Perfect in the English tense system in contrast to the value of the *Perfekt* in the German tense system. The view that every linguistic sign is part of the system and has no existence outside of it is an important reason for the structuralist position that every language system needs to be considered by itself.

primacy of synchrony and the system

value / *valeur*

According to Saussure, linguistics should solely be concerned with the systematic regularities of the abstract language system which is

langue–parole

shared by all members of a speech community (*langue*), and not with its concrete use by the individual (*parole*). What stands at the centre of structuralist linguistics is the determination and description of the individual elements of this system (on all structural levels: sounds, words and their components, sentences and their constituents), and the relationships existing between them on each of these levels. Within any system, there are two basic types of relationships between linguistic units which have to be distinguished: relationships of choice or interchangeability on the vertical axis (paradigmatic relationships), and relationships of "chain" or combination on the horizontal axis (syntagmatic relationships). A paradigmatic relationship holds between the initial sounds of *ban*, *can*, *Dan*, *fan*, *tan* and *van*, whereas the relationship between any of these sounds and the two following sounds is a syntagmatic one.

paradigmatic – syntagmatic
(choice)　　　(chain)

(1)

A	man	saw	my	horse
The	girl	loved	your	cat
This	visitor	hit	our	baby

(1) illustrates paradigmatic and syntagmatic relationships on the sentence level: a choice relationship holds among the words within any of the braced brackets, a chain relationship between the words in the immediately neighbouring brackets. These relationships are found on all structural levels of language (cf. Figure I.1):

object of study	branches of linguistics	
	form	function/meaning
sound	phonetics	phonology
word	morphology	(lexical) semantics
phrase, sentence	syntax	(sentence) semantics

Figure I.1
The structural levels of language

As far as these structural levels (sound, word and sentence structure) and the corresponding branches of linguistics are concerned, it is important to note that it is not always easy to determine the exact boundaries between them. Often we can observe interaction between the structural levels and, as a consequence, so-called "interfaces" between the relevant linguistic subdisciplines. When, for example, in the course of the derivation of the noun *pronunciation* from the verb *pronounce*, the sound shape of the root changes from /prə'naʊns/ to /prəˌnʌns-/, we are not only dealing with a morphological (more precisely: word formation) process, but also with a phonological one. The same holds true in the case of the regular English plural formation, where the plural marker is pronounced /s/ (*kits*), /z/ (*kids*), or /ɪz/ (*kisses*) depending on the final sound of the singular form of the respective noun. The interface relevant for these two examples is called "morphophonology" or "morphophonemics" (cf. chapter III.2). Other interfaces are, for instance, those between phonology and syntax, morphology and syntax, or syntax and semantics.

model of the linguistic sign

Saussure's model of the linguistic sign, i.e. his model of what constitutes the nature of words (cf. Figure I.2), is another of his groundbreaking contributions to modern linguistics. The linguistic sign consists of two parts which are as inseparably linked to one another as the two sides of a sheet of paper: a sound or, typically, sound sequence (*signifier; signifiant*) on the level of expression and a concept (*signified; signifié*) on the level of meaning. Two kinds of

signifiant - signifié

relations hold between *signifié* and *signifiant*: on the one hand a reciprocal relationship, which means that the sound sequence automatically evokes the concept linked to it and vice versa (therefore the arrows in Figure I.2). On the other hand – and much more important still – there is a relationship of arbitrariness and conventionality. Which *signifiant* is used for which *signifié* is solely based on an 'agreement', a kind of 'contract', as it were, between the members of a speech community; neither side of the linguistic sign has any special feature that would inevitably require the assignment of a particular signifier to a particular signified, or vice versa. That is why different languages have completely different expressions – all equally appropriate or inappropriate – for the same concept (for FLOWER just take /flaʊə(r)/ in English or /bluːmə/ in German), and why, conversely, the same sound image can refer to completely different concepts in different languages (consider /ɡɪft/, which denotes the concept PRESENT in English as opposed to TOXIC SUBSTANCE in German).

Figure I.2
Saussure's model of the linguistic sign

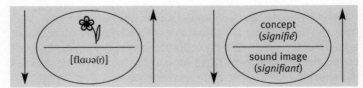

The crucial point about the linguistic sign is its arbitrariness, i.e. the lack of a motivated link between signified and signifier. According to the theory of signs by Charles Sanders Peirce (pronounced /pɜːs/), the linguistic sign therefore qualifies as a symbol, in contrast to the two other major types of signs he distinguishes, namely indices and

16

icons. The characteristic feature of indices is an existential or physical effect–cause or effect–reason relationship between the sign and what it stands for. Tears, for instance, are a sign of emotional turmoil (sorrow, disappointment, joy), smoke is a sign of fire, and slurred speech is a sign of drunkenness. The defining feature of icons is that there is a relationship of similarity between the sign and what it stands for. The nature of this similarity can be physical or imagic, i.e. consist in visual similarity (e.g. the pictogram of a telephone indicating a public telephone, or the pictogram of a running person indicating an emergency exit) or in phonetic similarity (e.g. *bow-wow* for barking, or *cuckoo* for the bird). However, icons can also display a rather abstract relationship of similarity: this kind of (so-called "diagrammatic") iconicity holds, for example, between maps and the regions of the earth they represent, or between the order in which, on a list of topics for presentations and term papers, the topics are listed and the chronological sequence in which they are to be presented in the seminar. Iconicity thus is a special kind of motivation. Although in human language, symbols are by far the most important and best researched type of signs, it should not be overlooked that there are definitely also words which, besides qualifying as symbols, are partly iconic (e.g. so-called "onomatopoetic expressions" like *bow-wow, moo, cuckoo*) or partly indexical (e.g. *here* and *today*, part of whose meaning refers to the here and now of the speaker; cf. chapter VII.2).

iconicity

onomatopoetic expressions

From the perspective of the theory of signs, human language is a (rather complex) sign system and, as a consequence, linguistics a semiotic science. Semiotics is the science of the linguistic and non-linguistic signalling systems and signing processes. Traditionally, it considers its object of study from three angles: (a) the relation(s) between signs (syntax); (b) the relation(s) between signs and their meaning(s) (semantics); (c) the relation(s) between signs and their users (pragmatics). The subdisciplines exploring these three kinds of relations in the scientific study of signs therefore also belong to the central areas of linguistics.

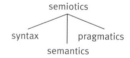

The importance of structuralist thinking as we find it in Saussure's *Cours* and, generally, in linguistics of the 1920s until the 1950s is largely undisputed in present-day linguistics. Just think of American structuralism à la Leonard Bloomfield, which is even more rigidly empirical and form-orientated than Saussure's vision of structuralism was, or of the Prague School of functionalism, which was primarily interested in the function(s) of language and linguistic elements (cf. also I.3.2). The crucial difference, however, is that ever since the 1960s

Leonard Bloomfield

Prague School

development of the discipline from the 1960s until today

(starting, above all, in sociolinguistics) and especially since the 1970s (with the advent of pragmatics) and 1980s (especially due to cognitive linguistics; cf. chapter VI.4), linguistics has significantly gone beyond the description of a linguistic system and the search for purely system-inherent explanations for linguistic phenomena. Rather, as will be detailed in section I.2.3, it has given priority to social, functional, and cognitive aspects, as well as aspects of language (use) grounded in communicative behaviour. Typically, these new approaches do not compete, but rather complement each other very well. What all these 'post-structuralist' approaches have in common is that the most important Saussurean dichotomies are increasingly critically reflected, and that linguists start to emancipate, or already have emancipated, themselves from these dichotomies. In the course of the renewed interest in processes of language change, for example, the strict separation between synchrony and diachrony has largely been abandoned (which makes sense especially if we consider, for example, the immediate link between language variation and language change; cf. section I.3.2 and chapter VIII.6). It is furthermore no longer import-ant to give priority to the system and to reduce linguistics to the study of the formal aspects, i.e. the structure, of language, which was typical of 20th century linguistics until the 1960s. Since then, research into language use (i.e. *parole* or *performance*) as depending on the individual speaker, the relevant communicative situation, and the relevant communicative goal(s) has gained significantly in import-ance. Therefore, at the turn of the 21st century, sociolinguistics and pragmatics also need to be counted among the disciplines constitu-ting the core of linguistics. A third example of the emancipation from Saussure concerns his sign model, more precisely the central role he attributes to arbitrariness. Especially since the 1980s, it is increasingly acknowledged that, both on the level of words and grammar, iconicity plays a bigger role than is traditionally assumed in Saussurean struc-turalism. Fourth, there is a general tendency in current linguistics that the idea of dichotomies (e. g. synchrony – diachrony, language system – language use, vocabulary – grammar, written – spoken language) and sharp category boundaries (e. g. main verb versus auxiliary) can be accepted only as idealizations which are pedagogically useful, but which, apart from that, should better be given up in favour of interfaces and fuzzy boundaries (thus the growing importance of so-called "gradients", "clines", or "continua").

emancipation from Saussure

18

2.2 Formalism / Generative linguistics

Both the emancipation of linguistics from traditional structuralist ideas, and the central status which especially pragmatics and sociolinguistics have developed over the last four decades can also be seen as reactions to probably the most influential school of thought in the second half of the 20th century, namely generative linguistics. Noam Chomsky initiated this approach to the study of language at the end of the 1950s and has remained the key intellectual and major shaping force of generative linguistics during its various phases and its various guises until the present day. "Generative" (Latin *generare* = generate) refers to the generation of language, more exactly to the full and precise description of syntactic structures by means of a limited (or: finite) inventory of rules. On the one hand, this inventory of rules allows linguists to make explicit statements concerning the grammatical well-formedness of a given phrase or sentence. On the other hand, it provides the theoretical and descriptive apparatus for predictions concerning the grammaticality (in the sense of grammatical well-formedness) of all possible grammatical sentences (and smaller syntactic units) in a language, or at least in its core grammar. The beginnings of generative linguistics mark the second fundamental paradigm shift in 20th century linguistics. Within a few years, it came to be one of the most influential schools in linguistics; in the US (unlike in Europe) it is even the predominant approach, both in research and teaching. One of the crucial distinctive properties of this approach is a high standard of explicit and stringent theory-formation and argumentation. This and other essential features of the generativist (alternatively known as "formalist") paradigm as well as some of its major contributions to linguistic theorizing will be presented in this section. The reader may note right away, though, that in none of the other chapters of this book will generativist positions play a role. For example, semantic and pragmatic issues (especially the study of word and utterance meaning, and how the latter is negotiated in context) and, in particular, sociolinguistic and contrastive issues are for the most part ignored or represent no more than a sideline in mainstream generative linguistics because, given its overall aims, they are simply of little or no interest. Mainstream formalist research and theory development has always focussed on the study of syntax and phonology.

Generative linguistics, probably still best-known as and equated with Transformational Grammar (the approach characteristic of Chomsky's 'classical' period in the 1960s, which has, however, gone

Noam Chomsky

mental grammar

competence vs. performance

out of use quite a long time ago), was and still is exclusively concerned with language as a mental phenomenon, more exactly with competence (as opposed to language use, performance). What is understood by competence is the entire (unconscious) mental knowledge an ideal native speaker (and hearer) has at his or her disposal. This knowledge allows him or her to be creative in the native language and to constantly (and successfully) produce and process new sentences according to the rules of that language. A grammar of a given language, for Chomsky, thus is a theory of what constitutes the ideal native user's competence of that language. In Chomsky's view, this aim can be achieved without analyzing large amounts of authentic linguistic data; indeed, given the often fragmented and/or ungrammatical structure of, for example, utterances in face-to-face interaction and spontaneous spoken language, the empirical analysis of natural language data is considered almost detrimental to the goals of generativist theory-formation. Therefore, generative linguistics still primarily relies on introspection, i.e. the linguist's intuition.

language acquisition device

The two central questions formalism is interested in are: How is this linguistic knowledge represented? and, above all, How is this linguistic knowledge acquired? In other words, the primary point of interest for generative linguistics is (child, first) language acquisition. What matters here in the first place, however, is not so much the documentation and detailed empirical study of the concrete processes and phases of language acquisition, but the question of how it is possible that, no matter into what speech community a child is born and in what surroundings it grows up, it develops enormous linguistic skills in an amazingly short amount of time. Chomsky's hypothesis is that humans are genetically predisposed to learn language, just as it is part of our genetic endowment to grow arms and legs. Indeed, Chomsky postulates the existence of a Language Acquisition Device (LAD). This raises the all-important research question what kind of information is contained in this device, which is common to all human beings and thus universal. Or put differently: What constitutes

Universal Grammar

Universal Grammar (UG)? Thus, when generative linguistics is said to search for universals, what is meant are not surface features common to all or at least a great number of languages, but the invariable, highly abstract innate properties and principles of the postulated language acquisition device. The reason why these properties and principles must be innate is that they are considered to be too abstract to be discovered, i.e. picked up or learnt, by the child in the process of language acquisition.

Two types of UG universals are typically distinguished: substantive universals and formal universals. Substantive universals are the grammatical categories which are universally available and necessary for analysing a language, e.g. the different word classes (nouns, verbs, etc.), their phrasal expansions (noun phrase, verb phrase, etc.), and the relevant grammatical categories which can be marked on them (for instance, case and number on nouns, tense on verbs). Formal universals are statements on the form the rules of a grammar can take like, for example, structure-dependency. This means that knowledge of language relies on structural relationships in the sentence rather than simply on the sequence of words. According to this universal, it is impossible for a language to turn a statement (e.g. *This is the good friend Alison met at the airport.*) into a question by simply using the reverse word order (yielding an ungrammatical sentence like **airport the at met Alison friend good the is this?*). Consider, by contrast, a language like English in which, for this purpose, only the order of subject and predicate is changed, as in *Is this the good friend Alison met at the airport?* Other candidates for UG universals include the structural means for referring to real-world entities (reference) and saying something about them (predication), for keeping track of referents and predications which are repeated in a certain stretch of discourse (reference tracking), for quantifying (e.g. via numerals or elements like *all, some, few, every*, etc.; quantification), and for allowing speaker and hearer to exchange roles easily and rapidly, e.g. in face-to-face interaction (speaker-hearer symmetry). In sum: the ultimate goal of linguistic theory from a formalist point of view is to provide a precise formal (and, by necessity, highly abstract) characterization of these and other constitutive elements of Universal Grammar and thus to define 'a possible human language'.

universals
substantive   formal

2.3 Functionalism

Whereas in formalist research the significance or impact of a linguistic study is ultimately determined by the extent to which it helps illuminating the nature of Universal Grammar, the corresponding all-important criterion in functionalist research is to what extent the relevant study is able to show

- why, in a particular domain of its structural system, language, a given language or set of languages is the way it is,
- what, in a particular context, motivates the choice of native users

of a given language between two or more semantically equivalent alternative constructions, and/or

- how communicative functions may help shape language structure.

function

The key notion in answers to these questions is function, a concept which oscillates between what may be paraphrased as "task, job", on the one hand, and "meaning", on the other hand. This key notion will be detailed below, along with other pillars of what constitutes the basic philosophy of functionalism, which is the second major theoretical framework, or research tradition, of late 20th century and current linguistics. The reader will soon notice that functionalism is incompatible, or at least in conflict, with most of the central assumptions as well as the ultimate goal of formalist linguistics. A summary of the relevant points will be provided at the end of the section.

external vs. internal functions

Two broad types of functions can be distinguished: the overall functions of language in communication (so-called "external functions") and, language-internally, the varied set of communicative (so-called "internal") functions served by different linguistic phenomena in individual, or partly even all, languages (e.g. referring to people and entities in the real world, placing situations on the time line, expressing ongoing as opposed to completed events, coding known as opposed to new information, or directly observed information as opposed to information for which no or only indirect evidence exists). Famous typologies of external functions were suggested by Karl Bühler and Roman Jakobson. In his organon model of language (Greek *organon* = implement, tool), Bühler distinguishes between three functions, or tasks, in the overall communication process which language serves: a referential (or: representational) function (as it allows us to talk about the world), an expressive function (as it allows the addresser, i.e. the speaker or writer, to express his or her beliefs, attitudes, and emotional state), and an appellative function (as it allows us to make an appeal to the addressee, i.e. the hearer or reader, e.g. formulate a request or issue a command).

organon model of language

external functions

To these three tasks served by language, Roman Jakobson adds another three, one for each of the three new dimensions he adds to the model of communication: message, code, and contact. One function of language may lie in the way the message is formulated (poetic function, which is not to be understood as applying exclusively to use in literary texts), a second one in talking about language (metalingual function, which is the typical function of everything in this book or, for that matter, in any linguistics publication or discourse

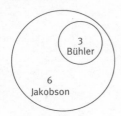

in a linguistics class), and a third function in establishing contact between addresser and addressee, be it psychological contact (especially a social relation of some kind) or physical contact (dominant in many doomed-to-fail telephone conversations involving the use of mobiles in a tunnel or when commuting on trains, which regularly trigger questions such as "Can you hear me?" or "Are you still there?").

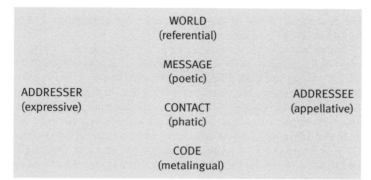

WORLD
(referential)

MESSAGE
(poetic)

ADDRESSER
(expressive)

CONTACT
(phatic)

ADDRESSEE
(appellative)

CODE
(metalingual)

Figure I.3
External functions of language

It is crucial to note that language typically fulfils several of these tasks simultaneously, but that, depending on the central communicative goal in a given communicative situation or piece of discourse, one of these external functions tends to predominate. For example, a statement like "What lousy weather we've had for days now" surely has a representational function, but in the context of a social get-together like a cheese and wine party, the primary function of this utterance is a phatic one, i.e. it counts simply as an attempt at establishing social relations with another person by engaging in small talk (or: social noise). Similarly, an utterance like "Quite a draft in here, I must say" serves a representational as well as an expressive function, but its primary function may well be an appellative one, namely when intended as a request to do something against the draft, such as closing the door or window (for further details cf. chapter VII.3 on indirect speech acts). Correspondingly, text types can be classified according to their predominant function, e. g. advertisements, cooking recipes or manuals as appellative texts, newspaper reports as representational texts, and private letters to close friends as expressive texts. More generally, this discussion of the external functions of language shows that, from a functional point of view, the entire communication process is relevant for linguistic analysis. Functionalists acknowledge that language is not something sterile, not something

focus on language use

that takes place in a vacuum, and that it can thus not be investigated independently from the primary function it serves, namely communication, from the participants involved in the act of communication, and from the general (e.g. social and cognitive) conditions in which communication takes place. In other words, the use component (as opposed to an exclusively system-centred approach to the study of language as advocated by formalists and structuralists) is part and parcel of these models of the external functions of language and of functionalism, in general.

internal functions

Compared with the external functions of language, the range of internal functions is much wider and more varied. But, essentially, they all boil down to functions which individual linguistic units (down to the sound level), constructions or domains in grammar play in (spoken or written) discourse and the overall communicative process. The most important of these functions are those which enhance the ease and efficiency of online production and processing, for example by guaranteeing that a given sentence or utterance is organically embedded into a given piece of discourse. What is meant by "organic embedding" here is that any sentence or utterance is typically part of a text or conversation. As a consequence, the way we formulate a sentence or utterance, the choice we make between structural options which English, for example, offers us is at least partially determined by the information which has been established earlier in the text/conversation and may also be determined by what we intend to write or say in its later parts. Relevant choices include the use of pronouns as opposed to common or proper nouns, the use of the indefinite article (*a, an*) as opposed to the definite article (*the*), active vs. passive, or the choice between *It was Alison who bought the book* and *What Alison did was buy the book*. A crucial function of pronouns, for example, is to help create a coherent text (which is why, from a functional point of view, they qualify as important cohesive devices): a pronoun indicates that it refers to the same person or entity as some noun phrase introduced in the prior discourse (cross-reference). Pronouns thus typically are an instruction to the reader or hearer to search for the referent in the previous discourse; at the same time, pronouns signal that the speaker/writer takes the information they provide for granted, that it qualifies as old, known, or given information. The same applies to definite articles. Besides creating a coherent discourse, a smooth integration into the information flow of a given piece of discourse (in the sense of given and new information) is a second central aspect of what was loosely called "organic embedding" above.

Examples (1) to (4) will make clear what the difference in outlook is between a functionalist, a formalist, and a structuralist when confronted with the following constructions in English grammar. The major contrast between the first two examples is one of active (1) vs. passive voice (2). The constructions in (3) and (4) are so-called "cleft constructions". Those in (3) are called "it-clefts" and those in (4) "wh-clefts" or "pseudo-clefts" (cf. also V.2.2):

(1) John smashed the bottle with a hammer.

(2) a. The bottle was smashed by John with a hammer.
b. The bottle was smashed.

(3) a. It was John who smashed the bottle with a hammer.
b. It was the bottle which John smashed with a hammer.
c. It was with a hammer that John smashed the bottle.

(4) a. What John did was smash the bottle with a hammer.
b. What John did with the hammer was smash the bottle.
c. What John smashed was the bottle (not the glass).

Structuralists will largely content themselves with describing each of these constructions of English grammar. Formalists will concentrate on formulating the rules for the syntactic operations generating the constructions in (2) to (4) from an underlying structure which most likely closely resembles the active sentence in (1). Functionalists or, in this case, functional grammarians will go one step further and ask in which contexts the individual structural options would be used, thus trying to motivate their choice. They include the use(r) perspective and are not simply interested in making statements on the grammaticality or well-formedness of a given sentence. They are primarily interested in the appropriateness of the individual constructions in (1) to (4) given the communicative situation (participants, setting, topic, its predominant communicative purpose). Communicative competence thus clearly takes priority over the grammatical competence formalists are solely interested in. Relevant in this respect is, for example, information packaging, i.e. the distribution of information of parts of sentences with different information status in terms of given and new information (or: information recoverable or non-recoverable from the prior discourse). Example (1) can be a neutral description of a situation

communicative competence

given vs. new information

(given a neutral intonation contour), but could also be used in a context where John was the topic of the previous discourse. (2a) would rather be preferred when the bottle was the topic, for example when answering the question "What happened to the bottle?" An additional advantage the passive voice offers is that, as in (2b), we need not specify who was responsible for the relevant situation (i.e. the doer, the agent). Compared with the neutral description in (1), the *it*-clefts in (3) all have in common that the highlighted, new information is given in the first part (*it was* ...), whereas the relative clause which follows contains the given information (e.g. (3a) could be an answer to the question "Who smashed the bottle with a hammer?"). In the pseudo-clefts in (4), on the other hand, it is the old information which comes first (*what John did/smashed*) and the new information which follows (e.g. (4a) could be an answer to the question "What did John do with the hammer?").

In other words, it is a hallmark of functionalist thinking that, in a given context, the choice between competing, semantically equivalent constructions is not random, but can be functionally motivated and that this knowledge also forms part of the native language speaker's competence, namely his or her communicative competence. Motivation is indeed a key notion in functionalism since, ultimately, discourse functions cannot only be argued to determine the choice between alternative ways of coding a certain piece of information, but also the shape of language structure itself, i.e. of individual constructions. This assumption of an often motivated link between the form and meaning/function of grammatical constructions does of course go against the basic structuralist (and also formalist) assumption of the arbitrariness of language (cf. I.2.1 above). Functionalists do not shy away from operating with the notion of iconicity (i.e. some sort of, typically highly abstract, resemblance between form and meaning). They hypothesize, for example, iconic relationships between cognitive and structural complexity, i.e. the more cognitively complex a given state-of-affairs is, the more structurally complex and often explicit (in the sense of more and/or more transparent coding material) the construction will be that is used to code it, or between cognitive relevance and structural distance (e.g. the more tightly two states-of-affairs are cognitively or semantically related to each other, the more tightly will the constructions coding these two states-of-affairs be interwoven).

The former type of iconic relationship, i.e. the complexity principle, can be illustrated with the help of adverbial (or: interclausal semantic) relations like simultaneity ('when', 'while'), anteriority ('after', 'since'),

motivation

iconicity

cause ('because'), condition ('if'), or concession ('although') and how they are explicitly signalled by adverbial subordinators (e.g. *when, after, if, because, although*) in English and many other languages. Adverbial relations can clearly be shown to differ according to the degree of world knowledge or context-substantiated evidence that is necessary before a given relation can plausibly be said to hold between two states of affairs (or: propositions). Establishing a causal link between two propositions, for example, requires more such knowledge or evidence than establishing an anterior link ('after', 'since'). A similar situation holds for concessive links ('although') compared with temporal links of simultaneity ('when', 'while'). Cause and, especially, concession thus have a considerably higher degree of cognitive complexity than temporal relations like anteriority or simultaneity. It is thus interesting to see that there is a pronounced tendency across many different and unrelated languages for adverbial subordinators (and other types of connectives) marking concession to be morphologically considerably more complex (consisting of two or more morphemes or even words) and transparent than, say, temporal markers, which typically consist of a single morpheme. Transparency means that the morphological structure of these concessive markers can easily be identified and in many cases still reflects their origin (e.g. English *all-though, never-the-less*, German *ob-wohl* 'whether/if-even', *ob-gleich* 'whether/if-even', Dutch *of-schoon* 'whether/if-already', Italian *sebbene* ‹ *se-bene* 'if-well', or Spanish *aun cuando* 'even when'). Another, clearly related cross-linguistic tendency is that, of all major adverbial relations, concession is that relation which needs to be explicitly coded by some lexical marker, be it, in the case of English, by an adverbial subordinator like *although* or by a concessive marker in the main clause like *nevertheless*. Given its cognitive complexity, concession is hardest to infer and thus requires explicit lexical support.

The examples in (5) illustrate the iconic distance principle, i.e. the iconic relationship between cognitive relevance and structural distance. In these examples, the cause-effect relation is most immediately or tightly coded in (5a), due to the use of the verb *sit* in a special, namely causative, meaning; the speaker (I) can almost be pictured as he or she physically puts a person in an armchair. In (5b) this relationship is less tightly, and in (5c) least tightly coded. Whereas the direct (in 5a even physical) responsibility for the caused action clearly lies with the speaker in both (5a) and (5b), this responsibility is less direct or loosened in (5c).

(5) a. I sat him in the armchair near the window.
 b. I made him sit in the armchair near the window.
 c. I caused him to sit in the armchair near the window.

3 types of autonomy

knowledge   nature of
of language   linguistic
                 knowledge
competence
        syntax grammar/
                language

Two other major differences between functionalism and formalism concern the notion of autonomy and how to approach the study of (first, child) language acquisition. Within formalism, autonomy is broken down into three facets. There is, first of all, the autonomy of competence, as opposed to performance, which was mentioned already and which is rejected by functionalists. The other two types of autonomy concern the nature of linguistic knowledge as opposed to other domains of human cognition. On a narrower scale, focussing just on the nature of syntactic knowledge, formalists postulate the autonomy of syntax as opposed to the meaning of language and language use in discourse, i.e. there is a set of elements constituting the syntax component of human language (and thus UG) which is held to be neither derived from nor to interact with the meaning component of language or with the use of language in communication. This claim does, of course, run counter to the functionalist position that function shapes form, i.e. that communicative needs may very well shape the language system. On a more general scale, the third type of autonomy formalists postulate is the autonomy of grammar or, essentially, language as an autonomous cognitive system. This part of the human cognition is thus taken to be independent from other cognitive systems of humans, such as the cognitive system of orientation in space or general principles of processing information (not just linguistic information, but also visual or auditory information like the distinction and perception of foreground and background, i.e. so-called "figure-ground constellations"). Again, just as functionalists believe in the interaction between syntax and other structural levels of language, they also assume interaction between language and the other systems of human cognition, a point which is particularly forcefully made within cognitive linguistics (cf., for example, chapter VI.4).

first language acquisition:
nature vs. nurture

Formalists and functionalists also entertain different views on how children acquire a language; as a consequence, they pursue different aims and research agendas when studying first language acquisition. At the centre of what is known as the "nature vs. nurture debate" stands the question how much weight should be attributed in child language acquisition to genetic conditioning (i.e. preprogramming), on the one hand, and social conditioning (as a process via communicative interaction with the child's social environment), on the other hand. More precisely, is it justified to make innate genetic structures (i.e., in formalist terms, the language acquisition device or Universal Grammar) alone (!) responsible for the child's ability to acquire a(ny) first language with ease (the nature or nativist position)? Or isn't it more realistic to assume, as functionalists do, that the child's ability to successfully acquire a language is to a large extent a result of the communicative interaction between the child and his/her family and wider social environment (the nurture position). Humans are, after all, social beings and the normal situation for children is to grow up in a social environment, with the family (including single-parent and patchwork families) at its core. Given the formalist assumption of the autonomy of competence, social conditioning, which inevitably involves the child's exposure to performance data, cannot explain how the child becomes a native speaker knowing how to produce and process all and only the grammatically well-formed sentences of its first language so efficiently and quickly. This is even more of a puzzle as it is assumed within the formalist paradigm that much of the linguistic input which children receive from their social environment is 'impoverished', i.e. often fragmented or even ungrammatical (the poverty of stimulus argument). Unlike formalists, functionalists are primarily interested in the process of language acquisition and the way in which the children's communicative interaction with the people around them, the linguistic input they receive, contributes to their acquiring a language. Recall that within the functionalist paradigm, language primarily involves communicative competence. From this perspective, the nature and structure of the genetically preprogrammed blueprint for acquiring language is only of minor interest. This does not mean, however, that such a genetic preprogramming is denied by functionalists (after all, language makes human beings unique among all species), or that functionalists may not also contribute to formulating hypotheses on the make-up of the language faculty we are genetically endowed with. The point is that functionalists will only take genetic factors to come into play when convincing 'nurture'-based facts, arguments or hypotheses can no longer be found or developed for explaining the language acquisition process. The main thrust of functionalist research in first language acquisition thus is on social conditioning (nurture), whereas the main thrust of the relevant formalist research is on genetic conditioning (nature).

The major contrasts between formalism and functionalism are summarized in Table I.1:

Table I.1 The major contrasts between formalism and functionalism

issues	formalism	functionalism
autonomy	(a) of grammar as a cognitive system	no separation of linguistic knowledge from general cognition; instead linguistic knowledge considered part of cognition
	(b) of syntax	syntax cannot be parcelled out from semantics and pragmatics
	(c) of competence	language is an instrument of interaction (communicative competence); language is a tool designed for a certain key purpose (communication), and this purpose continuously shapes the tool
language acquisition	'nature': genetically preprogrammed (innate language faculty; LAD)	'nurture': outcome of communicative interaction child – environment (but: genetic factors are not excluded)
universals	properties of Universal Grammar (formal vs. substantive universals)	functional typology: focus on search for universal tendencies rather than absolute universals and for correlations between properties of languages
explanations of universals	in terms of innateness (UG)	in terms of the usage-based factors determining their nature (e.g. online processing and production, communicative needs, external functions of language)
relationship between form and meaning/function	arbitrary	motivated (e.g. iconicity, metaphor, metonymy)
synchrony – diachrony division	sharp	fuzzy or 'soft' (panchronic approach)
method	deductive introspection reductionist, highly formal analyses	inductive strongly empirical (authentic data) non-reductionist analyses

There is only a handful of truly functionalist schools of linguistics which explicitly call themselves "functional". The first of these was founded in the late 1920s and is still highly respected for its work which continued until the 1960s and 1970s: this is the Prague School (of Functionalism; famous members include Vilem Mathesius, Nikolaj Trubetzkoy, Roman Jakobson, Frantisek Danes). All the other relevant schools were founded in the late 1960s or 1970s: the Amsterdam

School of Functional Grammar (founded by Simon Dik), (Systemic-) Functional Grammar (founded by Michael A.K. Halliday; especially important for English linguistics), and Functional Typology (founded by Joseph Greenberg). Positively formulated, the functionalism which is subscribed to and practiced in these schools and elsewhere in linguistics is characterized by a high degree of heterogeneity and pluralism. Negatively formulated, it lacks the coherence and rigidity which characterizes the considerably larger family of formalist-driven schools. Nevertheless, the views functionalists entertain on the various points in Table I.1 represent more than just a loose bundle of assumptions and attitudes concerning the study of language. All or at least a substantial subset of them constitute what may alternatively be called the basic philosophy, set of beliefs and convictions, or declaration of professional faith of many linguists working in many different branches of linguistics these days. Especially linguists working in pragmatics (chapter VII), cognitive linguistics (chapter VI.4), corpus linguistics (see section I.3.1 below) and most scholars working in sociolinguistics (chapter VIII) are natural-born functionalists, as it were.

Another factor which, not surprisingly, unites the large and heterogeneous community of functionalists is that they disagree in many fundamental respects with the corresponding set of assumptions and views of the formalist paradigm. These two research traditions are not totally incompatible, but certainly anything but easy to reconcile. The situation is different if we include in our discussion the third (and chronologically first; see Figure I.4) major research tradition of 20th century linguistics, namely structuralism. To a certain extent, structuralism can be said to mediate between functionalism and formalism. There are aspects of structuralism that functionalists subscribe to, and aspects of structuralism which formalists subscribe to, and these two sets of aspects partly overlap. As a consequence, someone can be a hard-core functionalist or a hard-core formalist and yet subscribe to certain basic structuralist ideas and positions. For example, the Prague School was at the same time a major structuralist school and the first functionalist-driven school of linguistics. But it is almost impossible, though not unheard of, that someone is at the same time a formalist and a functionalist. It thus has to be acknowledged that the two major research traditions at the turn of the 21st century follow largely different aims and avenues of research. It remains to be seen whether formalism and functionalism will continue to diverge, or whether at least for individual issues some of the findings and theories in one of these paradigms may also find their place in individual components of the other paradigm.

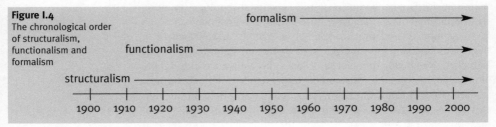

Figure I.4
The chronological order of structuralism, functionalism and formalism

I.3
Recent developments in 20th century linguistics

The developments sketched below have been in full swing only since the late 1980s and 1990s. They are a (to some extent natural) outgrowth of technological progress, more exactly the availability of the computer as a new major research tool, of the advances in linguistic theory and, simply, of the huge body of descriptive linguistic knowledge which has accumulated in 20th century synchronic linguistics, whether in language-specific or cross-linguistic studies. Furthermore, all of these developments are functionalist-driven: their focus is on language use, and the relevant scholars all subscribe to the view that function shapes form, i.e. that language use over time shapes the language system (or, in structuralist terms, that *parole* shapes *langue*; in formalist terms, that performance shapes competence).

3.1 Corpus linguistics

specialized meaning of
corpus

The meaning of the term "corpus" (Latin *corpus* = body; collection of facts') has undergone a significant specialization in the course of the last decades. In its wide, traditional sense the term "corpus" could be (and by some linguists still is) used for any finite set of authentic linguistic data compiled as an empirical basis for linguistic research (e.g. a collection of all *if*-clauses extracted from three novels by different authors may be called a "corpus"). In its narrower and dominant present-day sense, however, the term "corpus" is reserved for large finite bodies of natural texts (written and/or transcribed spoken data) which are available in machine-readable form, have been carefully compiled according to certain principles, and are often annotated with linguistic (for instance, syntactic) or non-linguistic (for instance, sociological) meta-information. What then defines a corpus linguist, beyond being an empirical linguist who is computer-literate and makes these large bodies of machine-readable data the basis for his or her research? Corpus linguists are interested in investigating language use. For this purpose they employ computers as a powerful research tool for linguistic analyses (especially for quantitative analyses) and thus need to be well-versed in statistical methods for evaluating the validity of the quantitative results arrived at. For English linguistics at the turn of the 21st century, the use of huge machine-readable corpora represents the new standard or will, undoubtedly, soon represent the standard of any kind of empirical research on the English language. In other words, the label "corpus linguist(ics)" will continue to lose the distinctive power it had during the pioneering period from the 1960s until the 1980s when it created identity among a rather small group belonging to the community of empirical linguists. Soon any empirical English linguist will be a practitioner of corpus linguistics, simply because this is the richest possible data source and most powerful method ever for investigating English language use (of increasing importance especially for the analysis of spontaneous spoken data). The same tendency can be observed in the empirical study of other major European languages. Thus, due to the technological revolution in the information age, corpus linguistics is or will soon be a standard method in 21st century linguistics. As a subdiscipline of linguistics, it may be useful to restrict this label only to those few who are involved in the compilation of new corpora and, shading already into computational linguistics, the development and application of new analytic and, for example, tagging software (e.g. automatically marking the part of speech on the individual words and word forms in a corpus).

method vs. subdiscipline

English linguistics was the cradle of corpus linguistics. It is here that around 1960 the first corpora for the study of British and American English were compiled. These were two parallel one-million word corpora consisting of 500 texts each from different registers (press, general prose, fiction, learned writing), with 2000 words from each text: the corpus of written American English compiled at Brown University (Brown Corpus) and the matching Lancaster-Oslo-Bergen Corpus (LOB) for written British English (see Table I.2 and Figure I.5 below). It was for the application to the first English corpora, too, that much of the standard corpus technology and the corpus linguistic toolkit (e.g. search software, concordancers) was developed. As a consequence, anyone working on Present-Day English or older periods of English is in an extremely privileged position. There is a wide and diverse range of partly huge corpora available which can be used for analyses on all structural levels (cf. Figure I.1. above), including even studies of inton-

English linguistics: the cradle of corpus linguistics

ation. This includes corpora for different national standard varieties, regional and social non-standard varieties, different historical periods, spoken and written English, different genres, different applications and professional fields, and the number and size of English corpora is constantly growing. Due to the technological revolution we have now reached the stage where English linguists can work with mega-corpora of 100 million words and more, putting scholars and even beginning students of English in a privileged position compared with fellow linguists working on other (even major) languages of the world. For English, we can explore and (often within seconds) even answer questions concerning language use, variation and change which specialists for other languages can barely dare to ask given the absence of a comparable array of large machine-readable corpora.

corpus-literacy

This enormous advantage of practitioners of English linguistics over linguists working on other languages is also increasingly felt in the academic education of undergraduates and graduates in English linguistics, where the standards and expectations concerning the use of electronic corpora are much higher than linguists studying other languages can currently afford them to be. Corpora and basic corpus-linguistic (combined with basic statistical) skills are, or soon enough will be, an integral part of the English linguistics curriculum throughout the world. The overall aim of turning students of linguistics into corpus-literates primarily involves the following aspects: knowledge of the availability of corpora; ability to choose the appropriate (part of a) corpus and the most appropriate evidence for the purpose, i.e. research question, at hand; ability to choose the most appropriate research tools, and to keep at all times a critical distance to the data and the quantitative results of the corpus analysis (notably by applying statistical tests for significance). What has loosely been called corpus-literacy here should not be taken too narrowly, though; everything that undergraduates and graduates learn with regard to existing corpora applies just as much to the selection, critical evaluation, and analysis of any other body of data which is available in electronic form and used as a data source in empirical studies. Just think of all the English language material which is available on CD-ROM (e.g. comprehensive text collections for older periods of English, text archives of newspapers) and, essentially, from the whole world of the internet, which these days gives us immediate access to, for example, authentic use of all sorts of varieties of English (written as well as spoken). Crucial to note is also the following: corpus-literacy requires just as much a solid knowledge of English structure and use, and a solid grounding in linguistic theories as before the advent of the computer as a powerful research tool and the compilation of corpora. Without a theoretical framework which allows us to formulate pointed research questions and put our results in perspective, the mountains of examples and statistics we can extract from corpora are worthless. It would be a grave mistake to consider wading in data and pure number-crunching as a purpose in itself. Any kind of corpus-based or corpus-driven research must be theoretically thought through, right from the very conception of the research questions to the interpretation and explanation of the research results.

In different formats, Table I.2 and Figure I.5 provide a survey of those major corpora of English, both for Present-Day English and older periods, which are accessible to the academic public and currently the most widely used corpora in English linguistics, especially for research on spoken and written Present-Day British and American English. The only exceptions in this respect are the following two still-in-progress collections: the International Corpus of English (ICE), which includes one-million word corpora of speech (60%) and written texts (40%) from different national varieties of English, and A Representative Corpus of Historical English Registers (ARCHER), which currently consists of more than 2 million words of written British and American English from different registers ranging from 1650 until 1990. Of all

major corpora of English

Table I.2 Major corpora of English						
		time slice	size (in million words)	BrE/AmE	spoken	written
Present-Day English Corpora of BrE and/or AmE	BNC	1990s	100	BrE	10%	90%
	LOB	1960	1	BrE	–	+
	FLOB	1990	1	BrE	–	+
	Brown	1960	1	AmE	–	+
	Frown	1990	1	AmE	–	+
	LLC	1960s	0.5	BrE	+	–
	CSAE	1990s	0.2	AmE	+	–
	Switchboard	1990s	2	AmE	+	–
historical corpora	Helsinki	800-1700	1.6	BrE	–	+
	Lampeter	1640-1740	1.1	BrE	–	+
	CEEC	1420-1680	2.7	BrE	–	+
	ARCHER	1650-1990	> 2.0	BrE & AmE	–	+

BNC	= British National Corpus	LLC	= London-Lund Corpus of Spoken British English
LOB	= Lancaster-Oslo-Bergen Corpus	CSAE	= Santa Barbara Corpus of Spoken American English
FLOB	= Freiburg-LOB Corpus	CEEC	= Corpus of Early English Correspondence
Frown	= Freiburg-Brown Corpus	ARCHER	= A Representative Corpus of Historical English Registers

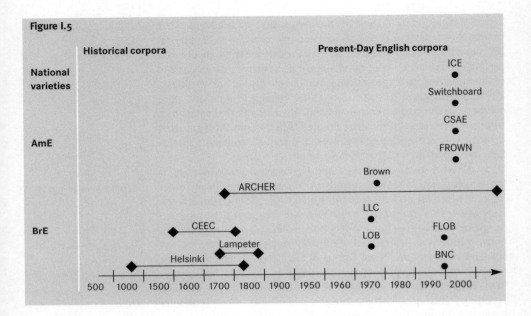

Figure I.5

Present-Day English corpora, the BNC World Edition currently is (and is likely to remain for several years) the most powerful corpus-cum-research software which is widely available for researchers and university students.

Beyond the corpora in this survey, the following corpora deserve mention. At present, however, they are either too expensive for a wide use in universities (Switchboard Corpus: about two million words of 2400 American telephone conversations recorded in the 1990s; discourse tagged, syntactically parsed, and in parts phonetically transcribed) or not publicly accessible (Bank of English: 450 million words of written British English and constantly growing; Longman-Lancaster Corpus: about 30 million words of written British and American English, different registers from the early 1900s to the 1980s). More information on these and dozens of other corpora (already existing, planned, or currently under construction, like the American National Corpus (ANC) as counterpart of the BNC) for research on the English language are available from Meyer (2002) and, especially useful for such a dynamic field, the following two regularly updated websites:

http://www.ldc.upenn.edu/ and http://www.devoted.to/corpora/.

3.2 The renewed interest in historical linguistics

The availability of large present-day and historical corpora has also had a shaping influence on English historical linguistics since the early 1990s. Essentially, three kinds of corpus-based historical studies can be distinguished: (a) truly diachronic studies investigating language change in real time, i.e. in different periods of English, on the basis of, for example, the Helsinki Corpus, the Corpus of Early English Correspondence, or ARCHER; on a much more modest scale, namely for a time slice of merely 30 years, diachronic studies are possible for late 20th century English by contrasting the 1960s parallel corpora for British and American English with their 1990s counterparts, i.e. LOB with FLOB and the Brown corpus with the Frown Corpus; there are plans for extending LOB and the Brown Corpus backwards by 30 year slots, yielding e.g. a pre-LOB corpus with material from 1930; (b) studies of language change in apparent time on the basis of a huge present-day corpus like the BNC: crucial is that sociological, especially age, information is available on the informants whose English is stored in the corpus. Innovations (like the use of such auxiliary verbs as *gonna* or *wanna*) can be traced especially in the younger and youngest age groups, whereas properties of the language which are on the way of being lost are most frequently encountered in the speech of the older informants; (c) comparative studies of different registers (or: genres) can be conducted on the basis of both present-day and historical corpora of English. By tracing and documenting the observable variation in different registers and age groups across different historical periods of English (and even within a single period), the historical linguist gains insights into the dynamics, i.e. the process, of language change. Especially important in this respect are the changing frequencies and distributions of a given word or construction across different registers in a corpus covering different periods of the language (or in separate period-specific historical corpora). Thus it is possible to determine where (i.e. in which register) a given change of English started and how (quickly) it spread in the language. Major results of this line of research include the following:

corpora in historical linguistics

real-time vs. apparent-time studies

register variation

- Language change, especially in the grammar of English, takes place at different speeds in different registers (e.g. personal letters and diaries tend to be most progressive, newspapers and fiction less progressive, scientific texts most conservative).
- Over the past 300 years (at least), there has been a tendency in English, across all registers, towards a more 'oral' style, i.e. towards

an increasing use of grammatical forms and constructions which are typical of (spontaneous) spoken language. Investigated for the second half of the 20th century with the help of newspaper corpora of British and American English, this has also been called the "colloquialization" of the norms of written English, reflecting the general social trend towards greater informality (cf. Mair 1998). This drift towards orality has made itself felt largely as a factor speeding up language change. Especially registers which are close to spontaneous spoken language (e. g. records of trials, personal letters or, these days, e-mail communication) are likely to show the earliest and greatest influence from spoken language, which is, after all, the motor of language change.

- In the second half of the 20th century the structure of British English has clearly been influenced by American English. Nevertheless one can say that grammar changes in both standard varieties develop in the same direction, only at slightly different speeds.

In other respects, too, historical linguistics is back on the stage, partly with old (or perhaps rather eternal) questions in the study of language change, but largely with new questions, methods, hypotheses and explanations, and on the basis of new types and quantities of data.

Since the 1980s and, especially, the 1990s, studies on the evolution of grammar have become extremely popular in modern historical linguistics, not just in the study of English. It is one special process of grammatical evolution, in particular, which has attracted a large amount of attention, namely the process of grammaticalization (cf. Hopper/Traugott 2003). This process takes as input formerly free (or: autonomous) lexical units (e. g. a noun or a verb) and yields as output a function word (e. g. an auxiliary or a preposition), which in turn may further grammaticalize into a bound morpheme, e. g. a suffix, or even disappear. In the course of this process, the relevant words or morphemes undergo a number of meaning- and form-related changes, with meaning-related changes (such as the loss or 'bleaching' of the original concrete lexical meaning and, either replacing the original meaning or as an additional meaning, the development of a more abstract, grammatical meaning) typically occurring earlier than form-related changes (such as two words merging into one, loss of morphological and phonological complexity; all three types of change are observable in *gonna < going to*). What is also typical is an increase in frequency of use in the course of the grammaticalization process, which is one reason for the popularity of corpus-based studies in

grammaticalization

38

grammaticalization research (and vice versa). The examples in (6) are instructive for a better understanding of the development which led to the genesis of the future marker *gonna*. Still a full lexical motion verb in (6a) and possibly still in (6b) and (6c), *going to* has clearly lost its motion meaning in all examples from (6d) onwards. In (6e) it even combines with the motion verb *go* (*I'm going to go...*), and it no longer requires an animate subject in (6f and g). In (6h and i), finally, it has additionally undergone a process of morphological and phonological erosion, i.e. from a two-word phrase with three syllables (*go-ing to*) to a single word with two syllables. The all-important step in this grammaticalization process has taken place in connection with examples as in (6b), where a *going-to* construction combines with an infinitival clause expressing purpose ("I am going in order to meet John."). For the evolution of the future marker *going to/gonna*, it was necessary that example (6b) was at some point in the history of English no longer analyzed as a complex sentence consisting of a main clause ("I'm going") and a subordinate purpose clause ("to meet John"), but as a simple sentence with *to* being part of the construction *be going to*.

(6) a. I'm going to London.
     b. I'm going to London to meet John.
     c. I'm going to meet John.
     d. I'm going to like John.
     e. I'm going to go to London (to meet John).
     f. There's going to be trouble.
     g. An earthquake is going to destroy that town.
     h. I'm gonna go to London.
     i. There's gonna be trouble.

The fascinating thing about grammaticalization is that the relevant change of paths (e.g. the development of future time markers from a motion verb like *to go*, as for *gonna*, or from a verb of volition like *will*) can be observed for many unrelated languages in different parts of the world. In other words, for many grammatical categories the same sources tend to be tapped across languages, i.e. serve as starting-points of the evolution of grammatical markers. It is thus not surprising that grammaticalization was put on the agenda of modern historical linguistics by typologists.

Grammaticalization research has also played a central role in re-awakening the interest in historical semantics, i.e. the study of

historical semantics

meaning change. After a period of approximately 50 years (from the 1930s until the early 1980s) during which historical semantics was no more than a sideline of historical linguistics, it was especially Elizabeth Closs Traugott who in the 1980s put historical semantics back on the research agenda of mainstream historical linguistics. Traugott was a pioneer in modern historical semantics in two respects (cf. Traugott/Dasher 2003). First of all, she demonstrated that many semantic changes are not random and unpredictable (as had been the dominant view in 20th century historical linguistics) but that regularities can indeed be found (not just in English, but often across many unrelated languages). All that is necessary is to look in the right place, namely grammar, more exactly at function words like auxiliaries, prepositions, conjunctions, or discourse markers. Secondly, she brought to bear pragmatic and cognitive concepts and theories in the study of meaning changes, especially those which accompany the evolution of grammatical markers. In other words, this paradigm shift in modern historical semantics is part of a more general cognitive and pragmatic re-orientation in the linguistic study of meaning since the 1970s (cf. chapters VI and VII respectively).

regularities of semantic change

Concerning regularities of semantic change, it turns out that if we look at the evolution of grammatical markers from formerly lexical markers, several widespread tendencies can be identified. The link between grammar and regularity in the context of semantic change may best be sought in the fact that there are far fewer grammatical meanings than lexical meanings (there is simply much more that can be talked about in the world than there is in grammar) and that within a given grammatical domain (e. g. tense or mood) there is far less semantic variation than in individual domains of lexical items (e. g. verbs of motion, hearing, understanding). In other words, within a given domain relatively few grammatical markers tend to vary along relatively few, at least fewer dimensions.

What exactly are the regularities that can be observed in the evolution of grammar? One widespread tendency in the world's languages is the change from markers of anteriority (meaning 'after', 'since') to markers of causality (as for the adverbial subordinator *since*, which has two meanings: the original temporal one and a causal meaning, as in *Since no one seems to be coming, I'll have to do it all by myself*, which developed later in the history of English). Other recurrently observable paths of semantic change in the domain of adverbial connectives include the following:

(7) a. simultaneity 'while' › contrast 'whereas' or concession 'although' (e.g. while, German *während* and *indessen*, Spanish *mientras que*, Italian *mentre*)

b. posteriority 'before' › preference 'rather than' (e.g. *before, rather than* ‹ Old English *(h)rathe* 'quickly, immediately', German *bevor* and *ehe*, Spanish *antes (de) que*, Italian *piuttosto che, prima che*)

For other grammatical domains too (e.g. modal verbs or, as mentioned in connection with the grammaticalization of *be going to*, future time markers), it emerges in language after language that the relevant grammatical markers developed from a restricted set of lexical sources, and that this typically happened by following only a limited number of paths of semantic change. There is also a general path of development which modal auxiliaries (e.g. *can, may, must, will, shall*) seem to have taken in the course of their evolution from formerly full verbs to the highly grammaticalized verbs they are now. They all developed deontic meanings first and epistemic meanings later. Deontic meanings have to do with necessity and obligation while epistemic meanings have to do with possibility and probability, i.e. essentially with knowledge and belief. Thus it can be documented that *must* in its obligation, i.e. deontic, meaning, as in *You must be back by ten*, developed first and *must* in its belief or conclusion meaning, as in *He left at six, so he must almost be there*, developed later. These and many more semantic changes accompanying grammaticalization all seem to have in common that they are unidirectional. Changes in the reverse direction, e.g. from epistemic to deontic meanings or from causal to temporal markers, are not (or only very rarely) documented. This puts us in a situation where we can now formulate constraints on semantic change, limits within which semantic change is possible.

constraints on semantic change

These widespread tendencies seem to be subcases of at least one of two more general tendencies in semantic change: (a) the change from concrete to abstract, and (b) the development from less inferential to more inferential meanings, i.e. to meanings based in the beliefs and attitudes of the language users. While the former development is basically triggered by metaphor, the latter essentially involves a mechanism which was indirectly introduced earlier on by means of the slogan "Today's semantics was yesterday's pragmatics" and is known as conventionalization of conversational implicatures (cf. chapter VII.4). What is behind this tongue twister is simply this. If we process words or utterances in a given context, most of us have the

metaphor: concrete › abstract

yesterday's pragmatics › today's semantics

tendency to 'read more' into what has been literally said, since often speakers and writers tend to mean more than what they say. Now, if over time an ever-increasing part of the language community 'reads more' into the meaning of a lexical item, thus giving up the previously existing contextual restrictions on this enriched interpretation, then what formerly was pragmatically inferred (alternatively called "conversational implicatures" or "invited inferences") may become part of semantics. Take again the cross-linguistically observable tendency for temporal connectives marking anteriority, such as *since*, to acquire an additional and, possibly, at a later stage exclusive sense of causality. This was possible because these connectives were given a causal interpretation in an increasing number of contexts by an increasing number of language users. Starting points for this semantic change were contexts as in (8a), where the connective can be given a causal interpretation beyond the basic temporal one:

(8) a. Since his wife left him, George has been a changed man.
b. Since no one seems to be coming, I'll have to do it all by myself.

pragmatic ambiguity ›
semantic ambiguity

At this stage the ambiguity between the temporal and the causal reading is still a pragmatic one; it would be no contradiction to utter (8a) and yet to add "But I don't want to say that this is because his wife left him". The situation is different as soon as *since* can be found in contexts where it can only have a causal meaning, i.e. where the temporal reading is impossible, as in (8b). What formerly was a pragmatic ambiguity has now turned into a semantic ambiguity of *since*. There are contexts in which from now on *since* may have solely a causal meaning. In other words, we have a completed semantic change and in a dictionary *since* needs to be listed with two meanings.

metaphor – subjectification

Our 'effort after meaning' when processing language in context is one aspect of what Traugott has called "subjectification", i.e. the pervasive tendency for grounding meanings in the speaker's subjective state of belief and attitude. This tendency gives us a powerful cognitive motivation for a wide range of very different semantic changes. Interestingly, the two central mechanisms underlying the semantic changes accompanying grammaticalization, i.e. metaphor and subjectification, seem to take effect in sequence. If a word has undergone more than one meaning change in its history, then the change from a less to a more inferential (or: more subjective, speaker-based) meaning will typically be found to have taken effect after, or at least never before, a change from concrete to abstract has taken place. Traugott also found that both regularities, subjectification as well as the change from concrete to abstract meanings, can be shown to underlie various domains of lexical items, too. Cases in point are mental verbs (e.g. *deduce, suppose, intend, understand, see, hold, grasp*) and speech act verbs, i.e. verbs used for describing different communicative acts (e.g. *admit, command, demand, promise, assert, insist, offer, suggest*). If we look at their etymology and the changes they have undergone before acquiring their present-day senses, many of them can plausibly be argued to have followed these two pathways of semantic change. Ultimately, then, historical semantics at the turn of the 21st century cannot only make predictions for regularities in the evolution of grammatical meanings, but also for regularities that may be valid in larger areas of the lexical vocabulary. This is largely a success of a cognitive-pragmatic paradigm shift in this field. Whereas formerly semantic change was primarily viewed as opening up the possibility for learning more about habits and attitudes in a particular society and culture, the study of semantic change is now increasingly regarded as one way of learning more about human cognition, about the way in which people experience and make sense of the world around them and structure their knowledge. This is, for example, why such basic cognitive mechanisms like metaphor and 'reading more' into word and utterance meanings, i.e. invited inferences, have played an important role in recent years. This explains also why contemporary historical semantics has a strong crosslinguistic orientation: if semantic changes can be motivated by a similar cognitive wiring of people, then it is only to be expected that many semantic changes can be observed in more than one language, even in languages whose speakers do not share the same cultural background. In addition, comparable changes in one language may provide the missing link(s) for semantic changes observable in another language.

cognitive-pragmatic paradigm shift

From modern historical semantics it is but a small step to historical pragmatics. In fact, given what was said above concerning the slogan "Today's semantics was yesterday's pragmatics" these two fields clearly blend into each other. However, the scope of historical pragmatics, an approach which was put on the map of historical, more exactly English historical, linguistics in the 1990s, is much more difficult to define (cf. Jucker 1995, 2000). Of all new late 20th century approaches to historical linguistics, it is clearly the one which is least focused and has the most heterogeneous research agenda. The reason for this is the extremely wide definition of pragmatics adopted

historical pragmatics

by the growing community of historical pragmaticists, namely pragmatics as the study of language use and the relationship between language and its users. This definition, which stands in the tradition of early 20th century semiotics (cf. section I.3.1 above), is much wider than the one adopted in this book, where pragmatics is defined as the study of meaning in context (and thus as a sister discipline of semantics, which is concerned with the study of meaning out of context; see chapter VII.1). Essentially, then, historical pragmatics starts out from (a) the vast and varied range of topics addressing language in use and (b) the theoretical and methodological apparatus developed in modern pragmatics (cf. chapter VII), and applies all this to language use in past periods of English. Besides the pragmatic approach to semantic change pioneered by Traugott, this includes, among other things, a study of changes in the communicative needs due to, for example, societal changes in different historical periods and how this is reflected in the structure and use of older stages of English. Which role, for instance, did politeness play and how did it influence the coding of speech acts like requesting, ordering, promising, or complimenting? In what ways have discourse conventions (and norms) changed in the course of time (both in writing and oral communication)? This may include the study of genre conventions in, for example, private letters, political pamphlets or texts for instruction (e.g. cooking recipes), genre-specific constraints on the extent and nature of code-switching (e.g. switching in the same text between English and French or Latin), or the way in which trials in the law court were conducted (e.g. who was allowed to say what to whom and when?) and recorded. To some extent, historical pragmatics continues the tradition of the philological tradition of linguistics by studying historical texts and data from the point of the context of their genesis: why and for what purpose was a given text drafted, by whom and for whom (i.e. which interests may have guided the author, for example in using particular formulations), what was the social and personal relationship between addresser and addressee (e.g. same rank, different rank; formal – informal), where was it produced, where was it read? In certain respects, the basic assumption that the use and change of language reflects (changes in) societal structure and the nature of social relations between addresser and addressee, historical pragmatics also shares interests with the last of the new approaches introduced in late 20th century historical linguistics presented here.

historical sociolinguistics Historical sociolinguistics (or: socio-historical linguistics) is an offspring of historical corpus linguistics, on the one hand, and modern sociolinguistics, on the other (more exactly, of variationist socio-linguistics as pioneered by the American William Labov ever since the early 1960s). Since the Labovian approach to the study of language variation and change will be discussed in detail in chapters VIII.4 and VIII.6, this ingredient of historical sociolinguistics will be addressed only in very global terms here. The basic challenge in historical socio-linguistics, which was put on the map of English linguistics by the Helsinki Research Unit for Variation and Change in English in the 1990s (cf. Nevalainen/Raumolin-Brunberg 2003), is how to transfer to histor-ical linguistics the sociolinguistic methods designed for the study of present-day variation. Some other differences between historical and modern sociolinguistics are summarized below:

	modern sociolinguistics	historical sociolinguistics
primary object of investigation	phonological variation and/or change in Present-Day English	grammatical variation and/or change in past periods of English
research material	spoken language	written language
	all people	only literate people (upper ranks, men)
	authentic speech; observation, elicitation, evaluation	randomly preserved texts
social context	society familiar, much data available	social structure to be reconstructed on the basis of historical research
standardization	significant element	significance varies
associated discipline	sociology	social history
length and result of the change	unknown	known

Among the greatest challenges of historical sociolinguistics as practiced by the Helsinki research group is the lack of social represen-tativeness in the Corpus of Early English Correspondence (2.7 million words, with texts from 1420 until 1680), which is primarily used for their studies. For example, since (by necessity) only written texts are included in this corpus, the language of the lower classes can hardly be represented; the vast majority of the population in the 15th, 16th and 17th century periods was illiterate. At the bottom of this social hierarchy of literacy at that time of English history, we also find women, since only few women were literate. Within these limits imposed by the nature of the corpus data, this approach has nevertheless yielded a number of interesting insights into morphological and, especially, syntactic change in Late Middle and Early Modern English, including the processes and steps leading to the rise of Standard English and the different degrees of conservativeness or progressiveness observable for members of different social classes. For instance, it seems to be especially the upper gentry which played a leading role in the spread of many syntactic changes. Moreover, in the 16th and 17th century the majority of morphological and syntactic features which were to become part of Standard English spread from the London region to the rest of the country.

traditional vs. modern historical linguistics

The re-awakened interest in language change and the innovative approaches sketched above may, as a convenient shorthand, be lumped together under the heading "modern historical linguistics". It is important to note, however, that traditional approaches to the study of language change have not been given up in contemporary linguistics. Neither have they become useless nor are they looked down upon. It is simply the case that additional approaches have been developed over the last few decades which the majority of the young(er) generation of historical linguists has adopted. Yet the dialogue with 19th century historical linguistics is continuing. The most important differences between modern and traditional historical linguistics as regards research focus and method are listed below:

traditional historical linguistics	modern historical linguistics
focus on documenting the facts of language change in past periods of a language or language family	focus on language change in progress, illuminating why and how language changes (cause/motivation and spread)
focus on internal factors of language change	focus on external (e.g. social) factors: variation in synchrony as a key to variation in diachrony: language change begins as variation
focus on language structure and language system	focus on language use and user (e.g. communicative strategies, functional needs, pragmatic inferences): discourse shapes grammar; speakers change language
focus on phonology and morphology (much less so on syntax and semantics)	phonology still going strong, but much increased interest in syntax and semantics as well as pragmatics
qualitative	qualitative and quantitative
written language only	written and spoken language

Despite these differences, there exist also important continuities 19th century continuities (or rather: rediscoveries of – partly mainstream, partly non-mainstream – 19th century forerunners). Among these continuities, the following figure prominently:

- the focus on language use and the language user (e.g. in the famous work by the neogrammarian Hermann Paul);
- functional and cognitive approaches (e.g. in 19th century work on historical syntax and historical semantics);
- learning about language change via the study of variation in language synchrony (which was the crucial motivation for the beginning of dialectology in the 19th century);
- the search for regularities (e.g. in phonology, semantic change, grammaticalization);
- a return to the philological roots of linguistics due to the renewed interest in historical text linguistics, historical discourse analysis, and the study of genre traditions;
- especially within the functionalist paradigm, an increasing acknowledgement of the parallelism between language structures and biological organisms; this includes, for example, acknowledging *functional adaptation* as the central shaping principle responsible both for the development of organisms in evolution and for change of the language system due to the pressures of language use; biology, in general, seems to be considered by an increasing number of linguists, functionalists as well as formalists, as the new kind of "guiding discipline" (German *Leitdisziplin*) of linguistics, a situation which is most familiar from the mid-19th century when there was an interplay between Darwin's theory of evolution of species and, for example, the family-tree model in historical-comparative linguistics (cf. sections I.2 above and chapter V.1 below).

Modern theories, findings, technologies and methods which developed in or emerged from various branches of synchronic linguistics during the last forty years of the 20th century have found their way into current diachronic linguistics. As a result, both completely new questions and old questions critically reconsidered in light of (especially late) 20th century linguistics can now be addressed to large, partly newly compiled bodies of historical data.

In conclusion, the following can therefore be stated: At the turn of the 21st century, the pendulum which in the course of the first half of the 20th century had swung (almost) all the way from the exclusive

Conclusion and outlook

turn of 21st century

diachrony   synchrony
(19th c.)   (20th c.)

turn of 21st century

Europe   US/Anglo-
(19th c. and   American
early 20th c.) linguistics
                (1950s until
                1980s)

pluralism

interest in historical developments in language(s) in the 19th century to the primary interest in language synchrony is currently on its way to assuming a balanced position in the middle between the synchronic and diachronic poles in linguistics.

At the same time, sticking with the image of the pendulum, we can observe that the centre of gravity of linguistics, which had clearly shifted from Europe (where it was firmly located until well into the first half of the 20th century) to the United States (since the 1940s or 1950s), is currently beginning to swing back to Europe. This is partly due to the renewed interest in historical linguistics, but also due to a strengthening of both formalist and, especially, functionalist linguistics on a firm empirical basis in Europe. Branches like contrastive linguistics, language typology, corpus linguistics, historical socio-linguistics, or historical pragmatics are going strong in Europe, in particular, and some of them were put on the map of linguistics by European linguists in the first place.

Linguistics at the turn of the 21st century has truly found its place as a respected autonomous academic discipline. It no longer needs to fight for recognition and acknowledgement. It is a very lively field, characterized by a much higher degree of pluralism than ever before. Different from the 19th and 20th centuries there is no single school of thought, research tradition, theoretical paradigm – whatever we want to call it – that can claim to dominate linguistic theorizing and practice today, by determining the research agenda and holding, as it were, the key to "the truth" or even to judging what does or does not count as an important research contribution in the field. The pluralism which is characteristic of present-day linguistics extends to topics, theories, and methods alike, and may (unfortunately) even lead to disagreement on the question what constitutes the core of the discipline. There is also pluralism concerning the question whether linguistics is part of the humanities (e. g. teaming up with the philologies and philosophy), of the social sciences (especially with sociology and anthropology as close partners), of the cognitive sciences (in tandem with cognitive psychology, in particular), or of the (natural) sciences (e. g. linguistics as a branch of biology, in close cooperation with genetics and the neurosciences). Not just individual linguists, even entire schools of thought and branches of linguistics hold different views on this rather fundamental question of self-definition, and yet happily coexist and see themselves rather as pursuing different, equally justified and relevant research goals, all of which in their own way contribute to illuminating the nature of language, individual (sets of) languages, and the way they are used in spoken and written communication.

This high degree of pluralism is not only a blessing. Especially for beginning and even for advanced students of linguistics, it makes life quite complicated. This is precisely where the present book wants to help, by focussing on (what the majority of linguists working in English and Linguistics departments consider to be) the core branches of linguistics, and by giving guidance concerning the essentials and, in a modest way, the state of the art within each of these branches. Beyond these essentials, there lies a fascinating universe of languages and linguistics waiting to be discovered (and, who knows, shaped) by anyone thinking of pursuing a professional career in or related to linguistics. So, all readers are warmly invited to join in and work through the essentials of the discipline! This will put you in the position to better understand and judge the continuities and changes in the future developments of 21st century linguistics and, maybe even, to be part of the future of the discipline!

Checklist Linguistics – key terms and concepts

apparent-time ↔ real-time studies
applied linguistics
arbitrariness
autonomy
British National Corpus
competence ↔ performance
contrastive linguistics
conventionality
corpora
corpus linguistics
descriptive ↔ prescriptive
dichotomy
empirical ↔ introspective
form ↔ function
formalism ↔ functionalism
function (internal ↔ external)
functional adaptation
general linguistics
generative linguistics
gradient
grammaticality

grammaticalization
historical pragmatics
historical semantics
historical sociolinguistics (or: socio-historical linguistics)
historical-comparative linguistics
icon
iconicity
index
language acquisition
language acquisition device
langue ↔ parole
linguistics
mental grammar
model of the linguistic sign
modern historical linguistics
morphology
nature ↔ nurture
onomatopoetic expression
paradigmatic ↔ syntagmatic
phonetics

phonology
pragmatics
Prague School
reciprocity
semantics
semiotics
sign
signifiant ↔ signifié
structuralism
symbol
synchronic ↔ diachronic
syntax
system ↔ use
system-based linguistics ↔ usage-based linguistics
transformational grammar
typology
Universal Grammar
universals (formal ↔ substantive)
well-formedness

1 Which of the following research topics call for a synchronic approach to the study of language?
   a. the fixing of English word order before 1600
   b. the topicalization of objects in Late Modern English
   c. the division of tasks between Present Perfect and Simple Past in EModE
   d. the evolution of the pronoun system of English
   e. the use of adverbial clauses in Early Middle English

2 Arrange the following terms in pairs. Note: some terms have no partner (see exercise 3):

signifier	symbol	nature	syntagmatic
prescriptive	arbitrary	parole	synchronic
expressive	conventional	formalism	empirical
competence	paradigmatic	introspective	appellative
nurture	icon		

3 a. For those terms lacking a partner in the list in (2), add the partner yourself.
   b. Try to associate as many of the pairs or individual terms in (2) and (3) as possible with the name of the relevant linguist(s) mentioned in this chapter.

4 a. Find the matching communicative dimension or external function for each of the following six terms: addresser, appellative, code, message, phatic, referential
   b. What is the predominant external function in the following utterances, types of discourse or communicative situations?
   • weather forecast
   • speech by politician during election campaign
   • small talk with people you don't know during your best friend's wedding party
   • Comment by another guest of the same wedding party: "I wouldn't say that they married. Rather SHE married HIM."
   • "Oh, damn!"
   • *Autumn* is clearly British English, while *fall* is preferred in American English.

5 Associate each of the following statements with one of the branches of modern historical linguistics sketched in section I.3.2:
   a. The much increased use of contractions like *isn't, haven't* or

didn't in newspaper language is a clear indicator of the colloquialization of the norms of written English.

b. This is a typical 18th century way of asking someone a big favour.

c. The upper gentry was responsible for spreading quite a number of grammatical innovations during the Early Modern English period.

d. Verbs of motion belong to the typical sources of future time markers in the languages of the world.

e. Euphemism is often responsible for pejoration (e.g. *smell* meaning 'bad smell, odour' in "What's this smell in here?").

6 Which of the following statements would be rejected by linguists working within a formalist framework?

a. Human beings are genetically endowed with grammatical knowledge and the ability to learn any (first) language with maximum efficiency.

b. Competence must be studied independently of performance.

c. Large-scale language comparison is necessary for identifying language universals.

d. There is no language change within the lifetime of the individual native speaker of a language. Language change takes place only between the generations.

e. Communicative competence does not offer a key to Universal Grammar.

7 Identify that corpus in each set which does not belong there.

a. LOB	FLOB	BNC	CSAE	LLC
b. Brown	CEEC	Helsinki	ARCHER	Lampeter
c. Switchboard	CSAE	LLC	Frown	LOB
d. CSAE	FLOB	BNC	LLC	Brown
e. Switchboard	Frown	Brown	FLOB	BNC

8 Which of the following statements are true, which are false?

a. Generative grammar is only interested in language production, not in language processing.

b. For icons there is a motivated link between signifier and signified.

c. Paradigmatic relations are relations of combination, syntagmatic relations are relations of choice.

d. Morphophonemics is a classic example of an interface in linguistics.

e. Grammaticalization is the process whereby formerly ungrammatical constructions and sentences turn grammatical over time.
f. Saussure's *parole* corresponds to Chomsky's *performance*, but Saussure's *langue* does not correspond to Chomsky's *competence*.
g. Formalists would agree with the statement "Linguistics is part of the social sciences."
h. The use of large machine-readable corpora is a standard method in formalist linguistics.
i. Regularities in semantic change have especially been observed in grammaticalization.
j. The study of formerly pragmatic ambiguities becoming semantic ambiguities can alternatively be considered as forming part of historical semantics or historical pragmatics.

9 This is an exercise in functional grammar. Consult a reference grammar of English (e.g. the chapter by Ward et al. in Huddleston/Pullum 2002) before tackling the tasks in (a) and (b). Both tasks are concerned with the following set of examples:

Exercises
Advanced

i   This one she forgot.
ii   He made without delay all the changes she wanted.
iii On board were three linguists.
iv   There is a dog in the pool.
v   It is obvious that he's a liar.
vi   That job I gave you, it's the best one you've ever had.
vii They're still here, the people from next door.
viii It was *Mary* who broke it.
ix   The car was taken by Kim.
x   What he did was crash the car.

a. Identify for each of the examples above the construction it represents. Choose from the following set (note: not all terms listed here are relevant for this task):

pseudo-cleft	preposing	mediopassive
postposing	preposition stranding	inversion
intonation	existential	ellipsis
extraposition	insertion	left dislocation
embedding	right dislocation	cleft
passive		

b. Which discourse-pragmatic function does each of the constructions primarily serve?

10 This task is concerned with the conflicting positions in the formalism-functionalism debate from a structuralist point of view (cf. section I.2.3). Try to determine in which respects structuralism is compatible (or clearly sides) with formalism, on the one hand, and/or with functionalism, on the other hand.

11 Find out more about the contribution of Leonard Bloomfield to the evolution of (especially American) linguistics in the mid-20th century. What, in particular, are major differences between American and European Structuralism (as represented by de Saussure and the Prague School)?

12 Try to write an essay of no more than 1,000 words on the major developments in 20th century linguistics. Make use of the pairs of terms in (2) and (3a).

Sources and further reading

Amsterdamska, Olga. 1987. *Schools of thought: The development of linguistics from Bopp to Saussure.* Dordrecht: Reidel.

Auroux, Sylvain et al., eds. 2001. *History of the language sciences: An international handbook on the evolution of the study of language from the beginnings to the present.* [HSK]. 2 vols. Berlin/ New York: de Gruyter.

Biber, Douglas/Susan Conrad/Randi Reppen. 1998. *Corpus linguistics. Investigating language structure and use.* Cambridge: Cambridge University Press.

Chomsky, Noam. 2004. *The generative enterprise revisited.* Berlin/ New York: Mouton de Gruyter.

Comrie, Bernard. 1989[2]. *Language universals and linguistic typology.* Oxford: Blackwell.

Croft, William. 1995. "Autonomy and functional linguistics". *Language* 71: 490-532.

D'Agostino, Fred. 1986. *Chomsky's system of ideas.* Oxford: Clarendon.

de Saussure, Ferdinand. 1983 [1916]. *Course of general linguistics.* edited by Charles Bally and Albert Sechehaye. London: Duckworth.

Harris, Roy. 1987. *Reading Saussure.* London: Duckworth.

Helbig, Gerhard. 1989[8]. *Geschichte der neueren Sprachwissenschaft.* Opladen: Westdeutscher Verlag.

Hopper, Paul J./Elizabeth C. Traugott. 2003[2]. *Grammaticalization.* Cambridge: Cambridge University Press.

Joseph, John Earl/Nigel Love/Talbot J. Taylor, eds. 2001. *Landmarks in linguistic thought.* Vol. 2: *The Western tradition in the twentieth century.* London: Routledge.

Jucker, Andreas H., ed. 1995. *Historical pragmatics: Pragmatic developments in the history of English.* Amsterdam/Philadelphia: Benjamins.

Jucker, Andreas H. 2000. *History of English and English historical linguistics.* Stuttgart: Klett.

Kortmann, Bernd. 1999. "Iconicity, typology and cognition." In: Max Nänny and Olga Fischer, eds. *Form miming meaning. Iconicity in language and literature.* Amsterdam/Philadelphia: Benjamins. 375-392.

Mair, Christian. 1998. "Corpora and the study of the major varieties of English: Issues and results." In: Hans Lindquist, Staffan Klintborg, Magnus Levin and Maria Estling, eds. *The major*

varieties of English: papers from MAVEN 97, Växjö 20-22 Novem-
ber 1997. Växjö: Växjö University. 139-157.

Matthews, Peter. 1994. *Grammatical theory in the United States from
Bloomfield to Chomsky*. Cambridge: Cambridge University Press.

Meyer, Charles F. 2002. *English corpus linguistics: An introduction*.
Cambridge: Cambridge University Press.

Nevalainen, Terttu/Helena Raumolin-Brunberg. 2003. *Historical
sociolinguistics: language change in Tudor and Stuart England*.
London: Longman.

Newmeyer, Frederick J. 1986. *Linguistic theory in America*. New York:
Academic Press.

Newmeyer, Frederick J. 1996. *Generative linguistics. A historical
perspective*. London/New York: Routledge.

Newmeyer, Frederick J. 1998. *Language form and language function*.
Cambridge, Mass.: MIT Press.

Paul, Hermann. 1995[10]. *Prinzipien der Sprachgeschichte*. Tübingen:
Niemeyer. 1888. *Principles of the history of language*. translated
from the 2nd edition of the original by H.A. Strong. London: Swan
Sonnenschein.

Pinker, Steven. 1995. *The language instinct. The new science of
language and mind*. London: Penguin.

Rohdenburg, Günter/Britta Mondorf, eds. 2003. *Determinants of
grammatical variation in English*. Berlin: Mouton de Gruyter.

Sampson, Geoffrey. 1980. *Schools of linguistics: Competition and
evolution*. London: Hutchinson.

Traugott, Elizabeth Closs/Richard B. Dasher. 2002. *Regularity in
semantic change*. Cambridge: Cambridge University Press.

Ward, Gregory/Betty Birner/Rodney Huddleston. 2002. "Information
packaging." In: Rodney Huddleston and George Pullum, eds.
The Cambridge grammar of the English language. Cambridge:
Cambridge University Press. 1363-1447.

Wunderlich, Dieter. 2004. "Why assume UG?". In: Martina Penke
and Anette Rosenbach, guest eds. *What counts as evidence in
linguistics? (Studies in Language)*. Amsterdam/Philadelphia:
Benjamins. 615-641.

II Phonetics and phonology: On sounds and sound systems

Introduction

The two branches of linguistics which deal with properties and functions of sounds are phonetics and phonology. They differ clearly, however, with regard to their research objects and the questions they ask. Phonetics is concerned with sounds (or: phones; Greek *phone* = voice, sound) as such, particularly with the substance of those sounds used in human communication, no matter in which language they occur. Relevant questions asked in phonetics concerning human speech sounds include the following: How are these sounds produced? What are their articulatory features (that is features determined by the speech organs)? What are their acoustic properties (in the sense of measurable oscillations)? How can sounds be described and classified using articulatory and acoustic information? How can sounds be transcribed, in other words be made visible in writing, with the help of a finite, manageable inventory of symbols?

phone [ ]

Unlike phoneticians, phonologists are solely interested in the function of sounds belonging to a given sound system: Does a certain sound have a meaning-distinguishing function within the system of a language or not? In other words, is the difference between two sounds of the same language distinctive, like the difference between the

distinctive
versus redundant

initial sounds of *lip* and *rip*, or not? An example of a non-distinctive (or: redundant) sound difference is the one between the so-called "clear l" in *lip* and the so-called "dark l" in *pill*. In English, there is no pair of words where replacing one of these two sounds with the other in an otherwise identical string of sounds would lead to a meaning difference. Or just think of the difference between the "trilled r" (*gerolltes Zungen-R*) and the "uvular r" (*Zäpfchen-R*) in German. We are clearly dealing with two different sounds here, which are therefore also represented by different symbols in phonetics, but it is irrelevant, at least from the meaning perspective, which one of the two we use, e.g. in German *rollen* or *Brot*. Phonology thus operates on a more abstract level than phonetics. Its research object is not the totality of all sounds actually uttered and processed in everyday life, but merely those units which constitute the sound system of a language, the so-called "phonemes" (Greek *phonema* = a sound). Thus in some varieties of English, notably RECEIVED PRONUNCIATION (RP), there is the phoneme /l/ with its phonetic variants (or: allophones) [l] in *lip* and [ɫ] in *pill*, and in German the phoneme /r/, which among others is realized by the allophones [r] and [ʀ].

phoneme / /

allophone

The major differences between phonetics and phonology can be described with the help of the following pairs of contrast:

phonetics	phonology
sounds as such	sounds as parts of a sound system
language use (*parole*)	language system (*langue*)
not language-specific	language-specific
substance	function (meaning differentiation)
concrete	abstract
phone [ ]	phoneme / /

Despite these differences, we must not fail to notice that phonetics and phonology are tightly interrelated, and ultimately cannot do without each other. Phonology can hardly do without the apparatus of phonetic description. Conversely, phonetics cannot find its research object without phonology; without reference to concrete phonological systems, sound segmentation would be impossible.

1.1 Transcription

Only a transcription system allows us to represent sounds in writing and thus to specify, for instance, the pronunciation of words in dictionaries. Phonetic transcriptions clearly show that spelling often do not tell us anything about pronunciation. Therefore they are of utmost importance especially for those languages with a large discrepancy between pronunciation and orthography. A prime example of this is the English language, the spelling of which often tells us more about the origin of the words or their pronunciation towards the end of the Middle Ages than about their present pronunciation. Concerning the divergence of spelling (in angled brackets) and articulation (in square brackets), we can roughly distinguish four types:

orthography ≠ pronunciation

(1) different spellings for the same sound:

[iː]	⟨ae⟩	Caesar	⟨eo⟩	people
	⟨ay⟩	quay	⟨ey⟩	key
	⟨e⟩	be, these	⟨i⟩	ski, police, fatigue
	⟨ea⟩	sea, tea	⟨ie⟩	field, yield
	⟨ee⟩	bee, sneeze	⟨oe⟩	amoeba, Phoenix
	⟨ei⟩	seize, receive		

(2) the same spelling for different sounds:

⟨ea⟩	[eə]	bear, tear (verb)	[ɑː]	heart
	[ɪə]	beard, tear (noun), hear	[e]	head, dead
	[ɜː]	heard, learn	[iː]	heat, mead

(3) silent letters:

know, honest, mnemonic, psychology, debt, listen, sword, column, bomb, sign, island; optional in the case of alright, often, sandwich

(4) missing letters:

[j] in use, fuse, cute, futile, stew, new (BrE)

Especially for learners and teachers of English, phonetic transcriptions are indispensable. Table II.1 gives an overview of the five currently most common transcription models for RECEIVED PRONUNCIATION (RP), the standard accent of southern – especially southeastern – British English (the more traditional upper-class or 'marked' variety which, however, is only spoken by 3% to 5% of the *educated native speakers*). The first four of these models have been developed specifically for the transcription of RP, thus they do not pay attention to whether a particular symbol might represent a different sound in the transcription of a different language. This is not the case for the

transcription models

IPA

quantity
quality

fifth model, the INTERNATIONAL PHONETIC ALPHABET (IPA), which has been developed by the *International Phonetic Association* for the transcription of any linguistic sound. The phonetic symbols listed in Table II.1 thus form the relevant subset of the overall inventory of IPA symbols for the transcription of RP. The main difference between the models by Gimson, Wells, and Upton, on the one hand, and Windsor Lewis and the IPA, on the other, is that the latter two do not use the colon as a diacritic for the long vowels (as in [siːt] *seat* or [buːt] *boot*). All models have in common that long and short vowels are treated differently, not only concerning their quantity (length), but also their phonetic quality. Accordingly, long and short vowels are transcribed by different symbols (e.g. [siːt] *seat* in comparison to [sɪt] *sit*). In this respect they differ from the original model by the London phonetician Daniel Jones, from which all the current models have developed. In this book it is the Wellsian model which will be used. As a successor of Gimson's model it is meanwhile the most widely used model for the teaching of English and English linguistics at schools and universities. Of no further importance, on the other hand, will be the transcription model that is frequently chosen in American publications on phonetics and phonology (see the last line in Table II.1). It differs strongly from all models introduced so far, apart from the fact that there are of course differences regarding the phoneme inventories and phoneme realisations between RP and GENERAL AMERICAN (GA), the standard accent of American English (cf. chapter VIII).

Tab. II.1 Transcription models*

	Key word	seat*	sit	set*	sat*	star*	soft*	sort*	stood	soon*	sum	sir*	suppose	say	so	sigh*	sow*	soil	steer	stare*	sure
RP	Upton	iː	ɪ	ɛ	a	ɑː	ɒ	ɔː	ʊ	uː	ʌ	əː	ə	eɪ	əʊ	ʌɪ	aʊ	ɔɪ	ɪə	ɛː	ʊə
	Wells	iː	ɪ	e	æ	ɑː	ɒ	ɔː	ʊ	uː	ʌ	ɜː	ə	eɪ	əʊ	aɪ	aʊ	ɔɪ	ɪə	eə	ʊə
	Gimson	iː	ɪ	e	æ	ɑː	ɒ	ɔː	ʊ	uː	ʌ	ɜː	ə	eɪ	əʊ	aɪ	aʊ	ɔɪ	ɪə	eə	ʊə
	W. Lewis	i	ɪ	e	æ	ɑ	o	ɔ	ʊ	u	ʌ	ɜ	ə	eɪ	əʊ	aɪ	aʊ	ɔɪ	ɪə	eə	ʊə
	IPA	i	ɪ	ɛ	æ	ɑ	ɒ	ɔ	ʊ	u	ʌ	ɜ	ə	eɪ	əʊ	aɪ	aʊ	ɔɪ	ɪə	eə	ʊə
GA	American textbooks	ij, iy, i	ɪ	ɛ	æ	ɑ, a	ɑ, a	ɔ	ʊ	uw, u	ʌ	ʌ, ə$^{+r}$	ə	ej, ey, e	ow, o	aj, ay	aw	ɔj, ɔy	(ɪ+r)	(ɛ+r), (i+r)	(ʊ+r)

* The asterisk indicates that for these vowels different symbols are used in the transcription models.

There is a simple reason why only the phonetic symbols for the vowels are listed in Table II.1. Concerning consonants there are no differences between the transcription models, again with the exception of the model widely used in North America, which uses the symbols [š, ž, č, ǰ, y] instead of [ʃ, ʒ, tʃ, dʒ, j].

phonetic/phonemic transcription

It is true that phonetic transcriptions are indispensable especially for languages like English. For the non-specialist, however, there are limits to the degree of precision that is still digestible. Most dictionaries and introductions to linguistics therefore refrain from using the fine-grained (so-called "narrow") phonetic transcription which represents even the most subtle phonetic features with the help of diacritic signs. Examples of this are the tilda for marking the nasalisation of vowels, which takes place regularly before nasal consonants (e.g. in *run* [ɹʌ̃n] or *wrong* [ɹɒ̃ŋ] in British English), and the superscript 'h' indicating the strong aspiration of some voiceless consonants, particularly word-initially (cf. [pʰĩn] or [tʰɪɬ]). Even the so-called "broad phonetic transcription", which provides different symbols for dark and clear /l/ or the various roll sounds, is mostly avoided outside of publications on phonetics. Much preferred, on the other hand, is the simplest type of transcription, the so-called "phonemic transcription". Not only does it dispense with diacritic signs (partly with the exception of the colon as a sign for length), but also with separate symbols for the various realisations of /l/ or /r/. In other words, this type of transcription takes into account only the phonemes of a language. For reasons of simplification, phonemic transcription will predominantly be used in the following parts of this chapter and book.

transcription

phonetic   phonemic

narrow   broad
ring [ɹĩŋ]   [ɹɪŋ]   /rɪŋ/
till [tʰɪ̃ɬ]   [tɪɬ]   /tɪl/

1.2 Speech organs

There are three branches of phonetics, each of which deals with one of the three phases of communication, namely sound production (articulatory phonetics), sound transmission (acoustic phonetics), and sound perception and processing (auditory phonetics). Acoustic phonetics is concerned with the measurable physical properties of

branches of phonetics

articulatory
acoustic
auditory

sounds; it falls primarily into the domain of physics and language processing by computers, e.g. automatic speech recognition. Auditory phonetics is of prime importance in medicine and psychology. Both branches will be of no further concern here.

articulators

Articulatory phonetics is of central importance in linguistics, especially for (prospective) language teachers. It is located at the interface between linguistics, on the one hand, and anatomy and physiology, on the other. A large part of its terminology is taken from the latter two domains, e.g. terms for the speech organs and for the description and classification of speech sounds.

The human speech organs (or: articulators) are shown in Figure II.1 (see inside of cover), and identified and illustrated in Table II.2. It is easiest to feel the speech organs in the upper part of the oral cavity (alveolar ridge, hard and soft palate) when, starting out from the back of the front teeth, we let the tip of the tongue slowly glide back along the roof of the mouth. Most of the speech organs are movable, thus so-called active articulators; only the upper jaw, the hard palate, and the back of the throat (or: pharynx) are relatively immovable and therefore called passive articulators. It should be noted, however, that the so-called "speech organs" do of course primarily serve biological and not linguistic functions.

Tab. II.2 Places of articulation and relevant English sounds (RP)*

	place of articulation	adjective	examples of sounds [ ]	examples
1	lips	labial	[p], [b], [m], [w]	puppy, Bob, mummy, word
2	teeth	dental	[θ], [ð]	throne, the
		labio-dental	[f], [v]	fan, van
3	alveolar ridge	alveolar	[t], [d], [s] [z], [n], [l]	turtle, dragon, superman, zeal, nasty, lollipop
		post-alveolar	[ɹ]	rap
		palato-alveolar	[ʃ], [ʒ], [tʃ], [dʒ]	shanty, illusion, chips, gipsy
4	hard palate	palatal	[j]	yuppie
5	soft palate/velum	velar	[k], [g], [ŋ]	ketchup, gorilla, prong
6	uvula	uvular		
7	pharynx	pharyngeal		
8	epiglottis			

Tab. II.2 Places of articulation and relevant English sounds (RP)*

9	glottis	glottal	[h], [ʔ]	hat, *in many non-RP-accents:* bottle [bɒʔl]
10	larynx	laryngeal	[ʔ]	*sometimes in RP before* /p, t, k/: popcorn ['pɒʔpkɔːn]
11	tip/apex of tongue	apical	[θ], [ð], [ɹ], [l]	throne, the, rap, lollipop
12	blade/lamina of tongue	laminal	[t], [d], [n] [s], [z] [ʃ], [ʒ], [tʃ], [dʒ]	turtle, dragon, nasty superman, zeal shanty, illusion, chips, gipsy
13	front of tongue	(medio-)dorsal	[j], [ɪ], [iː], [e], [æ]	yuppie, insect, leap, pet, pat
14	back/dorsum of tongue	(post-)dorsal	[k], [g], [ŋ] [ʊ], [uː], [ɒ], [ɔː]	ketchup, gorilla, prong foot, food, ton, tall

* The examples in the right column refer to the initial sound (unless indicated otherwise). In RECEIVED PRONUNCIATION there are no clear examples of the sounds in lines 6-8 and 10. An example of a uvular sound is the German [ʀ]. Pharyngeal sounds (line 7) are a characteristic feature of Arabic, laryngeal sounds are typical of Danish.

1.3 Types of sounds

The two main types of sounds in the languages of the world are vowels and consonants. This is one of the few cases in which we can speak of an absolute (i. e. exceptionless) universal. The main phonetic difference between these two sound types is that for vowels the air passes through the oral cavity relatively freely, whereas consonants are formed via a partial or complete obstruction of the airflow somewhere in the vocal tract. Moreover, vowels are generally voiced, that is the vocal folds (better known under the misleading term "vocal cords") are vibrating, whereas consonants can be voiced or voiceless.

In general, three criteria (or: parameters) are used for the description and classification of consonants:
- vocal fold action: yes (voiced) / no (voiceless),
- place of articulation,
- manner of articulation. Stimmart

The first criterion is about whether the vocal folds are approximating each other closely enough in order to be set vibrating by the airflow coming up through the windpipe. If they vibrate (Figure II.2), the result is a voiced sound. These vibrations can easily be felt: simply put the tip of your index finger on the Adam's apple (often more prominent with members of the male sex) and produce in turns of

vowels

consonants

Figure II.2

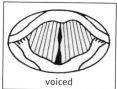

voiced

Figure II.3

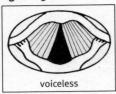

voiceless

homorganic sounds
obstruents

fricatives

plosives
affricates

three seconds [s] and [z] or, alternatively, [f] and [v]. (Another indicator of voiced sounds is that only these may be hummed or sung.)

Voiceless consonants, by contrast, result from the fact that the vocal folds are too far apart to be set vibrating (see the open glottis in Figure II.3). Voiceless consonants further differ from voiced ones in that the intensity of muscle tension and emission of air is considerably larger for the former. That is why the distinction between voiceless and voiced consonants often – in English generally – correlates with the fortis/lenis (strong/soft) distinction, which refers to the degree of muscle tension and breath pressure when producing consonants.

The second criterion (place of articulation) leads us back to the speech organs, in particular to Figure II.1 (see inside of cover) and Table II.2, and does not need any further explanation. Sounds which are produced at the same place are called homorganic sounds.

On the basis of their manner of articulation, the third relevant criterion, two major classes of consonants are distinguished: obstruents and sonorants. With obstruents, the airflow is strongly, sometimes even completely, obstructed at some place in the articulation channel. If the air is pressed through a narrow articulation channel, friction is produced, which again generates a certain type of sound, the so-called "fricatives" (e.g. [v] or [s]). If the airflow is completely blocked due to two articulators touching each other, and this obstruction is suddenly released, then the result is an 'explosive' sound due to the escape of the blocked airstream (so-called "plosives", e.g. [p] or [d]). A third type of obstruent are the affricates, as e.g. [tʃ] in *church* or [dʒ] in *judge*. For their production there is first – as for plosives – a complete obstruction of the airflow, which then, however, is not released abruptly but rather slowly. Due to the narrow channel which opens between tongue blade and the area between alveolar ridge and hard palate, the accumulated air escapes slowly and, due to friction, produces a sound similar to fricatives.

On the basis of the three criteria voiced/voiceless, place of articulation, and manner of articulation, we are now in the position of describing, for example, [p] as a voiceless (bi)labial plosive sound, or [v] as a voiced labio-dental fricative. We can also formulate generalisations on individual groups of consonants, making for instance statements only about voiceless obstruents, voiced alveolar sounds, or all plosives, fricatives, or affricates. Together with their different places of articulation, these three types of obstruents are illustrated in the first three lines of Table II.3, which contains all 24 consonant phonemes of English.

Tab. II.3 The English consonant inventory

place of articulation	bilabial		labio-dental		dental		alveolar		post-alveolar		palato-alveolar		palatal		velar		glottal	
manner of articul.	vl.	vd.	vl.	vd.	vl.	vd.	vl.	vd.	vl.	vd.	vl.	vd.	vl.	vd.	vl.	vd.	vl.	vd.
plosive	p	b					t	d							k	g		
fricative			f	v	θ	ð	s	z			ʃ	ʒ					h	
affricate											tʃ	dʒ						
nasal		m						n								ŋ		
lateral								l										
roll									r RP [ɹ] GA [ɻ]									
semi-vowels		w												j		(w)		

Obstruents do not only provide the majority of consonants. In comparison to sonorants they are also the more prototypical consonants. For example, almost all obstruents come in pairs (voiced/voiceless), whereas sonorants (at least in English) are usually voiced. As can be seen from Table II.3, there are different subsets of sonorants. Let us first turn to the nasals: similar to plosives, there is a complete obstruction of the airflow in the oral cavity for [m], [n] and [ŋ], but since the soft palate (or: velum) is lowered (see Figure II.4), the air can escape through the nasal cavity. Due to the similar manner of articulation, nasals and plosives are often also lumped together as "stops", but then divided into nasal and non-nasal (or: oral) stops.

On account of their combination of obstruction and simultaneous escape of the airstream, [l] and [r] are collectively referred to as *liquids*. The term laterals for the various /l/-realisations stems from the fact that the air escapes along the sides of the tongue here. "Rolls" (or: "trills") is the term used for, among other things, particular phonetic realisations of /r/; these do exist in the Celtic Englishes (Irish, Scottish, Welsh English), but not in the standard accents of British and American English (therefore the brackets in Table II.3).

For liquids, although the air is escaping in a relatively unimpeded way, there is still a contact between two articulators. This is different

sonorants

Figure II.4

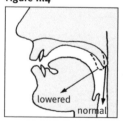

liquids

for the initial sounds of *we* [w] and *you* [j], which lead us right into the transitional zone between consonants and vowels and, at the same time, between phonetics and phonology. From the point of view of phonetics, these two sounds are rather vowels, more precisely gliding vowels, with the relevant articulators moving away from (for [w]) or towards (for [j]) the narrowing in the articulation channel. This is also mirrored in the terms that are commonly used for them, namely *semi-vowels* or *glides*. Only because of their distribution in syllables are they considered as consonants. They are exclusively located at the margins of a syllable, and thus, different from vowels, can never serve as the nucleus of a syllable, let alone constitute a syllable on their own. In other words, purely functional and thus phonological considerations (Which function do these two sounds fulfil in the sound system of English?) are responsible for the classification of [w] and [j]. In principle, even if not to the same extent, a similarly 'inaccurate' manner of proceeding from a phonetic point of view applies to the classification of liquids. Here, too, the air can escape relatively freely from the oral cavity so that there is no audible friction of the escaping airflow.

In phonetics, liquids and semi-vowels, in some accounts also [h], are therefore also grouped together as approximants (defining characteristic: two articulators approaching or touching each other without audible friction).

The biggest problem concerning the description and classification of vowels is that, different from consonants, we cannot feel what is happening in the oral cavity during their articulation. It is true that we can observe differences in the lip position (e.g. spread lips for [iː] in *tree*, lip rounding for [uː] in *true*). But the lip position is only a secondary feature of vowels, especially in English where, in contrast to German and most of the Germanic languages, there are no rounded front vowels like [yː] (German *Sühne*) or [øː] (German *Söhne*) (cf. chapter V). Tongue indeed is the key word: it is that speech organ on which everything in vowel production hinges. Both the quality and the quantity of vowels change depending on (a) which position (b) a particular part of the tongue remains in (c) for how long. On top of this, (d) the position of the tongue can even change in the course of the articulation of a vowel and thus produce a completely different vowel.

It is only with the help of detailed physiological studies in a phonetic laboratory that we can determine these four pieces of information, which are relevant for every single vowel sound. It was such a laboratory where the vowel diagram (or: vowel chart) was developed.

semi-vowels or glides

approximants

liquids   semi-vowels

vowels

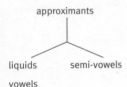

reference system

66

It serves as an invariable reference system for the description and classification of any given vowel of a language.

The relevant reference vowels (see the nodes in Figure II.5) are called cardinal vowels. These idealized vowels are constructs and do not occur in any language, which is why they are generally placed outside of the vowel diagram (also known as the "cardinal vowel diagram"). The primary cardinal vowels (1-8) are given in Figure II.5. The secondary cardinal vowels (9-16) follow from the reversal of the lip position for the primary ones (thus rounded lip position for the cardinal vowels 1-5 yields the cardinal vowels 9-13, and non-rounded lip position for the cardinal vowels 6-8 yields the cardinal vowels 14-16). Two closed central vowels complete the cardinal vowel system developed by Daniel Jones.

cardinal vowels

primary   secondary

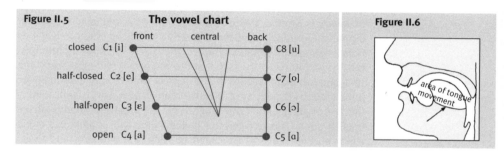

| Figure II.5 | The vowel chart | | | Figure II.6 |

The vowel chart

	front	central	back
closed C1 [i]			C8 [u]
half-closed C2 [e]			C7 [o]
half-open C3 [ɛ]			C6 [ɔ]
open C4 [a]			C5 [ɑ]

The vowel diagram is an abstracted representation of that area of the oral cavity where the vowels are produced (Figure II.6). The two axes of the diagram relate to the tongue as the all-important speech organ in the production of vowels. The horizontal axis indicates which part of the tongue (front, back, or central) is raised most during the production of a particular vowel; this is why we speak of "front" or "back vowels". The vertical axis indicates the degree of tongue raising (high – mid – low). The vowel [ɪ] in *sit* is thus called a (non-rounded) high front vowel, [ʊ] in *foot* a (rounded) high back vowel, and the schwa-sound [ə], which usually occurs in unstressed syllables only, is called a "mid central vowel". These three sounds have in common that the tongue remains in the respective position of articulation for a considerably shorter period of time than is the case for the vowels in *seat* [iː], *boot* [uː], and *sir* [ɜː]. Thus, how long the tongue remains in a particular position is a further relevant factor for the description and classification of vowels. Figures II.7 and II.8 show all short and long vowels of English; as we can see, and as is reflected in their tran-

front and back vowels

scriptions, short and long vowels do not only differ quantitatively, but also qualitatively, i.e. with regard to their tongue positions:

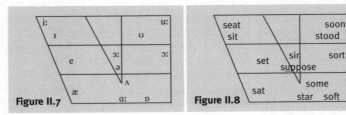

Figure II.7 Figure II.8

The vowels in these two figures are called "monophthongs" (or: pure vowels) in contrast to the diphthongs (or: gliding vowels) in Figures II.9-11. The crucial criterion for the distinction of these two types of vowels is whether the tongue largely remains stable in its position during the production of the respective vowel, or whether it glides from one position towards another. The latter is true for diphthongs, but it is important to stress that at the end of this gliding process, the tongue never quite reaches the position in which it would normally be if the second element were articulated on its own. This is indicated by the arrows in Figures II.9 through II.11. The eight diphthongs of the English sound system may be divided into two subgroups: those which end in [ɪ] or [ʊ] (so-called "closing diphthongs"), and those which end in the schwa-sound (so-called "centring diphthongs").

So-called "triphthongs" as in *fire, layer, royal, our,* and *lower,* where we have two position changes of the tongue, are generally considered as combinations of the respective (closing) diphthongs and the schwa-sound, and not as part of the English vowel system, which comprises 20 phonemes altogether.

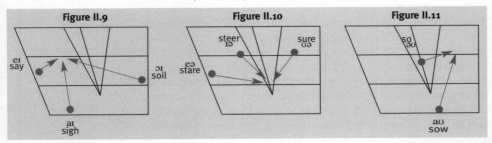

Figure II.9 Figure II.10 Figure II.11

In the classification of vowels, the main distinction is typically drawn between monophthongs and diphthongs, each with their respective subgroups. As Figure II.12 shows, however, it is just as well possible to give phonetic and phonological arguments for a different classification. In analogy to the fortis/lenis distinction for consonants, there is a tense/lax distinction for vowels. Tense vowels require greater muscle tension and are produced more peripherally; this is the case during the production of long vowels and diphthongs. The short vowels, on the other hand, belong to the group of lax vowels. This grouping cannot only be motivated by a phonetic, more exactly articulatory, criterion (degree of muscle tension), but also by the phonological criterion of distribution. Only tense vowels can occur in stressed open syllables, i.e. stressed syllables which do not end in one or more consonants (e.g. *fee* [fiː], but not [fɪ]); on the other hand, only lax vowels can precede the velar nasal [ŋ], e.g. [sɪŋ], but not [siːŋ].

tense/lax vowels

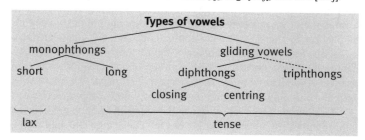

Figure II.12

2.1 On determining the phoneme inventory: Segmental phonology

II.2
Phonology

Unlike phonetics, phonology indisputably is an integral part of linguistics. It abstracts from the multitude of different sounds used in a language and is only interested in those sound units which fulfil a meaning-distinguishing (distinctive or contrastive) function within the sound system (therefore also the term "functional phonetics"). These abstract, idealized sound units are called "phonemes", and are defined as smallest meaning-distinguishing units of a language. They exist only in our minds, however, more exactly in our mental grammar; on the level of language use (*parole*), phonemes are always realized as phones.

There is almost always more than one phone which realizes a given phoneme. The relevant phones are called the "allophones" of the respective phoneme. Clear and dark /l/, for example [l] in *lip* and [ɫ] in *pill*, are the two best-known allophones of the lateral consonant phoneme of English; a third one is, for instance, the voiceless [l̥],

phoneme

allophones [l] [ɫ] [l̥]

which occurs regularly after [p] as the initial sound of stressed syllables (e. g. in *place* or *please*). To be more precise, the phonetic transcription of this allophone would need to look like this [pʰ], since at the beginning of a syllable the voiceless bilabial plosive is aspirated, especially when vowels follow. However, this is not the case for all allophones of the phoneme /p/; in syllable-final position, there is normally no aspiration (*lap, rap, tap*). If an additional [t] follows, as in *apt* or *captain*, the closure is not even released, as is normally the case for plosives: the resulting sound is the non-released voiceless bilabial plosive [p̚].

complementary distribution

In the vast majority of cases, it is predictable in which phonological environment which allophone of a phoneme will be used. This is known as complementary distribution of allophones, i.e. normally they never occur in the same environment; thus, a given allophone cannot simply be replaced by one of the other allophones. In contradistinction to these so-called "contextual variants", there are also numerous free variants of phonemes. For instance, voiceless plosives may well be aspirated in the final position of a syllable or word, too, as in [læp] and [læpʰ] for *lap*, or [ʃʌt] and [ʃʌtʰ] for *shut*. We are dealing with free variation of aspirated and non-aspirated allophones here.

free variation

The all-important method for determining the phonemes (versus (allo-)phones) of a language is the so-called "minimal pair test". Minimal pairs are pairs of meaning-carrying units which differ in exactly one sound, but apart from that have an identical sequence of sounds. More exactly, such pairs qualify as minimal pairs only if they additionally differ in their meaning. Since the meaning difference is only due to the sound difference, and thus the difference between the two relevant sounds is distinctive, these two sounds must be ascribed phoneme status. For example, on the basis of the minimal pairs in (5a) and the series of minimal pairs (minimal set) in (5b), the following phonemes of English can be determined: /t/, /p/, /r/, /f/, /e/, /æ/, /iː/, /ɪ/ and /aɪ/.

minimal pairs

(5) a. ten-pen, time-rhyme, try-fry   b. set-sat-seat-sit-site

A minimal pair test thus consists of (a) substituting exactly one sound in a sequence of sounds by another, and (b) answering the question whether this substitution has resulted in a change of meaning of this sound sequence, that is whether the result is a different word. If the answer is positive, we are dealing with a minimal pair, and a single minimal pair suffices for the identification of two phonemes. If, on the other hand, we look at phonetically contrasting pairs like [læp] and [læpʰ], or the post-alveolar /r/ of RECEIVED PRONUNCIATION and the retroflex /r/ of GENERAL AMERICAN, we are inevitably led to the conclusion that we are merely concerned with different phonetic realisations of the same phoneme here.

distinctive features

In connection with the distinction between phonemes and allophones, a further central term of phonology becomes relevant, namely distinctive features. Similar to the way we proceeded in the phonetic description of the various types of sounds, phonemes can alternatively be defined as bundles of distinctive features. The phoneme /p/ could thus be described as a bundle of the features [+CONSONANT, -VOICED, -NASAL, +LABIAL, +CLOSURE, +PLOSIVE], different from, for example, the nasal /n/ with its features [+CONSONANT, +VOICED, +NASAL, -LABIAL, +CLOSURE, -PLOSIVE]. In these two examples, the important aspects from a phonological point of view are that for /p/ aspiration does not figure as a distinctive feature (precisely because it is not distinctive, i.e. not capable of bringing about a change in meaning), and that for /n/ the feature [+VOICED] is superfluous (or: redundant) since all English nasals are voiced. This is important

phonological systems

because it applies to the English sound system, but not necessarily to the sound systems of other languages. In Hindi, for example, a language spoken in India, aspirated and non-aspirated /p/ are two independent phonemes forming minimal pairs. This shows that a (meaning-wise) redundant sound difference in one language can perfectly well be a distinctive sound difference in another language. As far as the English nasals are concerned, there is something else we can learn: a combination of certain distinctive features may be impossible in the sound system of one language (e.g. the feature [+NASAL] in combination with [-VOICED]), things can be totally different in another language, though. Thus, the phoneme system of Burmese includes, besides the 'normal' inventory of voiced nasals, the corresponding set of voiceless nasals, namely /m̥, n̥, ŋ̊/. Or take Welsh with its voiceless lateral phoneme /ɬ/, which is furthermore a fricative (e. g. in *Llewellyn*). In English, on the other hand, the combination of [+LATERAL] and [+FRICATIVE] is impossible, even for an allophone of /l/. The sound systems (or: phonological systems) of languages thus differ with regard to the combinatory possibilities of certain features, which necessarily leads to differences in their phoneme inventories.

phonotactics

Phonology, however, does not only deal with those restrictions which concern the combination of distinctive features, but also with restrictions concerning the combination of phonemes in a language (so-called "phonotactic restrictions"). Relevant examples are ⟨ps-⟩ – /s-/, as in *psychology*, or ⟨kn-⟩ – /n-/, as in *knight*. This branch of phonology is called "phonotactics" (Greek *phone* = sound, *taxis* = order). It essentially deals with the possible combinations of consonants (so-called "consonant clusters") at the beginning or end of a syllable or word.

The most general definition of the English syllable from a phonotactic point of view is the following: (CCC) V (CCCC), i.e. a syllable consists of a vowel as core or nucleus (/aɪ/ *I*, *eye*), which can be preceded by up to three consonants (/spraɪ/ *spry*, /stjuː/ *stew*), and followed by up to four consonants (/teksts/ *texts*, /glɪmpst/ *glimpsed*). Impossible at the beginning of a syllable (i.e. the onset) are, for example, /ŋ/ or combinations of a liquid /l, r/ or semi-vowel /w, j/ with other consonants; the same is true for /h, w, j/ and the RP /r/ at the end of a syllable (i.e. the coda). In general, longer consonant clusters are possible in the coda of a syllable in English than in the onset. Two types of syllables are distinguished: open syllables end in a vowel, whereas closed syllables end in a consonant.

2.2 Prosody: Supra-segmental phonology

Phonology not only deals with the phoneme system of a language, and the properties and possibilities of combinations of phonemes. It also deals with phenomena like stress (or: accent), rhythm, and intonation, which all belong to the domain of prosody. Prosodic (or: supra-segmental) phonology is concerned with those phonetic features that extend over more than one phoneme (segment). With regard to stress, rhythm, and intonation, the most important relevant features are breath pressure (or from a perceptual point of view: loudness), length and pitch. *Tonhöhe*

In English, fixed word stress exists only in the sense that, apart from a few exceptions (e.g. *advertisement*), a given word is always stressed on the same syllable. There is, however, no general rule of word stress placement according to which, for example, the (main or primary) stress of words is generally placed on a particular syllable, e.g. the first (Finnish), the penultimate (Welsh), or the last syllable (French). Instead word stress in English varies, even though partly according to predictable principles. Here, the so-called "mixed vocabulary" of English plays a major role (cf. chapter III), that is the fact that, besides its inherited Germanic word stock, English also borrowed many words and word formation elements mainly from French, Latin, and Greek. Thus, words of Germanic origin are frequently stressed on

Margin diagrams:

syllable
— open /tiː/
— closed /tiːm/

onset / coda = beginning / end of syllable

stress
— word stress
— sentence stress

the first syllable of the root (*'father*, *'fatherly*), which is mostly not the case for polysyllabic words of French and Latin origin (*pa'ternal*). Words with particular (borrowed) endings are always stressed on the last syllable before the ending (*a'tomic*, *develop'mental*, *natio'nality*), or even on the last syllable (e.g. *-ee* in *trai'nee*).

Another, more important property of English on the word level is that stress alone can be distinctive. As a consequence, there are quite many minimal pairs which are based solely on a difference in stress placement. Compare the noun/verb pairs in (6), the adjective/noun pairs or adjective/verb pairs in (7), as well as the examples in (8), where it is stress which distinguishes compounds from phrases in which an adjective precedes a noun (cf. also chapter III.3.2).

(6)	object N	/'ɒbdʒekt/	object V	/əb'dʒekt/
	subject N	/'sʌbdʒekt/	subject V	/səb'dʒekt/
	survey N	/'sɜːveɪ/	survey V	/sɜː'veɪ/
(7)	content A	/kən'tent/	content N	/'kɒntənt/
	invalid A	/ɪn'vælɪd/	invalid N	/'ɪnvəlɪd/
	alternate A	/ɔːl'tɜːnət/	alternate V	/'ɔːltəneɪt/
(8)	'blackbird N	versus	'black 'bird (A + N)	
	'blackboard N	versus	'black 'board (A + N)	
	'English teacher N	versus	'English 'teacher (A + N)	

As can be seen in the examples in (6) and (7), stress-shift typically goes hand in hand with a change of the vowel quality. In unstressed syllables, the vowel quality is reduced (or: weakened), mostly to a schwa /ə/, otherwise to /ɪ/, which is why these two are the most frequently occurring vowels in English.

This phenomenon is also typical of stress in connected speech. Reduction, and in extreme cases, the total omission (elision) of vowels is found particularly frequently for function words (e.g. auxiliaries, prepositions, conjunctions, pronouns). Especially for this group of words we need to distinguish between strong and weak forms. When reading aloud *and*, *of* and *some* as isolated dictionary entries, they would come out as /ænd/, /ɒv/ and /sʌm/, respectively. If, however, we listen closely to how these function words are actually pronounced in spontaneous speech, the relevant transcriptions would look as follows: for *some* /səm, sm/, for *of* /əv, v/, and for *and* /ənd, ən/ or /n/ – clearly to be seen in *Guns 'N Roses,* the name of a famous rock band in the late 1980s and 1990s. From a phonetic perspective, function

strong/weak forms

words share the properties that they mostly consist of only one syllable and that (in so-called "unmarked utterances") they are normally unstressed. Of course, it is also possible to put heavy stress on these words, as in *Frank AND George went to the cinema*. Such cases of contrastive stress are rather the exception, however. The appropriate use of weak forms is important for a naturally sounding spoken English, and it has to be given special attention in the training of future teachers of English at university, particularly when it comes to transcriptions.

The reduction of unstressed syllables resulting in weak forms immediately leads on to the perhaps most important property of English with regard to rhythm, namely "stress-timing". This term describes the tendency of two stressed syllables in an English utterance to occur at fairly equal intervals of time, no matter how many unstressed syllables there are in between. Alternatively, this phenomenon of isochrony can be described with the help of the term "foot". A foot is the basic rhythmic unit which exhibits various regular patterns of sequences of stressed and unstressed syllables. In languages displaying isochrony, a foot starts out with a stressed syllable and comprises all (unstressed) syllables up to the next stressed syllable. Isochrony therefore means that in the relevant language, feet are approximately of the same length. The most important means for achieving isochrony are the lengthening of stressed syllables and, above all, the reduction of unstressed syllables. For the sentence *Frank and George went to the cinema*, uttered at normal speech speed and with an unmarked intonation contour, it would thus be claimed that the polysyllabic feet /'fræŋk (ə)n/, /'went tə ðə/ and /'sɪnəmə/ are about as long as the foot /'dʒɔːdʒ/ taken by itself:

(9) //'Frank and/'George/'went to the/'cinema//

This, at least, is the perceptual impression a hearer of English gets. Isochrony is not measurable. It cannot be quantitatively proved in a phonetic laboratory; we therefore speak of "subjective" isochrony. For this reason, the classification of languages based on this parameter into stress-timed (e.g. English, Russian, less distinctly also German), and syllable-timed languages (e.g. French, Spanish, Italian) should be taken with a pinch of salt. In syllable-timed languages all syllables are said to occur at roughly the same intervals of time. However, all that is certain is that in such languages the syllable structure is simpler, that there is no tendency, for example, of condensing unstressed syllables (e.g. by means of reduction), and that word stress is not phonemic, thus not grammatically distinctive (i.e. there are no minimal pairs of the type '*abstract* noun/adjective – ab'*stract* verb).

While rhythm has to do with the distribution of stressed syllables in the normal speech flow, intonation (or: speech melody, pitch) relates to the distinctive use of pitch movements in an utterance and its organisation into prosodic units (or: tone groups).

intonation

The choice of a pitch movement fulfils a number of very important functions, especially grammatical, pragmatic, and attitudinal or emotional functions. The distinction between sentence types belongs to the grammatical functions, e.g. falling intonation in statements and exclamations (*She's a teacher. She's a teacher!*), and rising intonation in many interrogative sentences (as in an echo question like *She's a teacher?*). The organization into prosodic units often marks syntactic units (phrases, clauses, sentences), like the difference between restrictive relative clauses (*The man who was sitting behind the driver looked out of the window*) and non-restrictive relative clauses (*The man, who was sitting behind the driver, looked out of the window*; cf. chapter IV.2.3). As far as grammar is concerned, intonation plays a similar role in spoken language as punctuation does in written language. The central pragmatic function of intonation is information structuring, above all signalling the information status (new information versus information which is old or which can reasonably be assumed to be part of the general background knowledge; cf. also chapter V.2.2), primarily of course in close interaction with the placement of the sentence stress, i.e. emphasis put on a particular syllable in an utterance. Compare *SAMpras lost* (as an answer to the question: *Who lost the match?*) with *Sampras LOST* (as an answer to the question: *What about Sampras? Did he win again?*). Perhaps the most important function of the various pitch movements, however, is the expression of attitudes, moods, and emotions (e.g. enthusiasm, surprise, interest, sarcasm, impatience, compassion, rage). In this respect, intonation is a much more reliable key to the speaker's true attitude to particular facts than the literal (word and sentence) meaning of what has been said. Just compare the clearly rising intonation contour in the honest praise in (10a) with the clearly falling one in the sarcastic praise in (10b).

functions of intonation

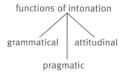

grammatical | attitudinal
pragmatic

(10) a. What a great iDEA! b. WHAT a great idea!

The unit of analysis in intonation research is the so-called "intonation" or "tone group", which on the grammatical level most often corresponds to a clause or a phrase. It consists of a syllable which carries the main stress, known as the "nucleus", and optionally of unstressed and less heavily stressed syllables preceding or following the nucleus. In (11a) the nucleus is framed exclusively by unstressed syllables, in (11b) three unstressed and two stressed syllables precede the nucleus:

(11)	a.	It's im	POS	sible!	
	b.	My 'mo ther 'ne ver	TOLD	me!	

As these two examples show, the nucleus normally falls on the last stressed syllable of an intonation group, thus it is only followed by one or several unstressed syllables. An important means of signalling the boundaries of intonation groups are those pauses which coincide with syntactic units, in particular with the boundaries between clauses (*When she saw me / she left*) and between subject, predicate, and adverbial complements (*The Prime Minister of Great Britain / will soon meet the German Chancellor / at Downing Street No 10*).

We can roughly distinguish between five main nuclear tones (nuclei) in English (marked by means of bold type in (12)), which again can be further differentiated. The most important points in this respect are the direction of the pitch movement (fall, rise, or level), and the possibility of a further change of the pitch direction after the nucleus, which leads to complex nuclear tones (e.g. fall-rise, or rise-fall). For a more precise description, the onset (high, mid, or low) is specified relative to the pitch range. Each of these main nuclear tones and their variants can roughly be assigned certain properties and functions:

(12) fall `

- *high fall:* contrastive sentence stress; strong emotional involvement
- *low fall:* most neutral nucleus, e.g. in affirmative clauses; cold and distanced
- *full fall:* emotionally involved (the higher the onset of the tone, the more involved is the speaker)

rise ´

- *high rise:* non-emphatic *yes/no*-questions, often used in echoing what has just been said, emphatic *why*-questions; mild query or puzzlement; in spontaneous narratives, increasingly also in affirmative sentences. *So we stand there for a long time* ↑ *and then wander into class* ↑ *about five minutes late.* ↑

⌐ *low rise:*	enumerations, requests, incomplete utterances
⌐ *full rise:*	emotionally involved (the lower the onset of the tone, the more involved is the speaker; 11a)
⌐ **fall-rise** ˇ	a strongly emotional tone; doubt, insecurity, hesitation, but also encouragement
⌐ **rise-fall** ˆ	strong emotional involvement; can express insecurity, enthusiasm, surprise, irony (11b)
⌐ **level** ⁻	boredom, irony, sarcasm; similar to *low rise*

These or similar types of nuclear tones should occur for all intonation languages (and thus essentially for all European languages). In general, the pitch contour in these languages is relevant only on the phrase and sentence level: It fulfils no distinctive function on the word level, i.e. it has no influence on the word meaning, or at least only in a relatively small number of cases (e.g. in Swedish). This is different in so-called "tone languages", which form the majority of languages in the world (e.g. in Chinese, in South-Asian and African languages) and where in many cases the pitch contour alone determines the word meaning. Thus, depending on the pitch contour, the phoneme sequence /ma/ in Mandarin Chinese can have as different meanings as e.g. 'mother' and 'horse'.

intonation languages

tone languages

2.3 Phonological processes in connected speech

At the end of this chapter, let us return to the weak forms of spoken English once more. They showed very clearly that it can make a big difference whether a word is pronounced by itself or as part of a phrase or whole utterance in a natural speech situation. As we have seen, vowel reduction and elision of sounds, in particular, are typical of weak forms. There are several more such phenomena in so-called "connected speech", i.e. utterances which consist of more than one word. The most important of these are assimilation, intrusion, and liaison. As far as elision is concerned, it is important to add that the regular omission of post-vocalic /r/ at the end of a syllable in RP (the so-called /r/-dropping in *car* or *card*) as well as the regular omission of /h/ at the beginning of a syllable in various regional accents (the so-called /h/-dropping, e.g. in Cockney *'otel*, *'is*) cannot be given as examples here. In both cases, the omission of the sound can already be observed in isolated, context-free pronunciation of words, and thus

connected speech

does not qualify as a phenomenon of connected speech but rather belongs to the domain of phonotactics.

assimilation

Things are completely different for assimilation. By assimilation we understand the process by which, especially in (rapid) spoken language, immediately neighbouring sounds are becoming more alike with regard to one or more articulatory features (partial assimilation in (13a)), in extreme cases even identical (total assimilation in (13b)).

partial assimilation

(13) a. width [wɪd̪θ], eighth [eɪt̪θ], tenth [ten̪θ], ten bikes /tem 'baɪks/
b. spaceship /'speɪʃʃɪp/, ten mice /tem 'maɪs/

In (13a) the first three are examples of dental allophones of the alveolar plosives /d/, /t/ and /n/, i.e. the tongue in these examples touches the back of the front teeth in anticipation, as it were, of the place of articulation of the following fricative. In the fourth example in (13a), the alveolar nasal in *ten* becomes a bilabial nasal due to the following bilabial /b/ in *bikes*. In (13b) the preceding sound even becomes completely identical to the following sound. All examples in (13) are characteristic of assimilation in English, in so far as in the great majority of cases assimilation is regressive. Alternatively, we also speak of anticipatory assimilation, since during the articulation of the preceding sound the speech organs already anticipate the articulation of the following sound. We are thus dealing with what is also known as coarticulation, which is essentially responsible for allophony, and ultimately founded in language economy (Least Effort Principle). On top of this, the examples in (13a) are characteristic, since in English assimilation usually affects the place of articulation; in other words, there is a clear tendency towards homorganic sounds. Besides regressive assimilation as the prototype of assimilation, there are also the rather rare types of progressive assimilation (/s/ to /ʃ/ in *lunch score* /'lʌntʃ ʃkɔː/) and reciprocal assimilation, where the two sounds concerned fuse and produce a third one (/t/ and /j/ to /tʃ/ in *don't you* /'dəuntʃʊ/ or /s/ and /j/ to /ʃ/ in *kiss you* /'kɪʃuː/).

anticipatory assimilation

coarticulation

progressive and regressive assimilation

Figure II.13

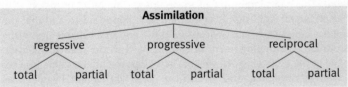

Assimilation					
regressive		progressive		reciprocal	
total	partial	total	partial	total	partial

While elision and assimilation are very widespread phenomena, only relatively few examples can be given for intrusion and liaison. The best-known cases of these two connected speech phenomena in English (above all in such accents as RP) are the so-called "intrusive" /r/ (cf. *law and order* /'lɔːʳən(d)'ɔːdə/, *Asia and America* /'eɪʒəʳən(d) 'ə'merɪkə/), and the so-called "linking" /r/ (in *My car is gone.* /maɪ 'kaːʳɪz'gɒn/). The two processes have in common that in connected speech a sound is added which is absent when the relevant word(s) is/are pronounced in isolation. Moreover, both processes prevent the core vowels of two immediately neighbouring syllables from directly following each other. Instead, an /r/ is added to the second (normally unstressed) syllable, by means of which the utterance gains in 'fluidity', as it were. The difference between intrusion and liaison is that in the case of intrusion this addition is justified neither historically nor orthographically.

Checklist Phonetics and Phonology – key terms and concepts

approximant (semi-vowel / glide, liquid)

articulator (active ↔ passive)

aspiration

assimilation (regressive / anticipatory ↔ progressive ↔ reciprocal; total ↔ partial)

cardinal vowels

coarticulation

complementary distribution ↔ free variation

connected speech

consonant (obstruent ↔ sonorant; roll, lateral; *fortis* ↔ *lenis*; consonant cluster)

contrastive stress

distinctive ↔ redundant

distinctive feature

elision

foot

homorganic sound

International Phonetic Alphabet

intonation

isochrony

linking /r/ ↔ intrusive /r/

manner of articulation

minimal pair (minimal pair analysis)

obstruent (affricate, fricative, plosive)

phone, phoneme, allophone

phonetics (articulatory, acoustic, auditory)

phonological system

phonology (segmental ↔ suprasegmental)

phonotactics

prosody

Received Pronunciation ↔ General American

reduction

rhythm (stress-timing ↔ syllable-timing)

sequential restriction

sonorant (liquids, nasal, roll, lateral)

stop (nasal ↔ plosive)

stress

stress-timing

strong form ↔ weak form

syllable

transcription: phonetic (narrow ↔ broad) ↔ phonemic

universal

velum

vocal folds

vowel (short ↔ long; front ↔ back; monophthong, diphthong, triphthong; tense ↔ lax; schwa; quality ↔ quantity)

vowel chart

1 Figures a-d illustrate four of the following places of articulation: alveolar, bilabial, dental, labio-dental, palatal, palato-alveolar, velar.

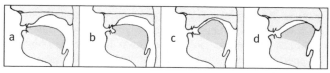

a. Identify the correct place of articulation for each of the four figures.

b. Provide for each place of articulation the phonetic symbol of two sounds which are produced at this place.

2 a. Provide a broad phonetic transcription of the noun *linguistics* and describe the consonants in their order of occurrence using the following four parameters: vocal fold action, state of the soft palate, place of articulation, manner of articulation.

b. Which of these consonants are homorganic?

c. Which of the sounds in linguistics are obstruents, which ones sonorants?

3 a. Identify the vowel sound(s) in each of the following words using Gimson's transcription model:

toad   tour   toy   tea   toe   tear   tray   tire
Teddy Timmy Tammy Tommy tummy

b. Classify the gliding vowels in these words.

4 a. Provide the phonemic symbols for those of the following descriptions that relate to sounds belonging to the sound system of RP:

a. voiced bilabial plosive   e. voiced velar nasal
b. voiceless velar dental   f. rounded high front vowel
c. lax high back vowel   g. voiced bilabial semi-vowel
d. voiced dental fricative   h. voiceless lateral fricative

b. Which description(s) is/are completely nonsensical?

5 a. Correct the errors in the following RP transcriptions (one error per word):

leave /liːf/   flash /fleʃ/   start /stɑːrt/
bingo /ˈbɪŋgəʊ/   unique /juˈnɪk/   other /ʌθə/
question /ˈkvestʃn̩/   emergency /ɪˈmɜːtʃənsɪ/ path /pæθ/

b. Which of these are errors most likely to be made by German learners of English? (More on this in chapter V.)

6 Which of the following words would be treated as minimal pairs?
ten, live, Maus, hippo, hen, tin, tale, leaf, pin, rose, lose, hippie,
house, tail, tooth, smooth, love, thief

7 In each of the following groups the phonemes share one or more
common properties; but in each group there is one phoneme
which does not belong to the group. Identify the phoneme and
specify in which respect(s) it is different from the rest of the group.

a. /f, p, m, θ, v, b/
b. /æ, uː, ɪ, e, ʊ, ə/
c. /z, v, s, ʒ, g/
d. /eɪ, aɪ, aʊ, ɔɪ, ɪə/
e. /m, n, g, d, p/
f. /l, r, w, ʒ/
g. /n, l, s, ʃ, z/
h. /ɔː, iː, ɪə, r, j, æ, l, ŋ, ɒ, aʊ/
i. /g, k, b, d, p, v, t/
j. /uː, iː, ɒ, ɔː, ɑː/

8 Which of the following statements are true, which are false?
a. Hard palate and vocal folds are active articulators.
b. [pʰɛ̃n] represents a narrow phonetic transcription of *pen*.
c. The majority of English sounds is produced with the velum
raised.
d. English lacks rounded back vowels.
e. Liquids and semi-vowels belong to the same large class of
sounds.
f. Voiced plosives are generally aspirated in syllable-initial
position.
g. One minimal pair is sufficient for establishing two given
sounds of a language as phonemes.
h. Stress in English is phonemic.
i. [s] and [ʃ] as realizations of the second consonant in *associate*
are instances of free variation.
j. In English stressed syllables tend to be compressed and
reduced.

Exercises
Advanced

9 We can perceive a noticeable difference in vowel quantity in the
following pairs:
tag – tack, league – leak, rude – root, ridge – rich, ride – rite,
plays – place, rib – rip, bud – but, love – laugh, use (V) – use (N)
a. Describe this difference.
b. Try to find a generalization concerning the environment which
seems to trigger this variation in vowel quantity.

10 Consider the realization of the negative prefix in the following words:

inadequate /ɪn'ædɪkwət/, incomplete /ˌɪŋkəm'pliːt/, impossible /ɪm'pɒsɪb(ə)l/, immobile /ɪ'məʊbaɪl/, illegal /ɪ'liːgəl/

a. Which process is responsible for this variation in form?

b. What exactly is responsible for the nasal and the following sound becoming more alike or even identical?

c. What do the above examples have in common with the pronunciation of *thin* /θɪn/ and *thing* /θɪŋ/?

11 Liaison and intrusion of /r/ are frequently observable in RP and other English accents without a postvocalic /r/, so-called non-rhotic accents. Can you imagine, though, why no intrusion is to be observed in any of the following cases? Could it be that there is a link between intrusion and liaison?

he is */hiːˈɪz/, true is */truːˈɪz/, way is */weɪˈɪz/, why is */waɪˈɪz/, toy is */tɔɪˈɪz/, how is */haʊˈɪz/

12 We said that English has a certain rhythm.

a. What exactly is this rhythm said to involve? Illustrate your answer with the help of the following example where stressed syllables are indicated by capitals.

When my MOther came HOME, she WENT into the KITchen, OPENED the FRIDGE and TOOK out a YOghurt.

b. Identify the intonation units in the example above and show that in English the nucleus tends to fall on the last stressed syllable.

c. Do you have any ideas as to the word class(es) which the word with this last stressed syllable tends to belong to? Can you make anything out of the so-called *Last Lexical Item* rule in English?

Sources and further reading

Anderson, Stephen R. 1985. *Phonology in the twentieth century*. Chicago: Chicago University Press.

Clark, John/Colin Yallop. 1995[2]. *An introduction to phonetics and phonology*. Oxford: Blackwell.

Cruttenden, Alan. 1986. *Intonation*. Cambridge: Cambridge University Press.

Crystal, David. 1997[4]. *A dictionary of linguistics and phonetics*. Oxford: Blackwell.

Giegerich, Heinz J. 1992. *English phonology*. Cambridge: Cambridge University Press.

Gimson, Alfred C. 1996[5]. *An introduction to the pronunciation of English*. Rev. by Alan Cruttenden. London: Arnold.

Goldsmith, John A. 1989. *Autosegmental and metrical phonology: A new synthesis*. Oxford: Blackwell.

Hardcastle, W.J./John Laver, eds. 1999. *Handbook of phonetic sciences*. Oxford: Blackwell.

Jacobs, Haike/Carlos Gussenhoven. 1998. *Understanding phonology*. London: Arnold.

Ladd, Dwight Robert. 1996. *Intonational phonology*. Cambridge: Cambridge University Press.

Ladefoged, Peter. 2001[4]. *A course in phonetics*. Fort Worth: Harcourt College Publishers.

Lass, Roger. 1984. *Phonology: An introduction to basic concepts*. Cambridge: Cambridge University Press.

Laver, John. 1994. *Principles of phonetics*. Cambridge: Cambridge University Press

O'Connor, Joseph D. 1988[2]. *Better English pronunciation*. Cambridge: Cambridge University Press.

Shockey, Linda. 2002. *Sound patterns of spoken English*. Oxford: Blackwell.

Upton, Clive/W.A. Kretzschmar Jr/Rafal Konopka. 2001. *The Oxford Dictionary of Pronunciation for Current English*. Oxford: Oxford University Press.

Wells, John C. 1982 [1995]. *Accents of English, Vol. 1: An Introduction*. Cambridge: Cambridge University Press.

Wells, John. C. 1990. *Longman pronunciation dictionary*. Harlow: Longman.

Windsor Lewis, J. 1972. *Concise dictionary of British and American English*. London: Oxford University Press.

III Morphology: On the structure and formation of words

Introduction

"Morphology" – incidentally a term coined by Johann Wolfgang von Goethe and originally used in the sciences for the study of the form and structure of living organisms – is concerned with the internal structure of words and with the various processes which allow us to constantly enlarge the vocabulary of a language. The basic morphological unit, however, is not the word, but the morpheme (Greek *morphe* shape, form), the smallest meaning-bearing unit of language. Thus, the word *singers* contains three morphemes: *sing*, *-er*, and *-s*. Each of these three morphemes adds to the overall meaning of *singers*: the verb *sing* makes the central contribution, while *-er* on its own means no more than 'someone who VERBs', and the *-s* merely gives grammatical information, namely plural. This simple example shows that we can distinguish between different types of morphemes. It is a widespread convention in linguistics to put morphemes in curly brackets, e.g. {SING}, {Plural}; however, most of the time this convention can be dispensed with without a loss of clarity.

On the level of morphology, morphemes are the exact counterpart to phonemes on the level of phonology. Just like phonemes, morphemes are abstract units which can be realized by more than one form. Just think of the plural morpheme in word forms like *kids, kits*, and *kisses*, where it is realised as /-z/, /-s/, and /-ɪz/ respectively. These concrete realizations of morphemes are called "morphs", and in analogy to the allophones of a phoneme we speak of the allomorphs of a morpheme (more on this in chapter III.2).

What is a word?

The example *singers* also shows how important it is to deal with the term *word* in a more differentiated way. Is *singers* a different word from *singer*? No, *singers* is merely a different form, a so-called "word form", of the noun *singer*. *Singer* itself, on the other hand, is not merely a word form of *sing* but a different, new word, which has been formed by affixation of -er to the verb. In this case, we speak of a new **lexeme** with a new dictionary entry which has been created by a specific derivational process. And what about *sing* itself: is it a word, a lexeme, or a morpheme? Three times yes: *sing* is a morpheme that can occur on its own (a so-called "free morpheme"); it denotes something in the extra-linguistic, i.e. real world, in this case a particular action or activity; it has an entry in the dictionary, and thus qualifies as a lexeme; and it is a word, if we adopt the prototypical use of *word* in everyday language. The example *sing* furthermore shows that words do not have to have an internal structure: it merely consists of one morpheme. The fact that *sing*, besides being monomorphemic, is also monosyllabic is irrelevant in this context: we need to keep syllable structure and morphological structure strictly apart. Just as monosyllabic words can consist of more than one morpheme (e.g. *sings, toys, loved*), polysyllabic words can perfectly well be monomorphemic (e.g. *finger, water, believe*). Morpheme boundaries are often not identical with syllable boundaries.

III.1
Types of morphemes

Essentially, morphemes can be classified according to three criteria:
• autonomy
• function/meaning
• position

autonomy

Autonomy relates to the question of whether a particular morpheme can occur on its own (*sing*), or whether it always needs to be attached to another morpheme (-*er*). According to this criterion we distinguish between free morphemes and bound morphemes (or: affixes).

function / meaning

The all-important question we have to ask ourselves in relation to the function or meaning of morphemes is whether they convey lexical or grammatical information (e.g. plural, case, tense). Depending on the answer, we distinguish between two kinds of bound morphemes: derivational and inflectional morphemes. The former create new lexemes via affixation (e.g. -er in *singer, painter, worker*), whereas the latter merely produce word forms (e.g. -s in *singers* or in *sings*; for more information on the English inflectional morphemes see chapter IV.1). Among the free morphemes, we have to distinguish between two major groups (cf. also chapter IV.2): on the one hand, there are free morphemes which belong to one of the so-called "lexical word classes" (essentially nouns, verbs, and adjectives), and, on the other hand, there are those kinds of free morphemes which belong to one of the grammatical or functional word classes (articles, pronouns, prepositions, conjunctions, auxiliaries, etc.). Lexical morphemes (or: content words) establish a relation between language and the world, among other things by denoting persons and objects (nouns), actions and situations of all kinds (verbs), and properties of persons and things (adjectives). Function words, on the other hand, have a purely language-internal (grammatical) meaning. This contrast is often also described in terms of "autosemantic" vs "synsemantic" words (Greek *autos* = self, *syn* = with, together with, *semainein* = to signify, mean). Moreover, these two types of word classes differ with respect to two further properties. The functional word classes are largely closed, i.e. the spontaneous creation of neologisms in this area is practically impossible, and it takes considerably more time to enlarge the inventory of function words than to coin new words in the lexical word classes. Besides, function words are typically not stressed in connected speech, so that the distinction between strong and weak forms (e.g. *and* /ænd/ - /ən/, *have* /hæv/ - /həv, v/) is mainly relevant for this type of free morphemes (cf. chapter II.2.2). Within limits, both of these differences between content and function words are also valid for derivational as opposed to inflectional affixes.

    The third main criterion for the classification of morphemes can only be applied to bound morphemes. It refers to the position of the relevant bound morpheme relative to the modified part of the word (base, root, or stem). If the affix precedes the base, it qualifies as a prefix (e.g. *inadequate, enclose*), if it follows the base, we are dealing with a suffix (e.g. *soften, sings*). English prefixes are exclusively used for the derivation of new lexemes, whereas suffixes are used for both derivation and inflection.

autosemantic terms
synsemantic terms

position

prefix

suffix

Figure III.1

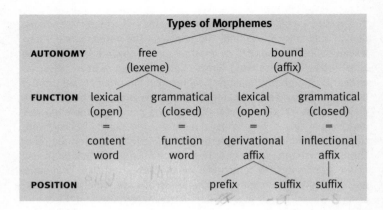

Types of Morphemes

AUTONOMY	free (lexeme)		bound (affix)	
FUNCTION	lexical (open) = content word	grammatical (closed) = function word	lexical (open) = derivational affix	grammatical (closed) = inflectional affix
POSITION			prefix suffix	suffix

special types

portmanteau morphs

With the help of the diagram in Figure III.1 we can capture the majority of morphemes. As always, there are a number of special cases. Among these are the following two: unique morphemes and so-called portmanteau morph(eme)s. We talk about "portmanteau morph(eme)s", a term which goes back to Lewis Carroll, author of *Alice in Wonderland*, in the rather frequently occurring cases in which a particular morph instantiates more than one morpheme at the same time, i.e. has several different meanings (similar to the way in which we can put more than one piece of clothing into a *portmanteau* 'suitcase'). The /-s/ in *he sings*, for example, indicates third person, singular, present tense, and indicative mood simultaneously. There are languages in which each of these four pieces of grammatical information is coded by a separate morph (see chapter IV.1). *His* is another example. Here, one morph provides three different pieces of information: possessive pronoun, masculine, and singular. The term "portmanteau morphs" does not, however, apply to homonymous morphs (cf. chapter VI.3.3), like *-er*, which serves both as a derivational suffix deriving nouns from verbs (*sing+er, work+er*) and as an inflectional suffix forming the comparative of adjectives (*quick+er, fast+er*).

unique morphemes

Another type of morpheme, or more exactly morph, which the diagram in Figure III.1 does not capture are unique morphemes – a particular type of bound morphemes. The probably most famous examples in this context are the underlined morphemes in *cranberry*, *huckleberry*, and *boysenberry*. It is true that in all of these three cases, the second element *berry* makes clear that these nouns denote various kinds of berries. However, it remains completely unclear exactly which contribution the underlined morphemes make to the

88

overall meaning of these four words. This is because *cran*, *huckle*, and *boysen* do not exist in isolation, that is as free morphemes; they only exist as morphemes which are attached to *berry*, and modify the latter. Their semantic contribution seems to lie merely in the distinction of these sorts of berries from others (e.g. *strawberry, gooseberry, blueberry, blackberry*). However, although they only appear as bound morphemes, they cannot be referred to as affixes, since the different *berry*-terms are clearly compound words (cf. section III.3.2). Therefore, the conclusion must be drawn that in the case of the bound morphemes in these so-called "cranberry-words" we are dealing with bound roots or bound bases.

compounds

This leads us to a last terminological question: How do we call the part of a word to which affixes are attached? Different terms are in use: "base"–"root"–"stem". The safest, because most general term is base (here: $base_1$). For more fine-grained differentiations, the following guidelines, illustrated for the word form *removals* in (1), may serve as an orientation. What remains once all inflectional suffixes are taken away is the stem; what remains when taking away all affixes is the root, which is the minimal lexical unit and cannot be morphologically analysed any further; what remains in each case if the derivational affixes are taken away one by one from the stem is called the base in the narrower sense (here: $base_2$) – which is still larger than the root.

```
            base₁
          /   |   \
      stem  base₂  root
```

(1) a. stem: <u>removal</u>-s   b. root: re-<u>mov(e)</u>-al-s
         c. base : <u>remov(e)</u>-als   d. base : <u>removal</u>-s, <u>remov(e)</u>-als,
                                                    re-<u>mov(e)</u>-als

Thus, *move* alone can be $base_1$ (1d), root (1b), and stem *(move-s)*; this applies to any inflecting monomorphemic word which also produces derived lexemes.

In language, nothing happens in isolation. It is often difficult to draw neat distinctions because many things interact and move along a continuum. This is why the different levels of linguistic analysis (e.g. phonology, morphology, syntax) cannot be totally separated from one another. Rather, there are frequently interfaces. In this and the following chapter, we will get to know various such interfaces where two structural levels of language interact, for example the interface between morphology and syntax (chapter IV.1). Here, only the interface between morphology and phonology will be of interest for which

**III.2
Morphophonemics:
Interface between
morphology and
phonology**

morpho(pho)nology

the following two terms are established: "morpho(pho)nology", preferred in European linguistics, and "morphophonemics", preferred in Anglo-American linguistics. This branch of linguistics is concerned with the systematic phonological realisations of morphemes and how they depend on their respective environments.

Just recall the distinction between morpheme and allomorph made at the beginning of this chapter. We noted that morphemes are abstract units (thus located on the *langue* level) which, on the *parole* level, can perfectly well be instantiated by more than one morph. As an example, the plural morpheme was cited with its three most frequent allomorphs /-z/, /-s/, and /-ɪz/ (*kids, kits,* and *kisses*). It is not by accident that precisely these three are the most frequent allomorphs of the plural morpheme – and also of the possessive marker (*Jill's, Jack's, Joyce's*) and the inflectional morpheme {3rd person singular present indicative} for verbs (*she runs, walks, blushes*): they are predictable. We do not need to learn when we have to use which of these three allomorphs, since the relevant allomorph arises rather naturally from the phonological environment, more exactly from the final sound of the word stem. The regularity underlying the complementary distribution of these three allomorphs can be described as in (2):

> **(2)** /-ɪz/: after sibilants (or: hissing sounds),
>   i.e. /z/, /s/, /ʒ/, /ʃ/, /ʤ/, /ʧ/ ⟹ *rest*
> /-s/: after all other voiceless consonants, i.e. not for /s/, /ʃ/, /ʧ/
> /-z/: after all other voiced consonants and all vowels
>   (except for /z/, /ʒ/, /ʤ/)

Thus, here we have allomorphs that are phonologically conditioned. Fortunately enough, this type of conditioning of allomorphs is the normal option for the vast majority of words. In most cases we do not have to learn the various realisations of a morpheme by heart; and even if we encounter a word that is completely new to us (e.g. the invented items like *sloy, strack, spish*), we can fairly safely predict what its plural form will be (in our cases /slɔɪz/, /stræks/ and /spɪʃɪz/).

There are, however, up to three further kinds of conditioning of allomorphs distinguished in the literature – morphological, lexical, and grammatical conditioning. All three are unpredictable – in other words, phonological criteria are irrelevant at least from a synchronic perspective – and thus have to be learnt together with the corresponding root morpheme. Among those morphologists who make use of all three terms, some do indeed use them synonymously for what is essentially irregular, i.e. non-rule-based, conditioning of allomorphs. Others consider morphological conditioning as the super-ordinate type, with lexical and grammatical conditioning as two of its subtypes. The most extreme case of conditioning yielding irregular allomorphs is lexical conditioning, since it is restricted to individual lexemes. Here a particular lexical morpheme determines the shape of an allomorph, as in all examples in (3), i.e. information on the appropriate allomorphs needs to be stored and retrieved together with all the phonological, semantic, and syntactic information concerning this particular lexeme:

lexical conditioning

(3)	root	plural form	not:
	ox	ox-en /-ən/	*ox-es /-ız/
	mouse	mice	*mouse-s /-ız/
	foot	feet	*foot-s /-s/
	woman	women	*woman-s /-z/

In the case of *oxen*, the lexeme *ox* determines the choice of the plural allomorph /-ən/. In the other examples in (3), the root (or, more generally, base) allomorph itself is affected by the process of plural formation. In the former case, just as in all examples in (2), we speak of "suffix allomorphy" or, more generally, "affix allomorphy", in the latter case (as well as in (4) and (5) below) of "base allomorphy".

In principle, even cases in which a base undergoes a morpho-logical process (e.g. plural formation) without any formal change (*one sheep – two sheep*) can be qualified as affix allomorphy due to lexical conditioning. In such cases, we also speak of a "zero allomorph" (Ø); as a linguistic construct, it belongs to the allomorphs of the plural morpheme, but with certain irregular verbs, for example, it also belongs to the allomorphs of the morphemes {Past} and {Past Participle}, e.g. in *He (had) hit me before.*

zero allomorph

If a particular morpheme demands a special allomorph of another morpheme it combines with, this is called "morphological condition-ing". Take, for example, the two allomorphs of *courage*: ['kʌrɪdʒ] in the free morpheme, and [kə'reɪdʒ] as the (obligatorily bound) base of the adjective *courageous*. Here, the derivational suffix {-*ous*} triggers the choice of the allomorph [kə'reɪdʒ]. Or consider the examples in (4) and (5), where only in the morphological contexts of past and plural marking a special base allomorph needs to be chosen. Such cases of morphological conditioning, where an inflectional affix conditions the

morphological conditioning

choice of another allomorph (typically the base allomorph), are sometimes called grammatical conditioning.

(4)	a.	weep	/wiːp/	wep-t	/wep-/ + /-t/
		sleep	/sliːp/	slep-t	/slep-/ + /-t/
	b.	take	/teɪk/	took	/tʊk/
		shake	/ʃeɪk/	shook	/ʃʊk/
	c.	wake	/weɪk/	woke	/wəʊk/
		break	/breɪk/	broke	/brəʊk/
(5)		wife	/waɪf/	wives	/waɪv-/ + /-z/
		leaf	/liːf/	leaves	/liːv-/ + /-z/
		loaf	/ləʊf/	loaves	/ləʊv-/ + /-z/

The conditioning processes in (4) and (5) are restricted to small sets of lexemes, and could thus be argued to be lexically conditioned. However, it is after all the case that here small sets of lexemes undergo the same morphological process, and not individual lexemes without parallels elsewhere in the lexicon. So there is at least some regularity in the overall irregular behaviour when judged against all verbs and nouns of English. In extreme cases, the allomorph resulting from grammatical conditioning neither bears any resemblance to the root morpheme nor is it etymologically related to the latter. Among the best-known examples of what is known as suppletion (Lat. *supplere* = substitute, fill up, complete) figure *buy – bought* or *catch – caught* as instances of weak suppletion, and *good – better*, *bad – worse*, *go – went*, and *be – was* as instances of strong suppletion.

For the morphological analysis of English, we may conclude that the preferable option seems to be the use of "morphological conditioning" as a cover term for all types of conditioning yielding irregular allomorphs of either base or affix. In all the relevant cases, it is not the phonological context, but a specific morphological context that determines the choice of an allomorph: either a particular free morpheme, i.e. base, demands the choice of a particular (form of a) bound morpheme (affix allomorphy) or, vice versa, a particular affix (be it derivational or inflectional) demands the choice of a particular form of the base (base allomorphy).

Tab. III.1 Types of conditioning of allomorphs in English		
cause	**regularity**	**type of conditioning**
phonological environment	regular, rule-based	phonological conditioning
morphological environment	irregular	morphological conditioning
a) involving grammatical categories, notably inflectional morphemes	moderately irregular (small paradigm still possible, e.g. {Past} for (*weep, keep, sleep,* etc.)	grammatical conditioning
b) involving lexical base morphemes	completely irregular, not rule-based	lexical conditioning

But let us return to the phonological conditioning of allomorphs. This kind of conditioning is of course not only found with inflectional suffixes. As mentioned before, there are two types of allomorphy – affix allomorphy and base allomorphy, with the former subdivisible into suffix and prefix allomorphy. Exercise (10) in chapter II, for example, dealt with a notorious case of prefix allomorphy, more exactly phonological conditioning involving the allomorphs of the derivational prefix {IN-}, namely /ɪn-/, /ɪŋ-/ and /ɪm-/ in *inadequate, incomplete,* and *impossible* respectively. In chapter II we dealt with this well-known *homorganic nasal constraint* under the heading of 'assimilation'. For free morphemes, too, phonologically conditioned allomorphs may exist, both for function words (e.g. the indefinite article: *a* before words that begin with a consonant, *an* before words that begin with a vowel) and for lexical words (cf. the examples in (6) and (7)):

[margin notes:] allomorphs of bases / affix allomorphy / base allomorphy

(6)	electric	/ɪˈlektrɪk/	electric-ity	/ɪˌlekˈtrɪs-/ + /-ɪtɪ/
	electric	/ɪˈlektrɪk/	electric-ian	/ɪˌlekˈtrɪʃ-/ + /-ən/
	invade	/ɪnˈveɪd/	invas-ion	/ɪnˈveɪʒ-/ + /-(ə)n/
	part	/pɑːt/	part-ial	/pɑːʃ-/ + /-(ə)l/
	infuse	/ɪnˈfjuːz/	infus-ion	/ɪnˈfjuːʒ-/ + /-ən/
	convulse	/kənˈvʌls/	convuls-ion	/kənˈvʌlʃ-/ + /-(ə)n/

(7)	angel	/ˈeɪndʒel/	angel-ic	/ænˈdʒel-/ + /-ɪk/
	miracle	/ˈmɪrək(ə)l/	miracul-ous	/mɪˈræk-/ + /-jʊləs/
	particle	/ˈpɑːtɪkəl/	partic-ular	/pəˈtɪk-/ + /-jʊlə/
	photograph	/ˈfəʊtəˌɡrɑːf/	photograph-ic	/ˌfəʊtəˈɡræf-/ + /-ɪk/

In all of these examples, the phonological shape of the base morpheme has changed with respect to one or two sounds in the course of a derivational process, i.e. the formation of a new lexeme by means of affixation (here more precisely: suffixation) of a derivational morpheme. The reasons for this change are diverse. In (6), co-articulation or progressive assimilation is responsible for the consonant change in the final sound of the base from /k,t,d,s,z/ to /s,ʃ,ʒ/ before /ɪ/ or /j/. Apart from the change /k/ › /s/, examples like those in (6) are processes of palatalisation (/ʃ/ and /ʒ/ are palato-alveolar consonants). These palatalisation processes are productive. Also productive are the changes affecting the base vowels in (7), which are merely a result of the stress-shift triggered by the derivational process: just recall what was said about full vowel quality in stressed syllables and vowel reduction in unstressed ones in chapter II.2.2. While in (6) and (7) we are dealing with synchronically transparent consequences of phonetic and phonological processes, the examples in (8) go back to different historical developments of English and are no longer productive.

(8)	pronounce	/prə'naʊns/	pronunc-iation	/prə,nʌns-/ + /ɪ'eɪʃ(ə)n/
	profound	/prə'faʊnd/	profund-ity	/prə'fʌndɪtɪ/
	divine	/dɪ'vaɪn/	divin-ity	/dɪ'vɪn-/ + /-ɪtɪ/
	profane	/prə'feɪn/	profan-ity	/prə'fæn-/ + /-ɪtɪ/
	appear	/ə'pɪə/	appar-ent	/ə'pær-/ + /-ent/

The examples in (6) to (8) once again draw our attention to a distinctive property of the English vocabulary: the frequently changing phonological form of base morphemes as a consequence of derivational or inflectional processes. For many base morphemes of English there exist so-called morphophonemic alternants, that is formally similar allomorphs which differ from each other in at least one phoneme. {ELECTRIC}, for example, has three morphophonemic alternants: /ɪ'lektrɪk/ in *electric*, /ɪ,lek'trɪs/ in *electricity* and /ɪ,lek'trɪʃ/ in *electrician*.

morphophonemic alternants

III.3
Word formation processes

Essentially, morphology comprises two branches: word formation and inflection(al morphology). Word formation is concerned with the processes that expand the vocabulary of a language, i.e. create new lexemes, and will be our concern in the remainder of this chapter. Inflectional morphology, on the other hand, is concerned with the formation of word forms and with all those morphemes and processes

94

that allow grammatical information to be coded directly on the stem, above all by means of affixation. This branch is already part of grammar and will therefore be dealt with in chapter IV.

morphology

word formation inflection
degrees of productivity

The word formation processes of English will be presented in two steps. Sections III.3.1 to III.3.3 will be concerned with the most productive word formation processes, that is with those that are responsible for the majority of neologisms. Essentially, these are derivation by prefixation (*ex-minister*) or suffixation (*friend<u>ship</u>*), compounding (*foot + ball* > <u>*football*</u>), and conversion (*elbow* > *to elbow*). Among the less productive word formation processes, which are, however, constantly gaining in importance, are the various types of shortenings, like clippings (*ad* < *advertisement*), back-formations (*to babysit* < *babysitter*), blends (*brunch* < *breakfast + lunch*), and acronyms (*laser* < *lightwave <u>a</u>mplification by <u>s</u>timulated <u>e</u>mission of <u>r</u>adiation*). These will briefly be presented in chapter III.3.4.

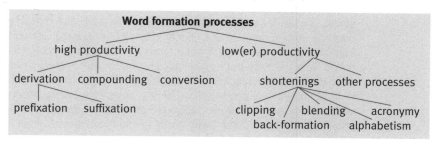

Figure III.2

In the remainder of this chapter we will work with examples that represent different stages of a newly coined lexeme with regard to its establishment in the vocabulary. Three such stages are widely distinguished:

- **nonce (or: ad hoc) formations**, e.g. *mega-multinationals*, *<u>people-choked</u> Tokyo*, *today's <u>Warholized</u> art world*, or *the director has <u>Gothicized</u> the tale*, that is formations which at least the word creator is convinced never to have heard or read before (although a model for such formations almost always exists). Due to the productive pattern, the meaning of a nonce-formation typically is largely transparent, i.e. its meaning can be deduced from the meanings of its component parts. Nonce-formations are particularly frequent in advertising and press language.
- **institutionalisation**, that is the neologism is also used by other members of the language community. Along with institutionalisation goes a gradual loss of transparency, and an inclusion of the

institutionalised word in one of the regularly published new edi-
tions of the dictionaries of a language.
- **lexicalisation**, that is the stage in which it is no longer possible for
a lexeme to have been formed according to the productive rules of
a language. Phonological lexicalisation, for example, is present in
(6), morphological lexicalisation in *length* (< *long + th*) and *breadth*
(< *broad + th*), semantic lexicalisation (and to a large extent a loss
of transparency) in *understand* and *blackhead*.

3.1 Derivation

derivation

prefixation   suffixation

We can distinguish between two major types of derivation – prefixation and suffixation – depending on whether the derivational affix
is a prefix (*a-, auto-, co-, ex-, semi-, sub-, super-*, etc.) or a suffix (*-er,
-ish, -ize, -ion, -ity, -ness*, etc.).

suffixation

In English, there are several interesting differences between these
two derivational processes, which can be reduced to the following
generalisation: for suffixation, most of the time more is happening
than the mere formation of a new lexeme with a meaning different
from that of the base. The lexeme formed by suffixation frequently
differs from the base both grammatically, that is with respect to its
word-class membership, and phonologically. Just recall the examples
in (6-8): in all these cases, suffixation (by, note, vowel-initial, never
consonant-initial derivational suffixes) has led to a change of the
phonological shape of the base, partly in combination with or as a
consequence of a shift of the main stress, triggered by the derivational
suffix. Moreover, there is a change of word class in examples (6-8).
Together with some further examples, this is illustrated in Table III.2:

Tab. III.2 Derivational suffixes changing word class

	> noun	> adjective	> verb
noun		part-ial partic-ular fashion-able boy-ish clue-less	woman-ize class-ify haste-n orchestr-ate
adjective	electric-ity tough-ness free-dom social-ist warm-th		modern-ize pur-ify activ-ate black-en
verb	infus-ion pronunc-iation develop-ment employ-er employ-ee	appar-ent hope-ful hope-less drink-able frighten-ing	

Among the word-class changing derivational suffixes, those forming nouns and adjectives constitute the two major groups. As for verb-forming suffixes, English possesses only a handful (-ize, -ify, -en, -ate). Of these, it is largely only the first two which are still productive. The best known adverb-forming derivational suffix is of course -ly, which forms adverbs from adjectives (quickly, strongly, hiply). Other adverb-forming suffixes include, for instance, -wards (earthwards, northwards) and the highly fashionable suffix -wise, which forms adverbs from nouns (weatherwise, moneywise, taxwise, theatrewise, holidaywise, etc.). Very similar to their German counterparts in -mäßig (wettermäßig, gehaltsmäßig, sportmäßig, studienmäßig, etc.), which also means 'with regard to X' or 'as far as X is concerned', the relevant adverbs often qualify as nonce-formations, whose productivity is nearly unlimited.

But not all derivational suffixes trigger a word-class change. As the examples in (9) show, nouns can frequently be formed from other nouns, and – even though only in relatively few cases – adjectives from other adjectives. There are, however, no derivational suffixes in English which form verbs from verbs:

(9)	a.	nouns:	tutor-ial, music-ian, orphan-age, doctor-ate, host-ess, child-hood, king-dom, pig-let
	b.	adjectives:	historic-al, green-ish, good-ly

prefixation

What is exceptional for suffixes, namely examples like those in (9), is the rule for prefixes: they neither trigger a change of word-class membership, nor a phonological change of the base, be it in the form of a morphophonemic alternation or a shift of the main accent. There are only few exceptions to this generalisation. A selection of prefixes that can bring about a change of word-class membership (more precisely: that can form verbs from nouns and, in some cases, also from adjectives) is given in (10) and (11):

(10) always changing the word class:
    be-: befriend, bedevil, bewitch, behead; belittle
    en-: enjoy, enlist, enslave; enlarge, enrich

(11) sometimes changing the word class:
    de-: debone, defrost, dethrone
    dis-: discourage, discolour, disillusion

borrowed affixes

An important property of the English language in the domain of derivation is the fact that most productive affixes are not of Germanic origin, but of Romance (that is, Latin and French) or Greek origin. This property neatly fits the characterisation of English as the prototype of a language with a 'mixed' vocabulary, that is, with an unusually high percentage of loan words and borrowed word-formation elements. But in this respect, too, prefixes and suffixes differ: While most prefixes of non-Germanic origin can be attached to any base, there is a much greater number of elements among the corresponding suffixes which can only be attached to bases of Latin or Greek origin (e.g. *-ity* or *-al*):

(12) *mind – mental* (not: **mindal*), *nose – nasal* (not: **nosal*)

limits of productivity

types of blocking

Derivation also serves to identify the limits of the seemingly unlimited possibilities of word formation. In particular, various types of blocking need to be mentioned at this point. By blocking we understand cases in which, due to the existence of another word, a new, mostly (more) complex word either is not formed at all or, as a consequence of low acceptance, is hardly used and in any event will

98

not be institutionalised. Thus, in spite of the extremely high productivity of the nominal suffix -er in English (singer, worker, writer), we do not, for instance, find the lexeme *stealer, because this slot is already taken by thief. There is also no reason to form the nouns *longness or *warmness by means of the nominal suffix -ness (cleverness, thickness, thinness), as the relevant meanings are already expressed by the lexicalised forms length and warmth (whereas there is no *thickth or *thinth). However, blocking can also be due to particular phonological, morphological, or semantic properties of an existing word. The fact, for example, that there is no productive derivation of adverbs by means of -ly from adjectives like friendly, stately, or miserly (more exactly: that this process has stopped being productive in the 18th century) is most probably due to their ending in -ly, which would lead to such tongue twisters as *friendlily or *miserlily. This is a case of phonological blocking. Or let us consider the following situation: two of the suffixes for the formation of abstract nouns, -ity and -dom, are practically in complementary distribution, with -ity attaching almost exclusively to bases of Latin origin and -dom (nearly as consistently) attaching only to bases of Germanic origin. This is a case of morphological blocking. Finally, why is it that words like unhappy, unwell or unoptimistic do exist, but *unsad, *unill, or *unpessimistic do not? This results from the fact that the negation prefix un- only attaches to those adjectives of a pair of opposites (so-called antonyms; cf. chapter VI.3.2) which have, in the broadest sense, a positive meaning. In other words, this is an instance of semantic blocking.

phonological blocking

morphological blocking

semantic blocking

3.2 Compounding

In terms of productivity, the only word-formation process playing in the same league as derivation is compounding, i.e. the stringing together of two or more free morphemes to one complex free morpheme, the compound. The prototype of an English compound can be characterised with the help of the examples in (13):

> **(13)** daylight, fingertip, girlfriend, water-bed, deathbed, bedroom, leg-room, cowboy, gameboy, game show, wallpaper, term paper, computer freak

The prototypical English compound is a noun consisting of two nouns, with the first modifying the second. From a semantic point of view, this modifier-head (or: determinans-determinatum) structure of compounds results in the fact that they mostly refer to something which is a special case or a subset of what is denoted by the head (e.g. a waterbed is a particular type of bed). A compound of this semantic type is called "endocentric" (or: "determinative"). Another characteristic of the majority of compounds is that their meaning cannot be fully deduced from the meanings of their parts, which means that they are, to varying degrees, lexicalised (contrast, for example, *bedroom* and *leg-room*, or *wallpaper* and *term paper*).

endocentric compound

Of course, there are also many compounds which do not correspond to this prototype. Table III.3 gives some examples both of non-nominal compounds (i.e. those which are, for example, adjectives or, though a much rarer type, verbs) and of nominal compounds which are not made up of two nouns. In the case of the latter, as is generally true for compounds consisting of free morphemes belonging to different word classes, it is usually the last free morpheme which determines the word class of the compound. Thus the rightmost free morpheme qualifies as the head also from a grammatical point of view:

syntactic types

Tab. III.3 Types of compounds with regard to word classes and combinations of word classes

	noun	adjective	verb*
noun	(13) PROTOTYPE	waterproof knee-deep sky-high airsick scandal-weary	proofread gatecrash babysit tailor-fit day-dream
adjective	small talk short story deadline wild card greenhouse	bitter-sweet deaf mute ready-made far-fetched short-sighted	fine-tune soft-land double-book free associate short-list
verb	talk show playboy cry-baby cutthroat pickpocket	fail-safe ?	sleepwalk freeze-dry

* The vast majority of verbal compounds have not been formed by compounding, but by back-formation or conversion from nominal compounds (e.g. *to babysit* ‹ *babysitter/babysitting* or *to short-list* ‹ *shortlist*). Thus they should rather be called *pseudo-compounds* (for more details cf. below and chapter III.3.4).

semantic types

As far as the semantic classification of compounds is concerned, there are three other types besides endocentric compounds:

(14) a. **endocentric compounds** (A+B denotes a special kind of B): *darkroom, small talk*; for more information cf. (13)

b. **exocentric compounds** (A+B denotes a special kind of an unexpressed semantic head, e.g. 'person' in the case of *skinhead* or *paleface*; these compounds often have metonymic character, when one part stands for the whole, e.g. *paleface* for 'a person with a pale face'): *egghead, blockhead, blackhead, birdbrain, redneck, greenback, paperback* = *%oupleuieur är*

c. **appositional compounds** (A and B provide different descriptions for the same referent): *actor-director, actor-manager, writer-director, maidservant*

d. **copulative compounds** (A+B denotes 'the sum' of what A and B denote): *bitter-sweet, deaf mute, sleepwalk, freeze-dry, Alsace-Lorraine*

From a contrastive perspective, endocentric compounds consisting of two nouns in English and German differ only in one respect, which leads us back to the discussion at the beginning of the chapter on how to define a word. Unlike in German, whether a string of free morphemes is written together or separately tells us relatively little about its word status in English. Consider the example of *word formation* with its alternative writings *word-formation* and *wordformation*. Whether written as separate words or not, whether with or without a hyphen, in all three cases we are dealing with the translation of the German compound *Wortbildung*. Likewise a string of words written together without a hyphen does not indicate a higher degree of lexicalisation than if it were written with a hyphen, nor does the latter indicate a higher degree of lexicalisation than a spelling in two words. So there it is again: our problem of how to define a word, which now however can be solved relatively easily. It is true that cases like *word formation*, *wallpaper*, or *small talk* consist of free morphemes, but each of them forms a lexeme. What is more difficult to resolve is the problem of how, especially in spoken language, we should distinguish compounds as in (15a) from syntactic phrases in (15b):

Compound or phrase?

(15) a. blackbird, darkroom, small talk, short story, no ball, yes-man

b. black bird, dark room, small talk, short story, no ball, yes man

The examples in (15) show that this problem especially arises with nominal compounds which have an adjective as their first element. It is, however, not restricted to this kind of compounds. Just consider *no ball*, a term taken from the world of cricket, and the opportunistic *yes-*

man and his notorious *yes-man behaviour*. Nevertheless, the following guidelines should take care of most problems of this kind:

- Compounds usually have only one main stress, namely on the first (or: left-hand) element (*a SHORT story* versus *a short STORY*).
- Compounds are not separable (cf. *a vivid SHORT story*, but not **a SHORT vivid story* as opposed to *a vivid short STORY* or *a short vivid STORY*).
- Compounds do not allow modification of their first element (**a very SHORT story*).
- Compounds are not fully compositional, that is, their meaning can not, or at least not completely, be deduced from the meanings of their component parts (cf. chapter VI.1); thus, they show different degrees of (semantic) lexicalisation.

hybrid formations or neoclassical compounds

A type of compounds which is extremely frequent not only in English but also in other languages are so-called "hybrid formations". These are compounds whose component elements stem from different languages, e.g. *bureaucracy* (*bureau-* French, *-cracy* Greek *-kratio*), or *spinmeister* (*spin-* English, *-meister* German). Since many of these elements (so-called combining forms) stem from Latin or Greek, the corresponding compounds are also called neo-classical compounds. The great frequency of formations like those in (16) fits the overall picture of English as a language with a mixed vocabulary:

(16) Anglophone, astronaut, barometer, biography, ecosystem, holograph, Francophile, psychoanalysis, technophobia, television, sociolinguistics

Here we enter the transitional area of composition and derivation. Incidentally, these two major word-formation processes are also linked historically by the fact that there are cases in which a formerly free morpheme has developed from the element of a compound into a derivational affix. Well-known examples are *-hood* (< OE noun *had* 'state, quality'), *-dom* (< OE noun *dom* 'verdict, jurisdiction'), *-ly* (< OE noun *līc* 'body'), and *-wise* (< noun 'manner'). Some people think that *man* is currently undergoing such a development, and that it develops an additional use as suffix-like word-formation element (semi-suffix or suffixoid). Take *Walkman*, for example: here the allomorph of *man* is not /mæn/, but /mən/; the plural is mostly formed according to the regular model for English nouns (*Walkmans*); and, finally, the semantic features [+ANIMATED], [+HUMAN], [+MALE], [+ADULT] can no longer be

compounding
↕
derivation

attributed to *man* in *Walkman*. Much more unusual is the reverse development, that is from a bound to a free morpheme. This can perhaps be claimed for *burger*, which does not only appear in all kinds of variants in analogy to *hamburger* (*cheeseburger, fishburger, onionburger, beanburger, veggieburger, muesliburger, nutburger,* etc.), but meanwhile also as an independent lexeme (e.g. in *Do they sell burgers?*), and as the first element in such compounds as *Burger King* or *burger bar*.

3.3 Conversion

While derivation and compounding have been the most productive word-formation processes since Old English, conversion has turned into a major word-formation process since Middle English (i. e. roughly since the 12th century) and particularly since Early Modern English (that is roughly since the 16th century). By conversion we understand derivation of a new lexeme from an existing one without a specific morphological marker indicating the change of word class and meaning. (Therefore, the term "zero-derivation" is sometimes used alternatively, reverting to the theoretical construct of the zero-morph(eme), only that in the context of the present section it has the function of a derivational affix.) In other words: without any overt changes, a free morpheme develops an additional usage as a member of a different word class and, as a consequence, can be used in entirely new syntactic contexts, and thus deserves a new dictionary entry. In principle, there are hardly any limits to conversion in English (e.g. *no more ifs and buts, this is a must, to up the prices, to down a beer*); however, the three word-class changes in (17) to (19) are by far the most productive ones:

(17) **noun › verb:**
bottle, butter, bicycle, carpet, father, knife, mother, mail, queue, ship, shoulder

(18) **adjective › verb:**
better, calm, clean, dirty, dry, empty, faint, idle, open, pale, right, total, wrong

(19) **verb › noun:**
cough, cover, desire, doubt, guess, love, rise, smell, smile, spy, turn, want

Especially verbs are formed with the help of conversion. Verb ›
noun conversion is clearly rarer than conversion in the opposite
direction. English thereby compensates for the fact that it can hardly
form denominal verbs by derivation; the only productive derivational
suffixes English has at its disposal for this purpose are *-ify* (*beautify,
codify*) and particularly *-ize* (*sympathize, containerize*).

Much less frequent among the productive conversion processes is
the one of an adjective into a noun. As many of the examples in (20)
show, this is only possible in a particular syntactic environment. Many
of these de-adjectival nouns are formed by omitting the head of a
phrase consisting of article, adjective, and noun (*a daily newspaper* ›
a daily, a regular customer › *a regular, the poor people* › *the poor*).

Once again, this leads us to a transitional area of word formation

> **(20) adjective › noun:**
> a (pint of) bitter, a crazy, a final, a gay, a natural, a red,
> a regular, a wet, a daily/weekly/monthly/ etc., the poor, the
> rich

**word-class internal
conversion**

and syntax. In fact, there are quite a number of further examples where
conversion rather ought to be considered as the result of a syntactic
process. This is particularly the case with word-class internal conversion, e.g. when non-count or mass nouns are used as count nouns
(*beer* › *two beers, coffee* › *two coffees*), or non-gradable adjectives as
gradable ones (*English* › *to look very English*). A type of conversion
which is particularly interesting in this context is the one illustrated in
(21). There are many cases in English where a verb which originally
could not take a direct object (i.e. an intransitive verb) developed an
additional transitive usage (21a), or vice versa, as in (21b), an
originally transitive verb is used intransitively (cf. also various
sections in chapters IV and V).

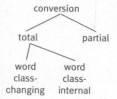

> **(21)** a. **intransitive › transitive verbs:**
> march › to march the prisoners, run › run a horse in the
> Derby, stand › to stand the bank robbers against the wall
> b. **transitive › intransitive verbs:**
> read › the book reads well, scare › I don't scare easily

There are also cases of so-called "partial conversion", where the
change of word class is not accompanied by a morphological, but by
a phonological change. Thus, the word-final sounds change from

voiceless to voiced fricatives in cases like those in (22a), or the main accent is shifted leftwards in cases as those in (22b) or (22c). The word-formation model in (22a) is no longer productive.

(22) a. the belief /f/ – to believe /v/, the use /s/ – to use /z/, the mouth /θ/ – to mouth /ð/
   b. to subJECT – the SUBject, to abSTRACT – the ABstract, to inSERT – the INsert
   c. to sit UP – SIT-ups, to take OFF – ready for TAKE-off, to show OFF – SHOW-off

Especially in view of the prototypical examples of conversion, i.e. instances of total conversion as in (17) to (19), the question naturally arises as to how we actually know which direction the word-class change has taken. This question cannot be answered definitively in all cases. However, sometimes certain formal features indicate the direction, e.g. typical noun endings of verbs are a rather clear indication of noun > verb conversion:

direction of conversion

(23) a. -eer: to pioneer, to mountaineer
   b. -or: to (co-)author, to doctor
   c. -ure: to lecture, to gesture
   d. -ion: to commission, to requisition, to vacation

Where formal indications are missing, paraphrasing the word meanings often helps determine the direction of conversion. Thus, probably no one will question the nominal origin of any of the verbs in (17) or the following verbs: consider *to wolf* in *He wolfed his meal down*, the verb *to data-bank*, or verbs derived from parts of the body like *head, face, eye, mouth, shoulder, elbow, hand, finger, foot* (*the bill*). Similarly obvious is the direction of conversion for the verbs in (18) and, after a little more reflection, for the nouns in (19). Of primary importance for determining the direction of conversion is the logical-semantic relationship between the original and the derived word, and not a chronology of the 'conversion history' of a word, as we only find it for a minority of cases in a historical dictionary like the *Oxford English Dictionary* (*OED*).

The great productivity of conversion is one of the characteristic features of the English language. This is related to the morphological language type English represents. Unlike Latin, Russian, German or also Old English, contemporary English has very few inflectional endings and thus qualifies as a highly analytical or isolating language (cf. chapter IV.1). English has undergone a radical typological change during and after the Middle English period. This change and its con-

English as a language type

sequences for the structure of modern English – especially in comparison with German – will be addressed on several occasions in this book.

3.4 Shortenings

The majority of word-formation processes which are much less productive (but constantly gaining ground) have one feature in common: their output is shorter than their input. Among these shortenings we can distinguish five groups. The first group is illustrated in (24):

(24) a. ad, bike, cig, deli (‹ delicatessen), exam, gas, gym, lab, mike, meg (‹ megabyte),
Net (‹ Internet), phone, porn, prof, pub, typo (‹ typographic error); hi-fi, sci-fi
   b. bus (‹ omnibus), plane (‹ airplane)
   c. flu (‹ influenza), fridge (‹ refrigerator), jams (‹ pyjamas), tec (‹ detective)

These are all instances of clippings (or: abbreviations), where part of a word, usually the final part (24a), is omitted. Only rarely is a lexeme shortened at the beginning (24b), or at the beginning and the end (24c). Many of these clippings are of a rather colloquial nature.

In the three following types of shortenings, two or more words are affected. In the case of blends two words are blended, typically the initial part of the first word and the final part of the second word (25a). There are also blends, however, where one (25b) or both of the underlying bases (25c) remain intact:

blends

(25) a. smog (‹ smoke + fog), motel (‹ motor + hotel), brunch (‹ breakfast + lunch), telex (‹ teleprinter + exchange), chunnel (‹ channel + tunnel), shoat (‹ sheep + goat), fanzine (‹ fanatic + magazine), sitcom (‹ situation + comedy), saunarium (‹ sauna + solarium), infotainment (‹ information + entertainment)
   b. rockumentary (‹ rock + documentary), breathalyze (‹ breath + analyze), paratroops (‹ parachute + troops), mor(pho)phonology
   c. slanguage (‹ slang + language), wargasm (‹ war + orgasm)

Particularly popular in professional jargons (e.g. politics, military, economy, computer sciences) are so-called "initialisms", which can be subdivided into the two classes of acronyms and alphabetisms. In both cases, a new term is formed from the initial letters of several words or, in the case of compounds, component parts of words. For acronyms, this term is also pronounced like a word (26), while alphabetisms are pronounced letter by letter (27):

acronyms

alphabetisms

(26) a. laser (Lightwave Amplification by Stimulated Emission of Radiation), radar (RAdio Detecting And Ranging), asap (As Soon As Possible), ALF (the TV-star: Alien Life Form), QANTAS (Queensland And Northern Territory Aerial Service)
   b. UNESCO (United Nations Educational, Scientific, and Cultural Organization), UNICEF (United Nations International Children's Endowment Fund), OPEC (Oil Producing and Exporting Countries), NAFTA (North American Free Trade Association), GATT (General Agreement on Tariffs and Trade)
   c. NATO (North Atlantic Treaty Organization), START (STrategic Arms Reduction Talks), SALT (Strategic Arms Limitations Talks)
   d. BASIC (Beginners' All-purpose Symbolic Instruction Code), ASCII (American Standard Code for Information Interchange), DOS (Disk Operating System), RAM (Random Access Memory), ROM (Read Only Memory), WYSIWYG (What You See Is What You Get)
   e. ERASMUS (EuRopean Action Scheme for the Mobility of University Students), TESOL (Teaching English to Speakers of Other Languages), TOEFL (Test Of English as a Foreign Language), COBUILD (COllins Birmingham University International Language Database), DARE (Dictionary of American Regional English)

(27) a. TV, CD, LP, DJ, PC (Personal Computer, but also Political Correctness), VIP, USA, UK, LA (Los Angeles), UCLA (University of California Los Angeles), ABC, BBC, CBS, CNN
   b. OED (Oxford English Dictionary), BNC (British National Corpus), IPA (International Phonetic Association/Alphabet)

Small letters in acronyms often indicate that this term has made it into the general vocabulary, i.e. has reached a higher degree of institutionalisation (*laser, radar, yuppy* (*Young Urban Professional*), or *dink(y)* (*Double Income No Kids*)). By far the greatest number of acronyms and alphabetisms, however, can only be found in special dictionaries, often compiled for particular subject areas.

All shortening processes presented so far have three things in common. They involve neither a change of word class nor of meaning, and they can be motivated by language economy. This is different for the fifth and last type of shortenings, namely back-formations, as in (28):

back-formations

(28) a. edit ‹ editor, commentate ‹ commentator, burgle ‹ burglar,
peddle ‹ peddler, scavenge ‹ scavenger, lase ‹ laser,
ush ‹ usher
b. donate ‹ donation, relate ‹ relation, televize ‹ television,
intuit ‹ intuition, attrit ‹ attrition; enthuse ‹ enthusiasm
c. contracept ‹ contraception, self-destruct ‹ self-destruction
d. babysit, window-shop, day-dream, sleepwalk, brainwash,
headhunt, hangglide, stage-manage, chain-smoke, lip-
read, sightsee, mindmelt

Back-formations result from taking away a real or putative derivational suffix. The output of this process, however, is a root or base
morpheme which did not exist prior to the longer form. This runs
counter to our expectations. After all, if there are derivational processes like *sing + er › singer, inspect + or › inspector*, or *inflate + ion
› inflation, insert + ion › insertion*, why should *editor* not originate from
edit, or *donation* from *donate*? Thus, back-formations demonstrate
two things very nicely: first, that the members of a language community have internalised productive word-formation rules; and second,
the power of analogy, which is one of the most important processes
and driving forces of language change, leading to greater regularity in
language. Not all back-formations, however, result from the reversal
of a derivational process. If this was the case, the 'back-formed' verbs
in (28c) would have to read as follows: *contraceive* (model *deceive ›
deception*) and *self-destroy* (model *destroy › destruction*). As the
examples in (28) clearly show, by far the largest group among back-
formations are verbs which have developed out of nouns. This goes
particularly for so-called "pseudo compounds" as in (28d), which have
been back-formed from nominal compounds (*babysit ‹ babysitter*).
But among back-formations there are also cases like those in (29):

(29) a. verb ‹ adjective: laze ‹ lazy, funk ‹ funky,
 underdevelop ‹ underdeveloped
b. adjective ‹ noun: surreal ‹ surrealism,
 autoimmune ‹ autoimmunization
c. noun ‹ adjective: paramedic ‹ paramedical,
 paraphysics ‹ paraphysical
d. noun ‹ noun: bioengineer ‹ bioengineering,
 aptitude ‹ inaptitude

Figure III.3

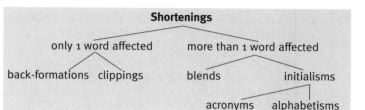

Finally, let us look at some examples of a word-formation process which does not belong to the group of shortenings, and is by far the least productive of all word-formation processes dealt with in this chapter:

(30) sandwich, Kleenex, Hoover, watt, to xerox, boycott, lynch

In all the examples in (30) a proper name has developed into a lexeme – thus the terms *words-from-names* or coinage. Either the name of a person (*sandwich, watt, lynch, boycott*) is used to denote an object, idea, activity, etc. which is linked to that person (cf. in German *röntgen, Röntgenstrahlen, Litfasssäule*), or a company or brand name is used to denote a particular product. German readers just need to think of everyday examples like *Tesa* instead of *Klebestreifen*, and *Tempo* instead of *Papiertaschentuch* in questions of the type "Have you got a _____ ?". Such neologisms can quickly then be used as input for further word-formation processes, e.g. conversion (*hoover › to hoover, sandwich › to sandwich*), compounding (*lynch law, sandwich board, sandwich course*), or clipping (*ampere › amp, wellington boots › wellies*). In general, we should not forget that there is often more than one word-formation process involved in the formation of many lexemes, e.g. compounding and conversion in *to kneecap*, or compounding, clipping, and derivation in *sitcomy* (e.g. in a phrase like *a sitcomy movie*). Thus, many neologisms are the result of different word-formation processes taking place one after the other.

coinage

Checklist Morphology – key terms and concepts

affix (prefix ↔ suffix;
  derivational morpheme ↔
  inflectional morpheme)
allomorphy (affix ↔ base)
base ↔ root ↔ stem
blocking (phonological,
  morphological, semantic)
coinage
complementary distribution
compounding; compound
  (endocentric ↔ exocentric,
  appositional, copulative
  compound; hybrid forma-
  tion / neo-classical compound; combining forms;
  modifier-head-structure)

conditioning of allomorphs
  (phonological,
  morphological, lexical)
conversion (total ↔ partial;
  word-class internal)
derivation (prefixation ↔
  suffixation)
free morpheme ↔ bound
  morpheme
head
institutionalisation
lexeme ↔ word-form
lexicalisation
lexical word-classes
  (autosemantic terms) ↔
  functional word-classes
  (synsemantic terms)

"mixed" vocabulary
morph, allomorph
morpheme (free ↔ bound,
  derivational ↔ inflectional)
morphophonemic alternant
morphophonology /
  morphophonemics
neologism
nonce formation
portmanteau morph(eme)
shortening (clipping, blend,
  initialism, acronym,
  alphabetism, back-
  formation)
suppletion (strong ↔ weak)
transparency
unique morpheme
zero (allo)morph

1   Fill in the blanks:
    A morpheme is defined as the smallest ......-bearing unit of lan-
    guage. ...... morphemes, for instance, add only grammatical mean-
    ing to the stem they are attached to. They create a new word-......
    (or: token). Lexical information, on the other hand, is added by
    ...... morphemes. The result of this kind of ....ation is a new lex-
    eme (or: type). Analogous to phonemes, which may be realized
    by a set of ......, called ......, there may be more than one ...... which
    instantiates a given morpheme. These are called the ...... of the
    relevant morpheme and are normally ...... conditioned.

2   a. Give a morphological analysis of *formalities* and *inconclusive-
       ness*. Make use of the terms *base, root* and *stem*.
    b. Give all morphophonemic alternants of the following free
       morphemes:
       {APPEAR} {LONG} {PHYSIC} {USE} {THIEF} {PHOTOGRAPH}

3   Give an account of the morphological status of *-en* on the basis
    of the following lexemes:
    earthen, wooden, widen, sweeten, deafen, oxen, silken.

4   By means of which word formation processes have the following
    lexemes been arrived at? (When two or more word-formation
    processes are involved specify their order.)
to enthuse	to netsurf	language lab	infotainment
laptop	campaigner	rockumentary	neocolonialism
judgmental	modem	sexist	exec
to breathalyze	sitcomy	weatherwise	

5   This question is concerned with the dominant types of English
    compounds in terms of (i) grammatical word-class of the com-
    pound, (ii) grammatical word-classes of the elements of nominal
    compounds, (iii) the logical-semantic relation between the ele-
    ments of nominal compounds, and (iv) the internal structure of
    compounds in terms of head and modifier. Now consider the
    groups of compounds in (a-d) below with respect to (i) – (iv)
    above respectively. In each group there is **only one** compound
    which represents the dominant type. Identify this compound:
    (a) *classroom, overeducate, leadfree, whenever*
    (b) *pickpocket, doormat, breakfast, bluebell*
    (c) *paperback, actor-manager, flower-pot, Alsace-Lorraine*
    (d) *Secretary-General, motor-car, court martial, poet laureate*

6 a. Identify all lexemes with prefixes exhibiting untypical properties from a grammatical point of view (hint: think of word classes)

counterintuitive aloud bewitch international empower encode miniskirt rebuild debark discourage archbishop

b. Give a morphological analysis of the following lexemes and identify the meanings of {-ISH}:

childish greenish feverish punish eightish foolish

7 This task is all about reconstructing the word-formation "stories" of the lexemes in bold print. Identify for each of the stories in (a-g) the corresponding sequence of word-formation processes from the set in (I-VII).

a. rap music › rap › to rap › **rapper**
b. rehabilitation › rehab › **to rehab**
c. vacuum cleaner › to vacuum-clean › **to vacuum**
d. campaign › to campaign › **campaigner**
e. tailor-fit › **to tailor-fit**
f. breathalyser › **to breathalyse**
g. brunch › **to brunch**

I. conversion – derivation
II. blend – conversion
III. compounding – clipping – conversion – derivation
IV. derivation – clipping – conversion
V. blend – back-formation
VI. compounding – back-formation – clipping
VII. compounding – conversion

8 Which of the following statements are true, which are false?

a. English has more derivational than inflectional morphemes.
b. Derivational morphemes produce word-forms of a single lexeme.
c. *Enslave* and *enshrine*, on the one hand, and *empower* and *embitter*, on the other hand, illustrate the phenomenon of lexically conditioned prefix allomorphy.
d. English has no inflectional prefixes.
e. Any monomorphemic English word will also be monosyllabic.
f. /ɪz/ in English /ɒksɪz/ is a phonologically conditioned allomorph of the genitive morpheme.
g. Back-formation always involves a change of word-class.
h. The majority of productive English affixes are non-Germanic.
i. All derivational affixes of English change word-class.

j. Two word-formation processes were involved in the formation of the verbs *to bus* and *to xerox*.

9 a. Give arguments why the underlined morphemes in the following sets of words are classified as unique morphemes:
   a. re<u>ceive</u>, de<u>ceive</u>, per<u>ceive</u>
   b. per<u>mit</u>, re<u>mit</u>, sub<u>mit</u>
   c. in<u>ept</u>, un<u>couth</u>, dis<u>gruntle</u>

   b. Why are *strawberry* and *gooseberry*, too, not entirely unproblematic if discussed in connection with unique morphemes?

10 Here are some more instances of so-called causative verbs like *widen*, *sweeten* or *deafen* in exercise (3): *madden, quicken, soften, whiten*. Now, if you contrast these verbs with those below, can you identify the phonological constraint on the derivation of causative verbs from adjectives with the help of the suffix *-en*?
*bluen, *concreten, *exacten, *greenen, *sanen, *slowen, *subtlen

11 a. What is a basic difference between vowel-initial and consonant-initial (derivational) suffixes?
   b. Find out about the difference between class I and class II affixes in a number of accounts of English derivation. Which arguments can be given against such accounts of English morphophonology?

12 Try to write a brief 'story' of fax from the point of view of the linguist. Use the following words (some of which are institutionalized, others nonce-formations), and try to reconstruct how everything started and which members of the *fax*-family came into existence by means of which word-formation process(es). Can you think of more family members?
   a. fax, facsimile, fax machine, fax number, faxable, faxworthy, unfaxable, speedfax, refax, faxer, faxability, fax addict, fax modem
   b. Can you fax me the bill, please?
   c. Sorry, Sir, this bill doesn't fax well.

Sources and further reading

Adams, Valerie. 2002 [1973]. *An introduction to modern English word-formation*. London: Longman.

Adams, Valerie. 2001. *Complex words in English*. Harlow: Longman.

Aronoff, Mark/Kirsten Fudeman. 2005. *What is morphology?* Malden, MA/Oxford: Blackwell.

Bauer, Laurie. 2002 [1983]. *English word-formation*. Cambridge: Cambridge University Press.

Bauer, Laurie. 2001. *Morphological productivity*. Cambridge: Cambridge University Press.

Bauer, Laurie/Rodney Huddleston. 2002. "Lexical word-formation." In: Rodney Huddleston/Geoffrey K. Pullum, eds. *The Cambridge Grammar of the English Language*, 1621-1721. Cambridge: Cambridge University Press.

Carstairs-McCarthy, Andrew. 1992. *Current morphology*. London/New York: Routledge.

Fischer, Roswitha. 1997. *Sprachwandel im Lexikon des heutigen Englisch*. Frankfurt a. Main: Lang.

Haspelmath, Martin. 2002. *Understanding morphology*. London: Arnold.

Katamba, Francis. 1993. *Morphology*. London: Macmillan.

Leisi, Ernst. 1975. *Das heutige Englisch*. Heidelberg: Winter.

Marchand, Hans. 1969[2]. *The categories and types of present-day English word formation*. München: Beck.

Matthews, Peter H. 1991[2]. *Morphology*. Cambridge: Cambridge University Press.

Plag, Ingo. 1999. *Morphological productivity. Structural constraints in English derivation*. Berlin/New York: Mouton de Gruyter.

Plag, Ingo. 2003. *Word-formation in English*. Cambridge: Cambridge University Press.

Schmid, Hans-Jörg. 2005. *Englische Morphologie und Wortbildung: eine Einführung*. Berlin: Schmidt.

Spencer, Andrew. 1991. *Morphological theory: An introduction to word structure in generative grammar*. London: Blackwell.

Stockwell, Robert/Donka Minkova. 2001. *English words: History and structure*. Cambridge: Cambridge University Press.

Welte, Werner. 1996[2]. *Englische Morphologie und Wortbildung*. Frankfurt: Lang.

IV Grammar:
The ground plan of English

What will take centre stage in this and the next chapter is the basic formal structure of English, or what could also be called "the ground plan of the language". The most important structural characteristics of English will be presented from two different perspectives: in the current chapter by way of introducing the key concepts and terms in grammar, and in chapter V as part of a comparison of English and another West Germanic (and thus genetically closely related) language, namely German. In both chapters, we will adopt what may be called an 'enlightened traditional approach'. This means that we will for the most part use the traditional, long established terminology (some of which is over two thousand years old), but in a critically reflected way, i.e. including the scientific insights and developments of recent research in the field of grammar. This approach is particularly suitable for teaching (foreign) languages at schools, colleges and universities; it is therefore the approach preferred for the linguistic training of future foreign-language teachers. A similar approach is used by Hurford (1994), Huddleston (1988), and the three currently most important English reference grammars namely Quirk et al. (1985), Biber et al. (1999), and Huddleston/Pullum (2002).

Introduction

Leaving aside *grammar* as language theory (as in *generative* or *transformational grammar*; cf. chapter I), the term "grammar" can usually mean three different things:
- the study of the rule-based structure (or: the ground plan) of a language
- the object of study itself, i.e. the system of rules according to which a given language may combine words and the morphemes they consist of into larger units
- the book in which these rules are formulated and described

grammar

inflectional-morphology   syntax

In the first sense, i.e. in terms of the study of the rule-based structure of a language, we can subdivide grammar into the grammatical structure of words (inflectional morphology, see section IV.1) and the grammatical structure of phrases, clauses and sentences (syntax, see sections IV.2 and IV.3). The linguistic units under investigation can be represented in the following hierarchy:

inflectional morphemes ‹ words (including word forms)
‹ phrases ‹ clauses ‹ sentences

descriptive – prescriptive

Examining some central aspects of English grammar from an 'enlightened' traditional perspective also means using a descriptive – as opposed to a prescriptive (or: normative) – approach. Among the grammarians of the 18th and 19th centuries, it was common practice to lay down rules – which often appeared to be arbitrary – for the correct or 'educated' use of English widely accepted among the higher social classes (how English should be spoken). This is not, however, the perspective taken in this book. We will instead be looking at English as it is actually spoken today, at the turn of the 21st century. The reader will not find any criticism on such phenomena as the so-called *split infinitive* (e.g. *to quickly go*), the use of *I will* instead of *I shall* as future-tense marker, of sentence-final prepositions or the missing use of *whom* (e.g. the latter two in *She's the woman who I'd like to talk to*). Note that this does not mean that descriptive grammars follow an 'anything goes' principle. It simply means that each variety of a language has its rules, but that these rules are not necessarily the same for each variety. Above all it must be noted that, from a linguistic perspective, no variety is inherently 'better' than, or superior to, other varieties (which is why we especially disapprove of terms like "sub-standard"). On the contrary: the reason why standard varieties enjoy a privileged status (cf. also chapter VIII.1) is that they enable people from different dialect areas to communicate with each other. The standard therefore seems especially suitable for use in the mass media, in schools and universities and in foreign language teaching (think of *TESOL–Teaching English to Speakers of Other Languages*). In this chapter, it is the structural core of the different standard varieties of English, notably British and American English, which will be examined in some detail.

Bound morphemes which are exclusively used to encode grammatical information are called inflectional morphemes. Only eight of the numerous inflectional morphemes found in Old English are still in use today. As mentioned in earlier chapters, English has developed into an isolating or analytic language. The few inflectional morphemes that have survived are used in the declension of nouns, the conjugation of verbs and the comparison of adjectives (see Table IV.1).

**IV.1
Inflectional
Morphology**

Table IV.1 English inflectional morphology				
word class	**kind of inflection**	**inflectional morphemes**	**examples**	**number of word forms**
noun	declension	{PLURAL}: {-s} {'GENITIVE'}: {-s}	two boy-s the boy-s toy	rule: 2 exception: 4
verb	conjugation	{3SG. IND. PRES}:{-s} {PAST}:{-ed} {PRES. PART}:{-ing} {PAST PART}:{-ed}	he work-s he work-ed he is work-ing he has work-ed	rule: 4 exception: 5 (8)
adjective	comparison	{COMPARATIVE}:{-er} {SUPERLATIVE}:{-est}	strong-er strong-est	rule: 3

As a result of the dramatic loss of inflectional morphemes in the course of the history of English, each of the three word classes mentioned above contains far fewer word forms in Present-Day English than, for example, in German.

If we consider only those lexemes that follow the productive pattern (again compare Table IV.1), we see that the English noun can occur in only two word forms (e.g. *boy, boy's = boys*), the English adjective in no more than three (*strong, stronger, strongest*), and the English verb in no more than four word forms (*walk, walks, walked, walking*). Even the irregular nouns and verbs – of which there are

English – a strongly analytic language

relatively few in English – have hardly more different forms. Irregular nouns can take on four – instead of two – word forms (e.g. *child, child's, children, children's*) and so-called "strong verbs" have five – instead of four – different forms (e.g. *sing, sings, sang, singing, sung*). Only the verb *to be* has eight forms (*be, am, are, is, was, were, being, been*). English has lost most of the inflectional morphemes it once possessed, resulting in a language in which each lexeme can appear in but a small number of word forms. It is therefore often characterized as a language of largely invariable words, i.e. as an analytic or isolating language (cf. also chapter V.2.1). Another peculiarity resulting from this development is a phenomenon called "conversion" (already mentioned in chapter III.3.3).

That English is indeed an analytic language also becomes clear from the many grammatical categories which can be formed synthetically (i.e. by using inflectional morphemes) as well as analytically. Take the comparison of English adjectives as an example. The decision whether the comparative and superlative of a certain adjective are formed by using *more* and *most* largely depends on the phonological complexity of the stem of the adjective (i.e. on how many syllables it has).

(1) Comparison of adjectives: synthetic or analytic?
   a. 1 syllable: usually synthetic (*old-older-oldest*); but some adjectives may also take the analytic strategy (*mad, brave*)
   b. 2 syllables: both strategies are possible (*polite*); inflection is preferred for adjectives with an unstressed final vowel, /l/ or /ə(r)/: *easy, narrow, noble, clever* (vs. *severe*)
   c. > 2 syllables: exclusively analytic (*beautiful, interesting*); exception: adjectives with the prefix *un-* (*untidy*)

In a similar way, possessive relationships can be marked either synthetically by using the so-called "genitive" (more adequately called "possessive") or analytically by using the *of*-construction (*my uncle's house* vs. *the house of my uncle*). The analytic nature of English becomes even more obvious when looking at other grammatical categories which are always formed analytically, i.e. by using so-called "periphrastic constructions". Periphrastic constructions, such as *he is working* (Present Progressive) or *he has arrived* (Present Perfect),

periphrastic constructions

consist of more than one word, at least one of which is a function word (e.g. an auxiliary or a preposition). It perfectly ties in with the overall picture that these two eminently important constructions (cf. IV.3.2) became obligatory only during the Middle English and Early Modern English periods, and that they have continuously conquered new territory, thus clearly qualifying as two strengthened grammatical categories of Late Modern and Present-Day English. On the other hand, all inflectional categories of the noun are weakened categories. From the relatively elaborate case system of Old English nouns only two cases have survived: the unmarked common case and the possessive. English has completely lost its grammatical gender distinction (in German: *der Baum, die Tasse, das Mädchen*), nowadays distinguishing nouns either by natural (e.g. *the boy – he, the girl – she, the tree – it*) or, marginally, metaphorical gender (e.g. *the sun – he, the moon – she, England – it/she, car – it/she*). Table IV.2 illustrates the marginal role inflectional morphology plays in the marking of grammatical categories in Present-Day English. We will take a closer look at the individual categories in sections IV.2, IV.3 and in chapter V.

strengthened – weakened categories

Table IV.2 Grammatical categories in English			
categories	**formal contrasts**	**kind of marking**	**marked on/ relevant for**
gender	masculine – feminine – neuter	no inflectional category neither synthetic nor analytic	only pronouns (*he-she-it,his-her-its*), natural gender (*the man-he, the girl-she, the table-it*) and metaphorical gender (*sun-he/it, moon-she/it, ship,truck-she/it*)
case	common case – possessive	synthetic; possessive also analytic	nouns (possessive: *the kids' toys – the toys of the kids*); some pronouns additional object case: *he-his-him, who-whose-whom*
number	singular – plural	synthetic	nouns, pronouns, verbs (*he put-s*, plural only for *be: are/were*)
person	1st/2nd/3rd person	synthetic	verbs: only 3SG ind. pres. active (*he sing-s, is/has/does*); only for be: also 1st and 2nd person: *I am, you are*
tense	past – non-past	synthetic	verbs (*walk-ed versus walk*)

Table IV.2 Grammatical categories in English			
categories	**formal contrasts**	**kind of marking**	**marked on/ relevant for**
aspect	(a) progressive – non-progressive (b) perfect – non-perfect	analytic	verbs (*be* + V-*ing*) verbs (*have* + V-*ed*)
mood	indicative – subjunctive	marginally synthetic, analytic	verbs: ind.; subj. only marginally (for *be: I wish I were…; I insist that he go/should go*)
voice	active – passive (– mediopassive)	analytic	verbs (*be* + V-*ed*)
comparison	absolute – comparative – superlative	synthetic, analytic	adjectives (-*er*, -*est*, *more*, *most*), adverbs (*more*, *most*)

interface morphology/ syntax

   Inflectional morphology is the link or interface between morphology and syntax. This is shown most clearly by the fact that it is syntax which makes certain word forms necessary:

> **(2)** a. Alice live_ in London, and ha_ live_ there all ___ life.
>   b. Yesterday Alice walk__ past Fred_ uncle_ house, one of many house_ along the way.

   The examples in (2) show that the most important function of inflectional morphemes is to establish agreement (or: concord), meaning the formal agreement between syntactically closely related units with regard to their grammatical categories. We have already observed two areas where inflectional morphology acts as the connecting link between morphology and syntax: the comparison of adjectives and the marking of the possessive case. Both can be marked synthetically as well as analytically, although in many cases only one strategy is possible (cf. (1) above). The close connection between inflectional morphology and syntax also becomes clear when considering the fact that English has one inflectional suffix which may be attached not to the stem of the noun it actually modifies but to the whole phrase containing the noun as its head:

> **(3)** a. the <u>Museum</u> of Modern Art's new Director
>   b. the <u>boy</u> next door's bicycle

This so-called "group genitive" is one of the rare instances where a suffix appears to have started to 'emancipate itself' and develop into a postponed preposition (i.e. a postposition like English *ago* or German *halber*). On the other hand, there is the opposite phenomenon (observed in many languages) of formerly free morphemes developing into bound morphemes. For example, it can be argued that the English negation suffix *–n't* is developing into a clitic which has started losing its independence and leans towards 'the left' to become the ninth inflectional suffix used with auxiliaries (as in *isn't, doesn't, don't, won't*). All of these examples illustrate that there are transition zones between (inflectional) morphology and syntax.

This becomes even more evident when comparing different languages. There are instances where a grammatical category which, in one language, is marked by inflection, can or even must be coded syntactically in another language. In Latin, for example, the perfect and future tenses are synthetic (*amavit* = he has loved, *amabit* = he will love), whereas English and German use analytic tenses (*he has loved, he will love*). Languages like Latin use inflection (more precisely case marking) to indicate which argument of the verb is the subject and which the direct object of a given sentence. The nominative case indicates subject function, while the accusative case marks the direct object (consider e.g. *puella videt puerum* = the girl sees the boy). In such languages, word order is relatively irrelevant or 'free'. The three sentences *puella videt puerum, puella puerum videt* and *puerum videt puella* have the same basic meaning. In analytic or isolating languages like English, this is totally different. Here it is through word order that we recognize the subject and object of a sentence (compare *the girl sees the boy* and *the boy sees the girl*). By fixing the word order (subject-verb-object: SVO), syntax assumes the function fulfilled by inflection in such languages as Latin. For this reason, Latin represents a language type diametrically opposed to English, namely a synthetic or inflectional language. We can therefore classify different language types according to their morphological characteristics. We call this "morphological typology". Pairs of contrasting properties are synthetic – analytic and inflectional – isolating. It should be kept in mind, though, that *synthetic* does not necessarily equal *inflectional*, and *analytic* does not necessarily equal *isolating*. Rather, inflectional languages are a special type of synthetic languages, and isolating languages can be seen as the most radical type of analytic languages. In the past, European languages have undergone a change from synthetic to analytic (e.g. French as compared to Latin, or the modern

languages in comparison

morphological typology

synthetic – analytic

inflectional – isolating

Germanic languages as compared to the Germanic languages used over a thousand years ago). German, too, has lost part of its inflectional system and has become more analytic. Even so, it is still clearly a synthetic language – consider the case marking in sentences like *Der Mann gab dem Jungen den Schlüssel* (subject – nominative, indirect object – dative and direct object – accusative). English, on the other hand, underwent a much more radical typological change, losing a large part of its former inflectional system. Compared to Old English, it is now a strongly analytic, almost isolating language where a single lexeme hardly ever exhibits more than one word form (see the "language of largely invariable words" mentioned above).

The basic properties of the different morphological language types are summarized in (4); the relationships between the different language types can be seen in Figure IV.1 (note that the language types are idealized types and the relationships between them are simplified). It goes without saying that there are fuzzy boundaries between the different language types, and that there are many languages which do not (or only to a certain extent) possess all properties of a given language type. In Figure IV.1 one more synthetic language type relevant for the European languages is introduced: agglutinating languages, such as Turkish or Finnish. The basic difference between inflectional and agglutinating languages is that in agglutinating languages every grammatical morph carries exactly one piece of information (i.e. there is a 1:1 relationship between form and meaning), whereas in inflectional languages one morph usually carries several pieces of information. The ending *-us* in Latin *dominus*, for example, signals not only nominative (case) but also masculine (gender) and singular (number). An agglutinating language would ideally use one inflectional morph for the encoding of each of these grammatical categories.

agglutinating languages

(4)	a. synthetic:	rich inflectional system; many word forms for each lexeme; subject-object marking by means of inflection; free word order
	a1. inflectional:	mapping of different kinds of grammatical information on one morph; often morphophonemic alternation (e.g. Latin *pater-patres*, German *gib-gab*); therefore no clear segmentation into morphemes possible
	a2. agglutinating:	1:1 relationship between form and meaning/function for grammatical morphs; transparent morphological structure (→ segmentation into morphemes easily possible)

b. analytic: poor inflectional system; few word forms for each lexeme; periphrastic constructions; subject-object marking by means of word order (→ fixed word order)

b1. isolating: complete loss of inflectional endings; no word forms; usually monomorphemic words

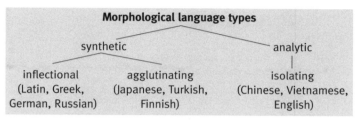

Morphological language types

synthetic — analytic

inflectional (Latin, Greek, German, Russian) agglutinating (Japanese, Turkish, Finnish) isolating (Chinese, Vietnamese, English)

Figure IV.1

Before concluding this section, let us return to the difference between inflectional and derivational morphemes. Chapters III and IV.1 have brought out a number of differences between these two types of morphemes and the corresponding morphological processes (see the summary in Table IV.3). Most of them are also valid for languages other than English, but they are not universal. There are languages, for example, which have a much greater variety of inflectional than derivational morphemes.

inflection – derivation

Table IV.3 Differences between inflection and derivation

inflection	derivation
part of the grammar	part of the lexicon
produces word forms (by means of suffixation)	produces lexemes (by means of prefixation or suffixation)
never changes word class	can change the word class
usually fully productive within one word class (e.g. possessive –s for all nouns)	only productive for subgroups of word-classes (e.g. *-ity* versus *-dom*)
very small inventory of inflectional morphemes with few very general meanings	large inventory with many relatively specific meanings
the meaning of the word form is predictable (e.g. *boys, walked, higher*)	the meaning of a new lexeme is not always predictable (*singer* = somebody who sings, but not *sweater* = somebody who sweats)

Table IV.3 Differences between inflection and derivation	
inflection	**derivation**
closed (two possible candidates for additional inflectional morphemes: negation and adverb-forming -LY)	more open (e.g. *-hood, -dom, -(a)holic* in *workaholic, chocaholic, shopaholic*)
further away from the root (only after the derivational suffixes)	closer to the root
strongly syntactically determined	hardly syntactically determined

IV.2
Syntax: Building blocks and sentence patterns

Syntax (from Greek *syntaxis* = <u>order, arrangement</u>) refers to both the study of the rules which make it possible to combine smaller linguistic units into well-formed (i.e. grammatically correct) sentences, and to the rule system itself. What is understood by *sentence* is the largest independent (!) syntactic unit of a language which is not embedded in any larger construction. The smaller building blocks sentences are formed of, their so-called "constituents", may vary in size and are hierarchically ordered:

(5)

constituents
- sentences — contain one or several
- clause(s) — contain one or several
- phrase(s) — contain one or several
- word(s) — contain one or several
- morpheme(s)

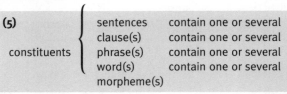

Sentences which consist of one clause only, i.e. sentences with no more than one simple subject-predicate structure (*The boy went to school*), are called "simple(x) sentences". Sentences with more than one clause may contain either several main clauses (compound sentences like 6a) or one main clause and at least one subordinate clause (complex sentences, as in 6b). The two main clauses in (6) are underlined in red, the subordinate clause in (6b) is underlined in black (also compare (9) below):

(6)　a.　<u>The girl went to school</u> and/but <u>her brother stayed at home.</u>

　　　b.　<u>The girl went to school</u> although her brother stayed at home.

The example in (7) illustrates a simplified syntactic analysis of a complex sentence. Each word is underlined, the phrases are put in square brackets, the clauses in angle brackets, and the sentence as a whole is indicated by curly brackets. The basic difference between phrases and clauses is that phrases have no subject-predicate structure:

(7) {<[A [very old] man] [left]> <after [the bus] [had arrived] [at [the station]]>}

a. clauses: *a very old man left* (main clause)
after the bus had arrived at the station (subordinate clause)

b. phrases: *very old* (adjective phrase); *a very old man, the bus, the station* (noun phrases);
left, had arrived (verb phrases);
at the station (prepositional phrase)

In what follows, we will present the most useful ways of classifying the syntactic units mentioned in (5). We will work our way up from smaller to larger units, starting with the classification of words. In section IV.3 we will then take a closer look at the most important phrase of the sentence, namely the verb phrase. In doing so the focus will always be on the special properties of the English verb phrase. In chapter V, these and further distinctive features of English syntax will be examined from a contrastive perspective by comparing them with German.

2.1 Parts of speech

The classification of words, or more precisely lexemes, into different syntactic categories (or: parts of speech) goes back to traditional grammars of antiquity, notably to the works by Aristotle and Dionysius Thrax. Their classifications and terminology are still widely used (*noun, verb, adjective, adverb, preposition,* etc.), but some of the basic assumptions underlying their classifications are no longer shared. Especially the mixing of purely formal (i.e. morphological and syntactic) and semantic criteria are nowadays rejected. If a noun is defined as "name of a person, place or thing", there is, for example, a problem for all abstract expressions (*freedom, permission*). By contrast, it is completely legitimate to classify a lexeme as a noun if it can be morphologically marked for possessive and plural, if it can appear as head in phrases like *many/much* _____ or *in the/a* _____, and if it can function as the subject or object of a verb (as in [*Many tourists*]$_S$

like [*a <u>drink</u>*]$_O$ *in the <u>garden</u>*). Similar arguments based on their morphological and syntactic behaviour, especially their inflectional properties and syntactic distribution, can be found for the classification of lexemes as verbs, adjectives, adverbs, articles, prepositions, conjunctions, etc. Several problems need to be taken care of, however.

problems with
determining word classes

First of all – and this is especially important for English – a word form can belong to more than one word class (*round*, for example, can be a noun, verb, adjective, adverb or preposition; cf. chapter III.3 on conversion). This means that multiple classifications are possible. Secondly, alternative classifications are also possible, which means that a certain lexeme or even a whole class of lexemes can be classified as belonging to either one word class or another. As will be shown later on, there are indeed reasons for relating function words like *after* or *before* not to three different parts of speech (*after school* – preposition, *after he left* – (subordinating) conjunction, *the day after* – adverb), but to one part of speech only, namely prepositions, which is subdivided into several groups. The third point to remember is that some parts of speech are more heterogeneous than others. This is especially true for adverbs, a part of speech which, due to its various modifying functions (notably as modifiers of verbs (*run <u>quickly</u>*), of adjectives (*<u>very</u> quick*) and of adverbs (*<u>very</u> quickly*)), has often been the 'waste bin' for those lexemes which could not be clearly assigned to any other part of speech. Just think of a group of adverbs as heterogeneous as *quickly, yesterday, here, very, rather, only* and *however*. But what is even more important to understand is that basically all parts of speech are heterogeneous in themselves, which means that <u>not all members of a certain word class exhibit all characteristics</u> <u>usually ascribed to that word class to the same degree</u> (especially not the semantic ones). If you compare, for example, the adjectives *quick, tired, top* and *asleep*, you will notice that only *quick* behaves like a prototypical adjective. It has a synthetic comparative (*quicker*) and superlative (*quickest*), it can be used attributively (*a quick man*) as well as predicatively *(the man was quick)*, and it can serve as the root for an adverb formed by adding the suffix {-ly} (*quickly*). As shown in Table IV.4, the adverbs *tired, top* and *asleep* behave differently. Compared to these three, *quick* can therefore be considered the 'best' (meaning the <u>prototypical,</u> most representative) adjective, while *asleep* is least prototypical.

Table IV.4 and the remarks above it point to a phenomenon that can be found on all levels of language and linguistics: there are

Table IV.4 The internal heterogeneity of the word class ADJECTIVE

	morphology			syntax		
	comp.	superl.	adverb in {-ly}	attrib.	predic.	*very*-intens
quick	x	x	x	x	x	x
old	x	x		x	x	x
top				x	x	x
asleep					x	

transitions and fuzzy boundaries between different categories, and there are gradations (from most to least representative) within categories. It is thus useful to represent the internal heterogeneity of categories with the help of continua or gradients (also termed *clines*; compare chapters I and VI).

gradients

Table IV.5 summarizes what has been said (including information in previous sections) on the various parts of speech and their most important properties. The most important criterion for the classification in this table has repeatedly been mentioned above: the distinction between lexical (open) and grammatical (closed) word classes. Interjections (like *Hey!, Ouch!, Golly!, Gosh!, Yuk!, Blast!*, etc.) have not been included here. Although they are traditionally treated as an independent word class, the status of interjections is often disputed due to their extremely idiosyncratic character.

Table IV.5 Lexical versus grammatical word classes

	lexical	grammatical (or: functional)
parts of speech:	noun, verb, adjective, adverb; in more recent syntactic theories also prepositions (incl. conjunctions)	articles, pronouns, numerals, auxiliaries; in traditional grammars also prepositions and conjunctions
phonologically:	at least one stressed syllable; nucleus of intonation unit	normally neither stressed nor nucleus of intonation unit; in connected speech: weak forms
morphologically:	open for neologisms; can be inflected (N, V, A); cf. Tab. IV.2	for the most part closed; no regular inflection
syntactically:	function as heads of phrases (NP, VP, AP, AdvP; cf. Tab. IV.2); depending on the theory: also prepositions (PP)	cannot function as heads of phrases; exceptions: some types of pronouns (NP)
semantically:	language-external, referential meaning (autosemantic terms)	exclusively language-internal, functional meaning (synsemantic terms)

2.2 Phrases and clauses

phrases with and without a head

The syntactic criterion mentioned in Table IV.5 leads us on to phrases. These may consist of either a single word (as in [John]$_{NP}$ [saw]$_{VP}$ [me]$_{NP}$) or of several words. In most phrases one central, obligatory element (the head) is extended by adding one or several modifying elements (modifiers). The whole phrase is classified according to the syntactic category of its head. The head of a phrase also determines its position in the sentence. A noun phrase, for example, has the distributional properties of a noun (compare _The man was reading a book_ with _John was reading Shakespeare_) while a verb phrase has the distributional properties of a (lexical, main) verb. Most phrases exhibit the same distribution as their heads; they are called _endocentric phrases_. Those phrases which, by contrast, have neither the same syntactic distribution as their head nor that of any other of their constituents are called _exocentric phrases_. The best example are probably prepositional phrases (_in London, at the station, on the roof_), where the phrase as a whole can take neither the position of the preposition nor that of the noun phrase it is in connection with:

(8) a. John sat in the garden.
     b. *John sat in.
     c. *John sat the garden.

Table IV.6 Types of phrases

	head	term	examples
ENDOCENTRIC	noun	noun phrase (NP)	Mary, she, the boy, a green apple, the man with the beard, the girl who stood at the corner
	verb	verb phrase (VP)	(has/was) asked, may ask, is asking, may have been being asked
	adjective	adjective phrase (AP)	(really) old, young and ambitious
	adverb	adverbial phrase (AdvP)	(very) quickly, right here
EXO-CENTRIC	preposition	prepositional phrase (PP)	at work, in the garden, on the roof, after the match, after the match had finished

The examples in Table IV.6 show that the complexity of phrases can vary quite considerably. At one end of the complexity scale there are phrases consisting of a single word, such as _Mary_ (NP) or _asked_ (VP), while at the other end we find phrases containing a whole clause. Relative clauses – as in *the girl who stood at the corner* – are almost always part of a noun phrase. Some prepositions can take not only arguments consisting of a single noun phrase but also arguments consisting of a whole clause (e. g. *after the match, after the match had finished*). This is one reason why, especially in more recent syntactic theories, conjunctions introducing a subordinate clause (subordinating conjunctions) are classified as a subgroup of prepositions.

Unlike phrases, clauses have a subject-predicate structure, with the predicate being either finite (tensed) or non-finite (non-tensed). Finite verbs are inflected and marked for agreement with the subject, as in (9a,b). The infinitive ((*to*) V), the present participle (V-*ing*) as well as the past participle (V-*ed*), on the other hand, are non-finite verb forms (see the verb forms in bold print in 9c-e). A finite verb can serve as the only predicate in a simple sentence, whereas non-finite predicates by themselves are possible only in subordinate clauses:

(9) a. <u>John leaves</u> and <u>Mary stays</u>.
    b. If John leaves, <u>I'll leave too</u>.
    c. <u>Someone wants</u> John **to leave**.
    d. **Leaving**, <u>I waved goodbye</u>.
    e. **Left** by John, <u>Mary was sad</u>.

As in (6), main clauses are underlined in red, subordinate clauses in black. In other words, (9a) is a compound sentence whereas (9b-e) are complex sentences (for details on the different types of subordinate clauses, see below and section IV.4).

2.3 Grammatical relations

In the preceding chapters we primarily focused on formal aspects when classifying the constituents of a sentence. What will stand at the centre of interest in the present section are the syntactic functions of individual phrases and clauses in a sentence, i.e. the grammatical relations they express in a sentence. Many of the relevant terms are familiar from school grammars: "subject, object (direct or indirect), complement, predicate" and "adverbial". The latter three terms require a few words of comment, especially the term complement, for which varying definitions can be found. Note that here this term will be used in the narrowest possible sense, namely as referring to predicative complements of either the subject ("subject complements", as in (10a)) or the direct object ("object complements", as in (10b)) without which the relevant sentence would be incomplete.

(10) a. My father is <u>a teacher</u> /<u>very old</u> /<u>as happy as a lark</u>.
b. I consider him <u>a hero</u> /<u>really witty</u>.

predicate

The term "predicate" will also be used more narrowly here than in traditional grammar. Typically, a predicate is one of the two indispensable core constituents of a sentence, containing all obligatory constituents except for the subject (i.e. the verbal nucleus, object(s), complement(s) and adverbial(s)). The assumption underlying this view is that every sentence consists of two parts: one part about which something is said (the subject) and the thing that is actually said (the predicate). The same view is adopted in more recent syntactic theories which favour a broader definition of the verb phrase, treating every sentence as a binary construction which can be divided (or: parsed) into a noun phrase (functioning as the subject) and a – sometimes very complex – verb phrase (i.e. the rest of the sentence):

(11)

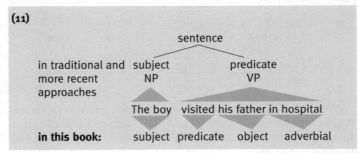

	sentence	
in traditional and more recent approaches	subject NP	predicate VP
	The boy	visited his father in hospital
in this book:	subject	predicate object adverbial

Below, the terms "predicate" and "verb phrase" will exclusively be used as referring to the verbal nucleus of the sentence. This nucleus can consist of up to five verb forms (cf. section IV.3), that is of up to four auxiliaries followed by one main verb (*he might have been being interviewed*$_v$), or one finite verb form followed by up to four non-finite verb forms (*he might*$_{fin}$ *have been being interviewed*). It can also consist of non-finite forms only (<u>*Having arrived*</u> *at the station, I bought a city map*). As far as adverbials (sometimes also known as *adjuncts*) are concerned, recall that, while this function can actually be served by adverbs (i.e. members of the word class 'adverb') (*We left <u>early</u>*), it is very often phrases (usually prepositional phrases as in *We left <u>in the morning</u>*, but also noun phrases as in *We left <u>the same morning</u>*) and clauses which function as adverbials (*We left <u>as soon as we had finished breakfast</u>*). Moreover, different from other grammatical functions, adverbials are often optional (as in *He (<u>always</u>) runs*

adverbial ≠ adverb

(*quickly*) (*along the river*)) – although certain verbs do of course require a special adverbial (e.g. a subject adverbial as in *She lives in Manchester*, or an object adverbial as in *He put the watch on the shelf*). Adverbials are usually considered part of the sentence periphery. This is also reflected by the fact that they predominantly occur at either of the margins, i.e. beginning or end, of sentences.

Having established this inventory of grammatical functions or relations, we are now in the position to describe the seven basic sentence patterns of English. In Table IV.7, the abbreviation "V" stands for "predicate" or "verb phrase" as defined above. The extent to which these sentence patterns are determined by different types of main verbs will be discussed in section IV.3.1.

7 sentence patterns

pattern	subject	predicate/verb	object(s)	complement	adverbial
SV	The girl	was sleeping			
SVO	Her mother	was dressing	the baby (O_d)		
SVC	Little James	seemed		very happy (C_s)	
SVA	He	was sitting			on the table
SVOO	Mrs Bates	gave	her children (O_i)		
			all her love (O_d)		
SVOC	Most people	considered	her (O_d)	a perfect mother (C_o)	
SVOA	She	had spent	all her life (O_d)		in the village

Table IV.7 The seven basic sentence patterns

A simple sentence consists of at least one subject and one predicate. In English, this 'minimal sentence' can be followed by a maximum of two obligatory constituents. If it is followed by only one obligatory constituent, this constituent can be either a direct object, a subject complement or an adverbial; if it is followed by two obligatory constituents, the first is an object and the second either another object, an object complement or an adverbial. In so-called *double-object constructions* (as *He gave the boy the book*) the indirect object always precedes the direct object. In English, there is thus a syntagmatic differentiation of the two objects, whereas inflectional languages use a paradigmatic strategy, i.e. different case-marking, to distinguish between direct and indirect object. Word order plays no role in these languages (compare German *Er gab dem Jungen$_{Oi}$ das Buch$_{Od}$* with *Er gab das Buch$_{Od}$ dem Jungen$_{Oi}$*). The basic ground plan of the English sentence can thus be reduced to the formula in (12).

This formula captures the word order (or more precisely the constituent order) in normal declarative sentences in English. In initial position (i.e. at the beginning of a sentence or as the first of the five constituents mentioned above) we find the subject, followed by the predicate which may or may not require further constituents (i.e. argument slots to be filled). If there are two constituents following the predicate, the first will always be an object. This is how we can typologically classify the English language as a language with a fixed word order, more precisely with an SV(O) pattern. This pattern may only be reversed in interrogative sentences and in a few other contexts which underlie very special and rigid restrictions. In such contexts, the subject follows the finite verb (*Did you know?*, *Never have I laughed like this*) – a phenomenon called "inversion". Except for *imperative sentences*, the subject slot in English sentences always needs to be filled, even if only by a so-called "dummy" element like *it* or *there*. As opposed to German (e.g. *Mir ist kalt* or *Jetzt wird aber geschlafen!*), English has no sentences without subjects. The SV(O) order in English does not only apply to main clauses but also to subordinate clauses. This is another remarkable difference compared with German (*Er ging nach Hause* vs. *Ich weinte, weil er nach Hause ging*; for more details see chapter V.2.2).

One reason why the basic sentence pattern in (12) is also valid for sentences that are more complex than those represented in Table IV.7, is that a clause or sentence can have several adverbials (as in [*Frankly,*]$_A$ [*as a child*]$_A$ he [*always*]$_A$ *ran* [*quickly*]$_A$ [*along the river*]$_A$ [*looking for dead fish*]$_A$). Each of these constituents can be much more complex. As already mentioned (see, for instance, the examples in Table IV.6), they can be extended by additional modifying elements (e.g. [*Most of the almost two thousand people in her village*]$_S$ [*considered*]$_P$ [*her*]$_{Od}$ [*an absolutely perfect mother loved and admired by her family*]$_{CO}$. Besides individual words or phrases, whole clauses (subordinate clauses) can function as the subject, object, complement or adverbial of a sentence. Depending on which grammatical function they express, they can be classified as either subject, object or complement clauses, on the one hand, or adverbial clauses, on the other hand. Because the first three have a grammatical function similar to that of noun phrases (13), they are subsumed under the heading of nominal clauses.

(12)
fixed word order SV(O)

$$SV \left((O) \left\{ \begin{array}{c} O \\ C \\ A \end{array} \right\} \right)$$

types of subordinate clauses

nominal clauses — adverbial clauses

relative clauses

Relative clauses, by the way, are excluded from our discussion here because they are always part of a noun phrase. Adverbial clauses specify the circumstances under which the situation described in the main clause takes place. Among others, we distinguish adverbials of time, place, manner, cause, condition, concession, result and purpose (14). The vast majority of adverbial clauses is finite and introduced by a subordinating conjunction (more precisely an adverbial subordinator, e.g. *while, if, because, although*). English is special among the Germanic languages in that it makes relatively frequent use of adverbial clauses in which the predicate is a participle, most frequently a present participle (so-called "adverbial participles" as in (14h); also compare (9d, e)).

(13) a. subject clause: That you are here is a miracle.
     b. object clause: We knew (that) he was a lousy driver.
     c. complement clause: The problem is how to stay away from trouble.

(14) a. adverbial of time: We left as soon as we had finished breakfast.
     b. adverbial of place: He waited where I had left him.
     c. adverbial of manner: She behaves as if she has problems.
     d. adverbial of condition: If you leave now, you'll still reach the train.
     e. adverbial of cause: I was angry because he came late.
     f. adverbial of concession: Although I love good food, I eat very little.
     g. adverbial of purpose: He came (in order) to help me.
     h. adverbial participle: Walking along the river, he watched the fishermen.

So far in this section, the building blocks or constituents of a sentence have been classified according to formal aspects (complexity, syntactic categories) and functional aspects (grammatical relations). In conclusion, it needs to be mentioned that different grammatical relations (sometimes also termed syntactic roles) are linked to different semantic (or: thematic) roles:

semantic roles

(15)
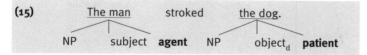
The man   stroked   the dog.

NP   subject   **agent**   NP   object$_d$ **patient**

In a prototypical active sentence, the subject is the element which carries out an action (the agent), while the direct object typically is the element affected by the action (the patient), the indirect object is the goal of the action and frequently also the element which profits from it (the recipient or benefactive). Adverbials often assume one of the semantic roles of time, place, source, goal or instrument. A comparison with a play may help illuminate the notion of semantic roles. One could say that they define the participants involved in a certain situation, the actors of a play, as it were. The number of actors and the parts they play are determined by the verb. A verb like *think* requires only one actor, namely a subject with the semantic role of an experiencer (speaking of an agent would be inappropriate in this case). The verb *give* requires three actors: a subject serving as agent, a direct object serving as patient and an indirect object assuming the semantic roles of recipient or benefactive. Once again, therefore, as pointed out in our discussion of the major sentence patterns of English, the verb turns out to be the dominating element, the anchor of any clause or sentence; in terms of the play analogy, we can say that it is the verb that gives the play its name or title. Note that concerning semantic roles, English has a special property. Frequently (at least much more often than in German), the subject is not an agent and the direct object not a patient. Just consider the examples in (16) and (17) (for more details cf. chapter V).

(16) a. The car burst a tyre. (possessor)
     b. The bucket was leaking water. (source)
     c. This tent sleeps ten people. (place)

(17) a. They fled the capital. (source)
     b. The seagull was riding the wind. (place)

Table IV.8 provides an overview of the various grammatical relations, including for each of them the prototypical syntactic category/-ies and the prototypical semantic role(s).

Table IV.8 Grammatical relations and semantic roles

grammatical relation	prototypical syntactic category	prototypical semantic role
subject	NP	agent
predicate	VP	
object (direct)	NP	patient
object (indirect)	NP	recipient, benefactive
complement	NP, AP	
adverbial	AdvP, PP	time, place, instrument

There are two reasons why the verb phrase deserves a section of its own. The first is of a general nature and valid for all languages: the verb phrase, more precisely its head, i.e. the main verb, is the central element on which the entire sentence hinges. It is the main verb that determines how many obligatory constituents there are in a sentence, that is whether, besides a subject, it is necessary to add one or two objects, a complement, or an adverbial. In other words, for any given English sentence the main verb is responsible for selecting the appropriate basic sentence pattern from those given in (12). The second reason specifically relates to English: both from a synchronic and from a diachronic point of view the verb phrase simply is the most interesting phrase. In no other phrase more has happened in the course of the history of English and currently is happening in terms of interesting innovations – from an English-specific as well as from a cross-linguistic point of view. Although the English verb, like other parts of speech, has experienced a loss of inflectional markers for certain grammatical categories (person, number, subjunctive), it is especially in the verb phrase where Present-Day English has developed the greatest number of so-called "strengthened categories" (especially the progressive and the perfect). It is here, too, where we can observe the development of new and the strengthening of old verb types and syntactic options which in part compensate for the dramatic loss of inflectional morphemes and the fixing of word order. The development of English into a strongly analytic language with a fixed word order is best illustrated with examples taken from the verb phrase. Not surprisingly this is also where some of the most important grammatical differences between English and German as well as between the different standard varieties of English can be observed (cf. chapters V and VIII).

The English verb phrase has a highly transparent modular structure. It consists of a maximum of five verb forms (typically fewer), the last of which is always the main verb, i.e. the head of the phrase, and the first of which is always a finite verb. The order of the auxiliaries preceding the main verb is strictly determined: the grammatical categories modality, perfect, progressive and passive are always marked in this order. Additionally, every auxiliary determines the form of the verb following it, which means that a modal verb (*may, must, can, could, would*, etc.) needs to be followed by an infinitive, a form of *have* by a past participle, and a form of *be* either by a present participle (when marking the progressive) or a past participle (when marking the passive). All examples in (18) follow this pattern:

verb = anchor of the sentence

strengthened categories in the verb phrase

structure of the verb phrase

(18)	modal aux	perfect aux (HAVE + past part.)	progressive aux (BE + pres. part.)	passive aux (BE + past part.)	main verb
			is	being	interviewed
		has		been	interviewed
	may	have			interviewed
	may	have	been		interviewing
	may	have	been	being	interviewed

In what follows, starting out from the distinction between main verbs and auxiliaries and the central role of the (main) verb in determining the basic sentence pattern, we will first present different types of verbs (IV.3.1) before giving an account of the most important grammatical categories of the English verb phrase (IV.3.2).

3.1 Verb types

main verbs versus auxiliaries

A fundamental distinction within the word class of verbs is the one between lexical and grammatical verbs, i. e. between main verbs and auxiliaries. It is one of the distinctive characteristics of English that, in the course of its history, it has developed an increasingly strict division between these two types of verbs. As a result, English auxiliaries nowadays form a separate group which – morphologically as well as syntactically – is very different from that of main verbs. The basic differences are summarized in Table IV.9:

Table IV.9 A comparison of auxiliaries and main verbs

	auxiliary verbs		main verbs	
the only verb in the sentence	no	(*He has), except in answers to questions of the type Has/Is/Does he ...?	yes	(He comes every day)
inversion (V_{fin} S)	yes	(Has he come?)	no	(*Comes he?)
negative contraction	yes	(isn't, hasn't, can't, mustn't)	no	(*comen't, *walkn't)
do-support				
in negations	no	(He hasn't come; not: *He doesn't have come)	yes	(He doesn't come; not: *He comes not)
in questions	no	(Has he come?; not: *Does he have come?)	yes	(Does he come?; not: *Comes he?)

136

Table IV.9 A comparison of auxiliaries and main verbs

for emphasis	no	(*He HAS come*, not: **He DOES have come*)	yes	(*He DOES come*)
in cases of ellipsis of main verb after first occurrence	no	(*John will come and so will ___ Mary*)	yes	(*John came and so did Mary*)

additionally:		modal verbs		main verbs
bare infinitive	yes	(*He can come*, not: **He can to come*)	no	(**He comes see me*; but: *He comes to see me*)
non-finite forms	no	(**to can, *canning, *canned*)	yes	(*walk, walking, walked*)
3rd sg. ind. pres. -s	no	(**he cans, *she musts*)	yes	(*he walks, she comes*)
past tense in simple declarative sentences has always past meaning	no	(*He could/might come tomorrow*)	yes	(**He came tomorrow*)

In some respects, of course, the distinction between these two verb types is not clear-cut. Thus it makes sense to place main verbs like *see, walk* or *jump* and modal verbs like *can, may* or *must* at the two opposite ends of a continuum, putting (modal) verbs such as *dare, need* and *used to* or so-called "semi-auxiliaries" like *have to* and *be going to* at the centre of this continuum. Clearly, the massive strengthening of English auxiliaries as a grammatical word class is closely linked to the development of English into an analytic language; it even needs to be seen as an important outcome of this development.

The term "auxiliary" goes back to the traditional grammar of verbs which have the same function as inflectional endings. This can be seen, for example, when considering the English perfect, progressive, passive, the analytic future formed with *will/shall* or English modal verbs, some of which have practically taken over the functions of the subjunctive formerly marked on the verb stem (for details see IV.3.2). Both as regards their semantics and, especially, their morphology and syntax (cf. Table IV.9), modal verbs differ from the second major group of auxiliaries: the so-called "primary verbs" *be, have* and *do*. The use of primary verbs is compulsory for the marking of different grammatical categories *(be, have)*, but also when forming questions and negating main verbs (cf. the so-called "do-support"). A further basic difference between modal verbs, on the one hand, and *be/have/do*, on the other hand, is the fact that only primary verbs may also be used as main verbs:

(19) a. Mary has a new car.
 b. Mary did nothing to help me.
 c. Mary is ill/a teacher/in the garden.

In (19c), *be* is a so-called "linking" or "copula verb" (or simply "copula"), i.e. a verb which establishes a link between the subject of a sentence and a certain property or attribute. That *be* in (19c) is not an auxiliary but has the formal properties of a main verb is easily shown by the fact that it can be combined with auxiliary verbs, and even with the progressive form of *be* (*Mary has been ill for quite some time, Mary will soon be ill, Mary is being a teacher*). Copula verbs form but a small group; they include verbs or certain uses of verbs like *seem, look, appear, become, remain, turn or grow* (*Yesterday she ..... ill*).

Copula verbs lead us straight back to our discussion of basic sentence patterns in section IV.2. It was repeatedly stated that sentences are formed around main verbs, and that main verbs therefore determine sentence patterns. Verbs determine both the number and the nature of their arguments by specifying their syntactic function in the sentence (i.e. their grammatical relation) as well as their semantic role. Copulas, for example, are responsible for the sentence pattern subject-predicate-complement because they require two obligatory arguments – a subject and a complement which attributes a certain property to the subject. In its spatial sense ('to be' somewhere) *be*, together with other spatial verbs such as *live, stay* or *lurk*, is also responsible for the sentence pattern subject-predicate-adverbial, the adverbial in these cases being one of place (*John is/lived/stayed in London, John lurked behind a tree*). The same sentence pattern (but with an adverbial of time) is required by another type of verbs, namely verbs which indicate duration (e.g. *It'll last/take five minutes*).

The other five basic sentence patterns found in English can all be explained by classifying verbs according to their "valency". This term (borrowed from chemistry) is used in linguistics to describe the ability, especially of verbs, to open up slots around themselves which must or can be filled. The two terms related to this property which are well-known from school grammars are "transitive" and "intransitive".

138

Margin notes:

copula verb

verb types and sentence patterns

valency

intransitive verbs

Intransitive verbs require only one argument, namely a subject (e.g. *John slept/snored/smiled*); they are therefore monovalent. Transitive verbs, on the other hand, normally require not only a subject but at least one more argument, namely a direct object (e.g. *John wrote/ read/forgot the message*), and can therefore be passivized (*The message was written by John*; for more details on the passive see the end of section IV.3.2). Transitive verbs which, apart from the direct object, require no further argument are monotransitive or divalent. But there are also trivalent verbs or uses of verbs; these require either an additional indirect object (ditransitive verbs as in *John gave/ passed Mary the message*), an object complement (*Mary considered/ called John a fool*) or an object adverbial (*Mary put/hid the message in her pocket*). Verbs like *consider* or *put* are sometimes described as "complex-transitive verbs".

transitive verbs

We have now derived all seven basic sentence patterns found in English from different types of main verbs (compare Table IV.10). For the sake of completeness, it needs to be mentioned that the minimal sentence pattern consisting of one subject and one predicate is not only required by intransitive verbs but also by so-called "avalent verbs", i.e. verbs with zero valency. Given their semantics, they do not even require a subject. In English, it is only due to the fixed word order that the subject slot of weather verbs such as *rain, snow, sleet, hail, drizzle* and *freeze* is filled, namely by the so-called "dummy it" (e.g. *it rains, it snows*).

Table IV.10 Verb types and sentence patterns

required arguments	valency type	transitivity type	examples	sentence pattern
0	avalent	–	rain, snow, freeze	SV
1	monovalent	intransitive	sleep, sit, walk	SV
2	divalent	– (copula)	be, become	SVC
2	divalent	–	live, stay, last	SVA
2	divalent	monotransitive	read, take, build	SVO
3	trivalent	ditransitive	give, offer, pass	SVOO
3	trivalent	complex-trans.	consider, call	SVOC
3	trivalent	complex-trans.	put, hide, spend	SVOA

Many English verbs can be grouped with more than one class concerning their valency or transitivity since they can be used either transitively or intransitively. Transitive verbs, for example, can be used

transitive/intransitive use of verbs

intransitively simply by leaving the second required argument implicit (as in *Mary was eating* or *John writes/drinks/plays*). This is usually the case with verbs of personal hygiene, so-called "verbs of grooming" such as *wash, comb, dress, shave*, etc., which are used reflexively, i.e. where the referent of the subject takes care of him-/herself (*Mary dresses, John shaves*). On the other hand, basically intransitive verbs can develop transitive uses, as in (20b) and (20d):

(20) a. The policemen stood, the bank robbers lay on the ground.
      b. The policemen stood the bank robbers against the wall.
      c. She ran.
      d. She ran a horse in the derby.

phrasal verbs

The meanings of the verbs in (20b) and (20d) can roughly be paraphrased as "make someone or something VERB". Such verbs are called *causative verbs*. *Stand* and *run* in the examples in (20) are instances of word-class internal conversion, a word-formation process which can be observed quite frequently in English (cf. also chapters III.3.3 and V.2.2).

The distinction between transitive and intransitive verbs is also valid for another English verb type, which has become more and more important over the last 200 years: so-called "phrasal verbs", such as look after, look up, take off, take in, give in, give up, give away.

(21) a. intransitive: John gave in. John looked up.
      b. transitive: Mary gave the secret away.
                      Mary looked the word up.

At first glance, phrasal verbs are very similar to prepositional verbs (e.g. *believe in, invest in, thank for, wait for, pull down*), but they differ from the latter in various respects (cf. Table IV.11):

Table IV.11 A comparison of phrasal and prepositional verbs		
	phrasal verbs	**prepositional verbs**
status of the particle following the verb:	adverb and/or preposition	preposition only
position of the particle:	(a) preceding or following the NP which follows the verb (*look the word up, look up the word*)	only preceding the NP (*wait for the rain, *wait the rain for*)

	phrasal verbs	prepositional verbs
Table IV.11 A comparison of phrasal and prepositional verbs		
	(b) if NP is a pronoun, only following the pronoun (*look it up,*look up it*)	only preceding the NP, even if the NP is a pronoun *believe in it*
	(c) not at the beginning of relativeclauses (**the word up which he looked*)	possible at the beginning of a clause (the rain for which I waited)
	(d) not at the beginning of questions (**Up what did he look?*)	possible at the beginning of questions (*For what did I wait?*)
stress on the particle:	usually yes (frequently nucleus of the intonation unit: *It was the word he had looked UP*)	usually no (**Here at last was the rain I had been waiting FOR*)

There is a subgroup of prepositional verbs (rather found in colloquial language use) which combine a phrasal verb with a prepositional
phrase. Examples of such phrasal-prepositional verbs are *put up with,
get away with, do away with, look in on, face up to* and *let someone
in on*. Note that in traditional grammar, the term *prepositional object*
usually refers to entire prepositional phrases (*Fiona believes in me*),
but it may also be used to refer only to the noun phrase following the
prepositional verb (*Fiona believes in me*).

3.2 Grammatical categories
The central grammatical categories of the English verb phrase are
tense and aspect. Simple sentences or main clauses obligatorily
require a finite verb, and finiteness is primarily defined by tense
marking (which is why the term "tensed verb/predicate" is sometimes
used instead of "finite verb/predicate"). By way of introduction, we
may consider the seemingly simple question: How many tenses are
there in English? There is more than one answer to this question,
depending on how wide or narrow our definition of the term "tense"
is. The lowest possible number of tenses is 2, the highest possible
number 16; but in the relevant literature we also find arguments in
favour of 3, 6, 8, 12 tenses and yet other values between 2 and 16
(compare Table IV.13 below).

tense/aspect

How many tenses?

Let us take a closer look at some of the possible values. If we regard as tenses only what can be marked inflectionally directly on the verb stem, English has no more than two tenses. In fact, English has only one inflectional suffix with an exclusively tense-marking function, namely the past-tense marker {-ed} (*walk-ed*). This word form stands in contrast to the unmarked form (*walk*), which is more adequately called "non-past" (instead of "present") because it can also be used to refer to both past (22a) and future events (22b):

(22) a. (Listen what happened to me yesterday.) This bloke walks up to me and says: ... (historical present)
b. The train leaves at six a.m. tomorrow.

If tense is not defined as a purely inflectional category, it makes sense to postulate three tenses for English, one tense each for placing a situation in the three time spheres past, present and future. In that case, the third tense is the future tense, coded by the analytic *will/shall* + infinitive construction. The *will/shall*-construction is the most neutral of the different constructions which are used to refer to events in the future. It is the one which is least restricted to a certain context, and therefore the most grammaticalized construction. All other constructions in (23) express slightly different meanings.

(23) a. The parcel will arrive tomorrow. (neutral prediction)
b. The parcel is going to arrive tomorrow. (future result of present action or intention)
c. The parcel is arriving tomorrow. (future result of an action that is already under way or is already completed)
d. The parcel will be arriving tomorrow. (future event as a matter of course)
e. The parcel arrives tomorrow. (future event is a fact, often a scheduled event)

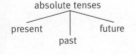

Since they take as an anchor point the here and now of the speaker, present, past and future tense are also called "absolute tenses". Tense thus qualifies as a deictic category (from Greek *deiknym-* = to show), i.e. as a grammatical category which locates a situation on the time line, always judging from the moment of utterance. We take a different view when assuming that English has more than these three tenses, for example six (adding the three perfect tenses Past Perfect, Present Perfect and Future Perfect). These perfect

perfect forms

tenses are often called "relative tenses" or "absolute-relative tenses", because they express anteriority to some reference point in the past (Past Perfect), in the present (i.e. the moment of utterance; Present Perfect) or in the future (Future Perfect; for more details see below).

relative tenses

(24) a. When my parents arrived we <u>had left</u> already.
b. Sorry, Mum. We<u>'ve left</u> already. (speaking from a car phone)
c. Mum, we're about to leave. When you arrive we<u>'ll have left</u> already.

Arguing in favour of English having six tenses therefore implies that tense is no longer considered a strictly deictic category, because the moment of utterance is no longer the direct point of reference for all tenses.

When combining these six constructions with the English progressive (*be* + present participle), we end up with twelve different 'tenses'. But if we decide to adopt this perspective, tense no longer exclusively defines the position of a situation as a whole on the time line, but also applies to the internal make-up of the situation, e.g. whether it is in progress at a given point in time or not. The meaning of the term "tense" would be watered down even more if we additionally included *would/ should* + infinitive constructions and their corresponding perfect and progressive forms. At least in direct speech, these constructions are no longer primarily responsible for situating events on the time line, but rather express different kinds of modality or speaker attitude (assumption, obligation, possibility, probability, necessity, etc.). If we included these constructions, too, English would end up being a language with 16 tenses; indeed, English is represented as such in many school grammars.

We should not, however, confuse the picture by lumping everything together, but rather try to bring out the modular structure of the English verb phrase and the possibilities of combining the different grammatical categories. An alternative way of arranging and classifying the 16 verb constructions discussed above differently is the following (also compare (18) above). The first step is to treat constructions with *would* and *should* (sometimes called "conditional tenses") as combinations of a modal verb and a grammatically marked (full) verb construction: *would have said* would thus be analyzed the same way as *must have said* or *may have said*. The second step is to classify

combinatorial options

the contrast between progressive and simple form (*he is singing* vs. *he sings*) not as a contrast in tense but as an aspectual contrast.

"Aspect" (from Latin *aspectus* = viewpoint, perspective) is a grammatical category that allows us to comment on the internal temporal make-up of a situation, where *situation* is used as generic term for conditions or states and different types of actions, events, etc. In English, the progressive form (also known as "expanded form") provides a grammatical means which allows, and sometimes even compels, the speaker to indicate explicitly whether he or she regards a certain action as completed or still in progress. Therefore, aspect – as opposed to tense – has a strongly subjective component. In many cases, however, it is not optional but obligatory, as can be seen in (25a):

aspect
progressive form   simple form

(25)	a.	John is walking to work.	(now, at the time of utterance)
	b.	John walks to work.	(usually, as a habit; not necessarily now)

It is not easy to identify a core meaning of the progressive. It is true to say, though, that the progressive describes a situation surrounding a certain point of reference (the so-called "temporal frame"), highlighting a certain phase of this situation – as if observing it through a magnifying glass or as if activating the frame-freeze function of a video recorder. The progressive therefore describes only part of the situation while the simple form covers the situation as a whole. The reference point indispensable for the progressive is generally introduced in the context, either by a time adverbial (26a,b) or simply by a tense marker (such as *looked* in (26c) or the present tense in (25a)). Since the progressive always needs a temporal reference (or: anchor) point, i.e. a point on the time line where we can place our magnifying glass, it can by itself never advance an action or, e.g. in a novel, the plot on the time line, and thus cannot be used for describing sequences of actions like the one in (26d):

(26)	a.	I was having a nap at three.
	b.	When she arrived, he was cooking dinner.
	c.	Jack turned and looked at his sister. She was laughing.
	d.	He opened the fridge, took out a pie and went back to his room.

The progressive has conquered a lot of new territory in the course of the history of English, and continues to do so, especially in spontaneous spoken (including all non-standard) varieties of English (cf. chapter VIII.3.1). As a result, it can nowadays be used in a much wider variety of contexts and for the expression of subtle differences in meaning (e. g. as future marker in (23c)), although not all of these uses can be attributed solely to the progressive interacting with different types of predicates (situation types, or so-called "aktionsarten"). Some effects resulting from this interaction between progressive aspect and the aktionsart of a verb occur regularly, though. Take, for example, the effect of rapid repetition when the progressive is used with momentary verbs (27a), or the effect of incompletion (27c) or not reaching the endpoint of an action (27e) when using the progressive with so-called "telic verbs" (from Greek *telos* = aim or goal), i.e. verbs with an inbuilt endpoint.

(27)			
	a.	John was knocking on the door.	(several times)
	b.	John knocked on the door.	(only once)
	c.	John was writing a letter.	(letter not finished yet)
	d.	John wrote a letter.	(letter is finished)
	e.	John was drowning.	(danger of drowning)
	f.	John drowned.	(drowned)

Excluding both the *would/should* and the progressive constructions, we are left with only six of the original sixteen candidates for English tenses. From these, we can subtract another three, namely the perfect forms. The contrast between *perfect* (as a cover term for Present Perfect, Past Perfect and Future Perfect) and non-perfect forms is often treated as a second aspectual contrast besides the progressive/ non-progressive one. This is primarily due to the contrast between Present Perfect and Simple Past. In contexts where the Present Perfect is neither obligatory (28a) nor impossible (28b), it depends solely on the view of the speaker which form is used to describe a situation in the past. Is the situation still relevant at the moment of utterance ('current relevance'; 29a), or is it considered completed (in the speaker's mind as well as in actual fact; 29b)?

Present Perfect versus Simple Past

```
            perfect
           /   |   \
    Present    |    Future
    Perfect    |    Perfect
               |
             Past
           Perfect
```

(28)		
	a.	adverbials of time which include the moment of utterance: *at present, so far, as yet, lately, before now, to this hour, for some time now, since Monday*, etc. (can never combine with the Simple Past)

b. adverbials of time which refer to a specific moment or period in the past preceding the moment of utterance: *long ago, yesterday, the other day, last night, at that time, then, on Tuesday,* etc. (can never combine with the Present Perfect)

(29) a. A. Will you come to the party?
    B. Sorry, I've broken my leg and have to stay in bed.
b. A. How was the weekend?
    B. Great! I broke my leg, my car was stolen and my girl friend left me.

Yet there are also good reasons for adopting a different view of the category perfect, namely as a third category, independent of both tense and aspect. The main function of this category is to establish a relationship of anteriority between a certain situation and a point of reference on the time line in the way described above. Similar to the category of tense, the perfect localizes an entire situation on the time line, but it does *not* use the moment of utterance as an immediate point of reference, and it *always* involves a relationship of anteriority. Similar to aspect, perfect is a non-deictic category which may depend on the speaker's perspective, but it does *not* give us any information about the internal structure of a situation. The differences and similarities of these three categories can be represented as in Table IV.12:

Table IV.12 The categories tense, perfect and aspect			
	tense	**perfect**	**aspect**
localizes a situation on the time line	yes	yes	no
deictic	yes	no	no
fixed sequence of situation and reference time	no	yes (anteriority)	no
focus on the internal make-up of a situation	no	no	yes (prog.)

Table IV.13 is an attempt at representing the complex tense and aspect system of English in its entirety. First, however, consider the three main uses of the Present Perfect in (30):

(30) a. (Would you shut the window, please?) I've (just) had a bath. (*resultative perfect*)

    b. Have you seen the Dali exhibition (yet)? (*experiential perfect, indefinite past*)

    c. I've known him for years. (*continuative perfect*)

Table IV.13 Tense and aspect system

nr. of tenses?	form	term	The 16 verb forms resulting from the combination of different categories:			
			tense (referential)	perfect (*have* +V-*ed*)	aspect (*be* + V-*ing*)	modal constr.
2	walk	present	x			
	walked	past	x			
3	will/shall walk	future	x			
6	have walked	present perfect	x	x		
	had walked	past perfect	x	x		
	will have walked	future perfect	x	x		
8	would/should walk	conditional I	x			x
	would/should have walked	conditional II	x	x		x
12	6+ 6 x be walking ... progressive		x	x	x	
16	8+ 8 x be walking ... progressive		x	(x)	x	x

All the grammatical categories discussed in this section so far (mood, tense, perfect and aspect) can be combined with each other without any problems. However, the complete meaning of the resulting complex constructions cannot always be derived from the categories involved; it is therefore not always easy to prove that the meanings of the complex constructions are fully compositional (cf. also chapter VI). It needs to be admitted that sometimes, after all, the meaning of the whole is more than a mere sum of the meaning of its parts. What is still missing in this system of combinable verb categories is the so-called "genus verbi" or "voice", which largely concerns the distinction between active and passive. Only transitive verbs have a passive voice (not all, but most of them), which, in English, is

compositionality

an analytic construction with either a form of the auxiliary *be* and a past participle (*Jerry was chased by Tom*) or *get* and a past participle (*He got (himself) arrested*). The *get*-construction is not quite as formal and is used to indicate that the speaker is emotionally involved in the situation he or she describes and/or that, especially when using a reflexive pronoun, the speaker considers the subject of the passive sentence as partly responsible for what has happened to him or her. The prototypical subject of a passive sentence has the semantic role of a patient (31a) or a benefactive (31b). Compared to other languages, English is special in that it cannot only convert the direct object (31a) and the indirect object (31b) of an active sentence into the subject of the corresponding passive sentence, but that it can do the same with the 'objects' of prepositions (31c,d). In English, it is even possible to passivize an intransitive verb if the verb is followed by a prepositional phrase functioning as an adverbial of place (31d):

(31)   a.   The award was given to the actor.
         b.   The actor was given the award.
         c.   This problem must be disposed of.
         d.   This bed has been slept in.

mediopassive

Also possible in many cases is the intransitive use of transitive verbs. In such mediopassive (or: middle voice) constructions the noun phrase functioning as the subject of the seemingly active sentence with an intransitively used verb is, from a semantic point of view, rather the direct object of a transitive verb, fulfilling the semantic role of a patient. In example (32a), it is not Kafka who translates something, but it is his work which cannot be (easily) translated. Bill in (32b) is not unable to scare other people but is not easily scared himself. In other words: in mediopassive constructions the supposed agent is affected himself. In English, this reflexive relationship between the actual grammatical subject and the "logical" direct object is not indicated by the use of a reflexive pronoun (as opposed to other Germanic languages; compare German *Kafka übersetzt sich nicht gut*, *Kafka lässt sich nicht (gut) übersetzen*).

(32)   a.   Kafka doesn't translate.   b.   Bill doesn't scare easily.

The opposition between dynamic and statal passive, corresponding to the opposition between the *sein* and *werden* passive in German, is usually marked by the formal contrast between progressive and simple form:

(33) a. Dinner is being prepared.
(still in preparation; dynamic passive)
b. Dinner is prepared. (dinner is ready; statal passive)

Further contrasts between the grammatical structures of English and German will be discussed in chapter V.

Checklist Grammar – key terms and concepts

adjective
adverb
adverbial
adverbial clause
agreement/concord
aktionsart
argument
aspect
attributive ↔ predicative
case
clause (main, subordinate,
declarative, interrogative,
imperative)
clitic
comparison
complement (subject, object)
compositionality
conjugation
constituents
declension
deictic category
descriptive ↔ prescriptive /
normative
distribution
endocentric ↔ exocentric
phrase
finite ↔ non-finite
gender
gradient

grammatical categories
(strengthened ↔
weakened)
grammatical relation/function
(subject, object$_{d/i}$,
complement$_{S/O}$, predicate,
adverbial)
group genitive
head
imperative
inflectional ↔ isolating
inflectional morphology
inversion
modality
morphological typology
(synthetic ↔ analytic,
isolating ↔ agglutinating
↔ inflectional)
nominal clause (subject,
complement, object)
noun
number
object (direct ↔ indirect)
passive (medio-)
perfect (present, past, future)
periphrastic construction
phrase (noun phrase, verb
phrase, prepositional
phrase)
predicate

preposition
progressive (form)
reference grammar
reflexivity
relative clause
sentence
compound sentence ↔
complex sentence
semantic role (e. g. agent,
patient, goal, benefactive)
situation
subject
subordinating conjunction
(adverbial subordinator)
syntagmatic differentiation
syntax
tense: absolute (present,
past, future) ↔ relative
valency
verb (auxiliary ↔ semi-
auxiliary ↔ main/full verb;
copula; modal; primary;
transitive ↔ intransitive;
causative; particle;
prepositional; telic verb)
voice (active ↔ passive ↔
middle/mediopassive)
word class
word form
word order

1 Which grammatical categories are marked on English nouns and verbs?

2 a. Identify in traditional terms all parts of speech occurring in the following sentence: *Then the boy rubbed the magic lamp and suddenly a genie appeared beside him.*
  b. *Round* belongs to as many as five different word classes. Give one example for each of them.

3 a. Provide the appropriate labels for the following phrases and state which of them do not have a head: *below the window, rather slowly, Tom and Jerry, has been saying, fast and expensive car.*
  b. Where else in this book did we talk about heads and modifiers? Can you make any generalizations about the preferred order of heads and modifiers in English?

4 Identify all phrases and their grammatical functions in the following sentences:
  a. He spends all his money on horses.
  b. John called me an idiot.
  c. Mary left the next day.
  d. They may be staying until next June.
  e. His face turned pale when he saw me.

5 a. Identify the adverbs and adverbials in the following sentence: *Honestly, I did see him briefly in the park yesterday when he was feeding the ducks.*
  b. Give typical properties of adverbials, and then specify what is unusual about the adverbial in the following sentences: *The whole thing lasted a mere thirty seconds.*

6 Underline and identify the different types of subordinate clauses in the sentences below:
  a. That cities will attract more and more criminals is a safe prediction.
  b. This shows how difficult the question must have been.
  c. Being a farmer, he is suspicious of all governmental interference.
  d. We knew that he was a lousy driver.
  e. I am very eager to meet her.
  f. The problem is who will water my plants when I am away.

g. No further discussion arising, the meeting was brought to a close.

h. I'll show you what you can open the bottle with.

7 There are two main types of relative clauses. *Restrictive* (or: *defining*) *relative clauses* provide necessary information about the head noun whereas *non-restrictive* (or: *non-defining*) *relative clauses* provide additional, but non-essential information. Identify these two types in the examples below and determine the structural differences between them.

a. My daughter, who studies medicine, will come and visit me today.

b. My daughter who studies medicine will come and ...

c. My daughter studying medicine will come and ...

d. The car she'll be using is our old Austin Mini.

e. *The car, she'll be using, is our old Austin Mini.

f. The car that she'll be using is our old Austin Mini.

g. *The car, that she'll be using, is our old Austin Mini.

8 Which of the following statements are true, which are false?

a. English is a language with grammatical gender.

b. Normally, only transitive verbs can be passivized.

c. Modal verbs lack participles.

d. All copulas have the valency zero.

e. English has no inflectional future.

f. Languages with little or no inflectional morphology need a fixed SVO order.

g. All verbs demanding an object complement also demand an object, but not vice versa.

h. The subjects of active and passive sentences differ with regard to their prototypical semantic roles.

i. English is relatively rich in mediopassive constructions and adverbial participles.

j. There is an inflectional subjunctive in the sentence *We insist that the director resign.*

9 a. Which of the following verbs are phrasal verbs and which prepositional verbs? *rely on, believe in, take in, take away, fill up, dispose of, blow up*

b. There are two possible syntactic analyses of prepositional verbs and the NP following them: either as an intransitive verb fol-

Exercises
Advanced

lowed by a PP (see A) or as a transitive verb followed by a direct object (see B):

A. [They] [trusted] [in a friend]
B. [They] [trusted in] [a friend]

If you consider the following sentences which is the preferred analysis? But note that there are also arguments for the alternative analysis: Try to find some of them.

a. A friend in whom they trusted.
b. In whom did they trust?
c. They trusted steadfastly in a friend.
d. *They trusted in steadfastly a friend.

10 The Progressive has constantly extended its territory in the course of the history of English. One example of this development is the construction in the sentences below. Describe this construction and specify its meaning. Can all types of adjectives be used with the progressive? Do different types of adjectives yield different effects when used in this construction? Note that noun phrases, too, can be used in this construction instead of adjectives. Give examples and specify the meaning of the relevant construction.

a. For once I am being practical.
b. I think you are being unfair to take these things up now.
c. I hope I'm not being unduly rhetorical.
d. I'm just being polite to Arthur.
e. I'm being very, very good.
f. I may be being a bit cynical about it.

11 Draw up a list of arguments taken from different domains of grammar which illustrate that English is a strongly analytic language.

12 The following text should make you say goodbye to English grammar with a big smile. But there is also a task connected with it. Try to spot all grammatical and otherwise language-related terms, and ask yourself what exactly it is that creates the humourous effect in the individual cases. So off we go with a stirring courtroom-drama: *The murder of the English language* – sometimes known as *The accusative case.*

Prosecution: Are you Very Quickly, adverbial phrase?
Accused: I am.
P: Very Quickly, you're accused of splitting an infinitive! Say, how do you plead: Guilty or not guilty?

A: Not guilty, not guilty.

P: A double negative. How then would you explain your past imperfect?

A: I was going through an awkward phrase. There's no substantive proof. Now and then I just colon friends for a quick imperative before lunch.

P: And is that all?

A: Well no, there is a rather pretty feminine gender in the case, a Miss Pronunciation, who lives in suffix with her grammar and grandpa.

P: When was your first dative?

A: I met her at a participle! There she was supine and in a passive mood. She was superlative, absolutely pluperfect.

P: Mr. Quickly, would I be correct in this preposition that you were aiming at an unlawful conjugation with this feminine gender? Answer the interrogative: How far did you get?

A: I made a parse at her, but she declined. She said her parentheses would object. And in many ways she's about to become a noun.

P: Was this news neuter you?

A: Affirmative.

P: Thank you. What nationality is she?

A: Italic.

P: Mr. Quickly, you're in quite a predicate I can tell you. Officer, put him in brackets! You are also accused of immoral earnings from prose – and even verse, evasion of syntax.

Judge: And now the sentence: Off with his prefix!

Sources and further reading

Biber, Douglas/Stig Johansson/Geoffrey Leech/Susan Conrad/Edward
Finegan. 1999. *The Longman grammar of spoken and written
English*. London: Longman.

Givón, Talmy. 1993. *English grammar: a function-based introduction*.
2 vols. Amsterdam/Philadelphia: Benjamins.

Greenbaum, Sidney/Randolph Quirk. 1990. *A student's grammar of
the English language*. Harlow: Longman.

Halliday, Michael A.K. 2004[3]. *An introduction to functional grammar*.
revised by Christian M.I.M. Matthiessen. London: Arnold.

Huddleston, Rodney. 1984. *Introduction to the grammar of English*.
Cambridge: Cambridge University Press.

Huddleston, Rodney/Geoffrey K. Pullum. 2002. *The Cambridge
grammar of the English language*. Cambridge: CUP.

Hurford, James R. 1994. *Grammar. A student's guide*. Cambridge:
Cambridge University Press.

König, Ekkehard. 1994. "English." In: Ekkehard König/Johan van der
Auwera, eds. *The Germanic languages*. London/New York:
Routledge. 532-565.

Leisi, Ernst/Christian Mair. 1999. *Das heutige Englisch*. Heidelberg:
Winter.

McCawley, James D. 1998[2]. *The syntactic phenomena of English*.
Chicago/ London: The University of Chicago Press.

Miller, Jim/Regina Weinert. 1998. *Spontaneous spoken language:
syntax and discourse*. Oxford: Clarendon Press.

Quirk, Randolph et al. 1985. *A comprehensive grammar of the
English language*. London: Longman.

Thomson, Audrey J./Agnes V. Martinet. 2001[4]. *A practical English
grammar*. Oxford: Oxford University Press.

Tallerman, Maggie. 2005[2]. *Understanding syntax*. Oxford: Oxford
University Press.

Trask, Robert L. 1993. *A dictionary of grammatical terms in
linguistics*. London/New York: Routledge.

V Contrastive Linguistics: English and German

Introduction

bundles of contrasts

The present chapter aims to give an overview of the most important structural differences between English and German. It will reconsider some issues discussed earlier in this book, albeit from a decidedly different point of view. It will be explored how the basic structural differences between English and German are related to each other. The focus of this chapter will thus be on clusters or bundles of contrasts, each of which can be derived from a fundamental structural difference between the two languages. The overarching objective, then, will be to show how it is possible to bring order to the large variety of superficially unrelated contrasts between English and German which, after all, are two otherwise closely related languages. Thus, we will increasingly take a bird's-eye view of the two languages: the task will be to work out their most essential characteristics and to trace back our findings concerning what they have and have not in common to general tendencies among the world's languages. One crucial insight is going to be that many of the differences between English and German are not restricted to these two languages but represent more general contrasts between languages which – like English and German – represent different language types. Along these lines, we will have to restrict ourselves to a few select grammatical structures (section V.2), yet the most important phonetic and phonological differences will be outlined, too, at the end of this section (V.3).

First, however, we will address the question: What is contrastive linguistics?, focussing on the following issues: what are its basic assumptions and premises, how did it develop, and how is it relevant to foreign-language teaching?

V.1 Contrastive Linguistics

pedagogical bias of early contrastive linguistics

Contrastive Linguistics (CL) traditionally refers to the synchronic comparison of two languages with respect to a large number of linguistic structures (or: parameters). Its objective is to work out not only what the two language systems have in common but especially in which respects they differ. The motivation for focussing on the differences between two languages lies in the basic assumption of early CL (1940s to 1960s) that, when learning a foreign language, a speaker will find those structures particularly difficult which are different in his or her native language. The aim of early CL was purely educational. The systematic comparison of two languages was expected to help improve foreign-language learning and teaching by, on the one hand, predicting potential sources of error and, on the other hand, incorporating contrastive findings into more effective learning and teaching materials. The educational approach of CL is based on the following premises: first, foreign language acquisition is different from first language acquisition. Second, a foreign language is always acquired against the background of a speaker's native language. Third, foreign-language learners usually find certain features of a foreign language easy to learn, while having difficulties with others. According to the so-called Contrastive (Analysis) Hypothesis (established by Robert Lado in 1957), speakers find those structures of a foreign language (L2) easy to learn which resemble equivalent structures in their own native language (L1). Differences between the two languages, on the other hand, may result in learning difficulties and are a major source for mistakes made by foreign-language learners. The contrastive hypothesis is therefore based on the idea of transfer, i.e. the tendency of foreign-language learners to transfer characteristic features of their mother tongue to the foreign language they are learning. Depending on whether this transfer supports or hampers the acquisition of a foreign language, we speak of "positive" or "negative transfer". Educationally oriented CL has of course always focused on negative transfer, so-called interference. From a contrastive perspective, the

transfer
positive   negative
                (interference)

156

most important types of interference are substitution (1a), over- or underdifferentiation (1b) and over- or underrepresentation (1c). Only the former two can actually lead to mistakes. Over- or underrepresentation, i.e. speakers using a certain native-language construction either too often or too rarely in a foreign language, may only result in unidiomatic language use and give the impression that a native speaker would have expressed the same content or issue differently. Unlike normal interference, which leads to errors, underrepresentation or the complete avoidance of certain structures of the target language is especially frequent among beginners and advanced learners.

types of interference

(1) a. **substitution:**
e.g. German /s/, /z/, /v/ for English /θ/, /ð/, /w/;
ich bekomme ein Bier > * *I become a beer; wenn ich ihn fragen würde, würde er ablehnen* > *if I would ask him, he would refuse* (not possible in Standard British English)

b1. **overdifferentiation:**
differentiation of L1 does not exist in L2 (e.g. German *Frucht/Obst* vs. *fruit*)

b2. **underdifferentiation:**
differentiation in L2 does not exist in L1 (e.g. *shade/shadow* vs. *Schatten, snail/slug* vs. *Schnecke*; Past Tense/Present Perfect vs. *Perfekt* as narrative tense, *simple/progressive form* in English vs. "simple form" in German)

c1. **overrepresentation:**
speakers use structures of their mother tongue more often than native speakers would do, e.g. finite subordinate clauses with introductory relative pronouns or adverbial subordinators. It can also be observed that advanced learners overuse foreign-language structures in L2.

c2. **underrepresentation:**
speakers use foreign-language structures more rarely than native speakers would do, e.g. shortened relative clauses (*The man sitting on the bench watched her all the time*), adverbial participles (*Sitting on the bench the man watched her all the time*) or mediopassive constructions (*This book won't sell*).

Figure V.1

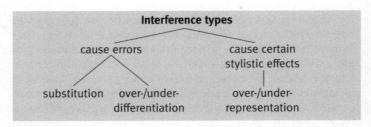

Interference types

cause errors — cause certain stylistic effects

substitution / over-/under-differentiation

over-/under-representation

a critical look at "pedagogical" contrastive linguistics

From what is known today, some of the basic assumptions of CL – and hence its objectives – must be taken with extreme caution. Learning difficulties and mistakes, for example, might not always result from differences between a learner's native language and the target language; on the contrary, these can also be due to similarities between the two languages. Consider the perfect in German and English. Both languages have very similar constructions (although Standard English has no equivalent of the German *sein* 'be'-perfect any longer: *Ich bin gekommen* but **I am come*). Nevertheless, the correct use of the English Present Perfect presents a major difficulty for many German learners. In German, especially in spontaneous speech, the perfect is almost exclusively used as an (absolute) past tense. It can, without any problems, replace the Simple Past *(Präteritum)* and is generally used as a narrative tense (see (2a)), whereas in English a story can not be told in the Present Perfect (2b). There is a strict division of tasks between Present Perfect and Simple Past, and there are many adverbials of time which can only be used with one of the two tenses (cf. chapter IV.3.2).

(2)　a.　Gestern Abend sind wir erst im Kino gewesen. Dann sind wir zu Luigi gegangen und haben noch ein Eis gegessen. Dann ist es auch schon ziemlich spät gewesen, und Tim hat uns nach Hause gefahren.

　　　b.　*Last night we've been to the cinema. *Then we've gone to Luigi's and have eaten an icecream. *Then it's been rather late already, and Tim has driven us home.

We should also be careful concerning the predictive power of contrastive analyses. Extensive empirical studies of errors made by foreign-language learners have shown that some errors predicted by CL were very rare or did not occur at all, whereas some frequently made mistakes had not been predicted. Especially in grammar this can frequently be observed, whereas in phonetics and phonology predictions made by CL are more reliable. Most importantly, however, the proportion of errors resulting from differences or similarities between two language systems, i.e. errors due to transfer, must not be overestimated. Although transfer is indeed responsible for a large number of errors (on average about 50 %), there are many additional factors which need to be taken into consideration.

To cut a long story short: the Contrastive Hypothesis and its basic assumptions about foreign-language acquisition have turned out to be too strong. The catalogue of errors which CL predicts because of the structural differences between two given languages only partially coincides with the errors actually occurring. CL must therefore be seen as having a relatively limited prognostic potential. Its strength lies in its use as a diagnostic tool which, by considering different language systems, can explain a considerable amount of errors. Similarly disappointing has been CL's role in improving learning materials. Among the teaching materials of the last few decades, there are very few which have incorporated CL findings. Moreover, there is no empirical evidence that learning and teaching materials based on CL findings are superior to traditional materials.

role of CL:
prognosis → diagnosis

By the 1970s, after realizing that its applicability must not be overestimated, linguists ceased to view CL primarily as a branch of applied linguistics and started regarding it as a branch of theoretical and descriptive linguistics instead. Even though they are not directly relevant to teaching practice, the insights obtained from non-pedagogical CL are valuable in themselves, especially for advanced foreign-language students and (future) foreign-language teachers. CL can therefore be considered as one out of several branches of comparative linguistics (cf. Figure V.2).

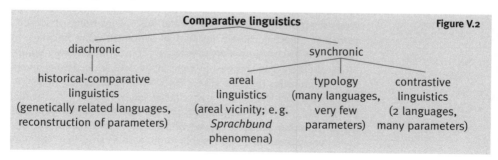

Comparative linguistics — **Figure V.2**

diachronic — synchronic

| historical-comparative linguistics (genetically related languages, reconstruction of parameters) | areal linguistics (areal vicinity; e.g. *Sprachbund* phenomena) | typology (many languages, very few parameters) | contrastive linguistics (2 languages, many parameters) |

The oldest branch of comparative linguistics is historical-comparative linguistics (or: comparative philology), the dominant linguistic approach of the 18th and especially 19th century. Its goal is to establish family relationships by comparing different languages (e.g. English and German as West Germanic languages, or Danish and Icelandic as North Germanic languages) and to reconstruct older stages of given languages or even the proto-languages from which different language families developed (e.g. Proto-Germanic as the 'mother' of all Germanic languages, where "proto" stands for "reconstructed, without written records"). The probably best-known fruit of historical-comparative research are language family trees. Areal linguistics (or: areal typology) uses a synchronic approach; it investigates languages which, in the course of time, have in certain respects become more and more alike due to their geographical proximity, even though they are not related genetically. One famous example of such a linguistic convergence area is the Balkan *Sprachbund*. The languages forming the core of this group (Modern Greek, Albanian, Romanian, Bulgarian and Macedonian) have a number of linguistic features in common (e.g. postposed definite articles, loss of the infinitive) which, say, Romanian does not share with any other Romance language, or Bulgarian and Macedonian do not share with any other Slavonic language. Of all comparative approaches, typology is the only one which matters in CL. Its goal is to identify patterns and limits of variation among the languages of the world and to distinguish different language types via the empirical analysis of a multitude of languages which are neither historically, genetically nor geographically related. To this purpose, typologists study representative samples of the more than 500 languages spoken worldwide focusing on only a few parameters, typically only one. Well-known examples of such variation parameters are the type and complexity of inflectional morphology (which yields the morphological language types described in chapter IV.1) or the basic word order of subject, verb and object in simple declarative sentences. One hallmark of typology is its constant effort to establish correlations between properties of different languages. In most languages, for example, where the verb precedes the object (so-called "VO-languages" as English or French), prepositions and relative clauses follow their nominal heads. Conversely, most OV-languages (like Turkish and Japanese) have postpositions and relative clauses which precede their nominal heads. Such generalizations are preferably formulated as so-called "implicational universals", e.g. "A language which has SOV as its canonical word order is very likely to have postpositions."

language typology (margin note)

Since the 1980s, CL has been increasingly inspired by typology, adopting new methods, asking different questions, offering new explanations, and adopting a whole new framework for classifying the contrasts and similarities observed between the languages under investigation. Above all, typologically oriented CL tries to establish correlations between structural differences which appear to be completely unrelated at first sight. It then bundles these differences into sets of contrasts, not only attempting to explain these by invoking properties of the structural systems of the relevant languages, but also setting out to predict to what extent we may expect these differences (but also the similarities) to occur among other languages of the same types. Section V.2 will illustrate what such an approach looks like.

There are also links between typology and foreign-language acquisition. For example, the greater the difference between the language types two languages represent, i.e. the greater the typological distance between two languages, the longer it will take a native speaker of one of these languages to learn the other language, or to achieve a high degree of proficiency. A different type of typology-based prediction regarding potential difficulties in foreign-language acquisition is concerned with those domains in which a learner's native language differs from the foreign language to be acquired. It has been shown that foreign-language learners experience special difficulties in those cases where the target language is (more) marked as compared to their mother tongue, i.e. instances where the target language is typologically unusual and does not follow a universal tendency (*Markedness Differential Hypothesis*; see section V.3 for a phonetic example). Thus modified, the Contrastive Hypothesis regains its relevance.

Before investigating some of the most important grammatical differences between English and German, it should be added that there are, of course, quite a number of structural features they have in common. Since German and English are two closely related languages, this does not come as a surprise. Together with Dutch, Frisian, Afrikaans and Yiddish, they form the branch of West Germanic languages. With these, as well as with the slightly more remote North Germanic (or: Scandinavian) languages, English and German share a number of morphological and syntactic properties, for example:

new orientation: CL ↔ typology

V.2
The most striking grammatical differences between English and German

- the distinction between strong verbs (e.g. *sing–sang–sung, gehen–ging–gegangen*) and weak verbs (e.g. *work–worked–worked, lieben–liebte–geliebt*)
- only two tenses which are marked by inflection of the verb stem, namely past (or preterite, marked) and non-past (or present, unmarked)
- verb-second position (V/2), i.e. in simple declarative sentences the predicate containing the finite verb usually comes second
- use of word order to distinguish between the basic sentence types (V/2 in declarative sentences and V/1 in questions)
- historically: increasing analyticity due to the loss of various inflectional morphemes

In what follows only the most central grammatical contrasts between English and German will be considered. As far as possible, they will not be discussed independently of each other or of the overall ground plan of English. Rather, they will be related to the language type English represents with regard to different parameters: morphology (V.2.1), word order (V.2.2) and the mapping between form and function (V.2.3). In each of these three sections, one set of contrasts will be presented, always starting out from a fundamental typological difference between the ground plans of English and German which will then open the door to a variety of other (contrasting) properties. Note though that there are, of course, causal links between these sets, and that some of them overlap. In English, the loss of inflectional morphology (V.2.1) has resulted in a more rigid word order (V.2.2), which, in turn, is the cause for the loosening of the mapping between semantic structure and grammatical form (at least in a number of central areas of grammar (V.2.3)). In other words: the structural differences between English and German will be considered from three different perspectives – which will help us see the wood for the trees. Finally, section V.2.4 offers an account of the most important structural contrasts which can not be easily subsumed under one of the three sets of contrasts.

2.1 Morphology

One important set of contrasts between English and German is related to the fact that English has travelled a long way from a strongly inflectional language towards an isolating language (cf. also chapter IV.1) while German has stayed rather conservative, also compared to the other Germanic languages. From this fundamental typological contrast between a near-isolating language (English) and a still strongly inflectional language (German) arise, for example, the following morphological and syntactic differences.

contrasts within the NP

English has an eroded case system. Nouns can only occur in two different forms, either not marked for case (common case) or marked for the possessive. Pronouns can have an additional object form (e.g. *he – his – him, who – whose – whom*), but the object form of the relative and interrogative pronouns is being used more and more rarely – at least in informal English – and most speakers prefer the unmarked form (*who*) or the zero pronoun in sentences like the following:

(3) a. The man whom/who/Ø I met yesterday
       is a professor of linguistics.
    b. Whom/Who did you give the money to?

English articles and adjectives are not marked for case at all. There is, then, no concord in English noun phrases, i.e. no formal agreement between the nominal head and the constituents which modify it. Also, English sentences lack government, i.e. there are no sentences where, for example, the preposition or the verb require that the nominal argument they precede is marked for a certain case. German, on the other hand, has both of these properties, marking not only gender by means of inflectional morphemes (masculine/ feminine/ neuter) but also marking nouns, pronouns, articles and adjectives for nominative, genitive, dative and accusative case (as well as gender):

concord/agreement – government

(4) a. concord: ein-Ø alt-er Mann-Ø   (nominative masc. sg.),
                     ein-es alt-en Mann-es (genitive masc. sg.),
                     ein-em alt-en Mann-Ø (dative masc. sg.),
                     ein-en alt-en Mann-Ø (accusative masc. sg.)
    b. government: *gedenken* + genitive, *bezichtigen* + genitive;
                     wegen + genitive /dative, *durch* + accusative,
                     in + dative (place/location: *er wanderte in
                     dem Wald*),
                     in + accusative (direction: *er ging in den
                     Wald*)

If the adjective is attributive, i.e. if it serves as a premodifier, German additionally distinguishes between 'strong' and 'weak' inflection (*ein toll-es Buch / ein-e toll-e Woche / ein toll-er Tag* vs. *das toll-e Buch / die toll-e Woche / der toll-e Tag*). English has completely lost this distinction.

grammatical relations

Another reason why case marking is so important in German is that it is the only means for indicating grammatical functions: the subject is nominative, the direct object is accusative, and the indirect object is dative. In this respect, German is the most conservative among the modern Germanic languages. In English, on the other hand, grammatical functions are determined by word order, which is relatively fixed: the canonical word order is subject – verb – (indirect – direct) object, in main as well as subordinate clauses (for further details see V.2.2).

contrasts within the VP

In the verb phrase, German has retained its numerous inflectional endings to mark mood (indicative – *sie komm-t*, Konjunktiv I – *sie komm-e*, Konjunktiv II – *sie käme*), number and person, all of which have either been lost completely in English or are retained in no more than a rudimentary form. In English, the distinction between indicative and subjunctive, singular and plural, as well as first, second and third person is hardly ever made except in the present tense where it is all expressed by one morpheme: the third person singular indicative {-s} (*she sing-s*). The verb *to be* is the only one with a separate subjunctive form (e. g. *if I were you*), which is however on the way out (e. g. *if I was you*). In all other cases, English uses other forms to indicate subjunctive mood (compare (5)):

(5) a. We demand that he leave. (infinitive without *to*)
    b. If he left, we would all be happy. (Simple Past)

In addition, there is a preference for constructions with modal *would* or *should* (e. g. *We demand that he should leave*), i. e. periphrastic constructions where inflectional languages would use, or at least may use, verb inflection (e. g. *er sagte, er käme morgen* vs. *er sagte, er würde morgen kommen*). This behaviour reflects a basic property of the English verb phrase, namely its high degree of

high degree of analyticity

analyticity and the stronger grammaticalization of periphrastic constructions as compared to German. This holds true for all auxiliaries (a group of verbs clearly distinguished from main verbs both morphologically and syntactically, see IV.3.1) as well as the tense and aspect system. Consider, for example, the Progressive, of which (at least written Standard) German has no equivalent, or take the use of the Present Perfect which is much more restricted than the German *Perfekt* (in English, it is only used to mark anteriority, never as a narrative tense), or the strongly grammaticalized *will/shall*-construction used to express future tense (for more details cf. V.2.4).

2.2 Word order

As a result of its almost complete loss of inflectional morphology, English has experienced a dramatic typological change from a language with a relatively free word order to a language with a relatively fixed word order. German has not changed in this respect: its word order is still as free as it used to be a thousand years ago, which means that the order of subject, object and verb can vary considerably (within certain limits, of course). All the German sentences in (6) are grammatically correct, but English only allows the word order used in (6a):

(6)   a.   Der Mann versprach dem Kind eine Überraschung. (SVO$_i$O$_d$)
      b.   Dem Kind versprach der Mann eine Überraschung. (O$_i$VSO$_d$)
      c.   Eine Überraschung versprach der Mann dem Kind. (O$_d$VSO$_i$)

But one thing has changed in both languages: the position of the verb. Like all other Germanic languages, both English and German have developed from verb-final to verb-second languages, with the important difference that English, once again, underwent a more radical change than German by changing its word order not only in main clauses but in subordinate clauses, too. In the latter German has retained the old SOV order (*er sah das Haus* vs. *..., weil er das Haus sah*). Additionally, English has not only changed into a verb-second language but has also developed a fixed word order of subject-verb-object, the first two constituents of which are always obligatory. This means that, in English, every sentence has to have a subject, which is why we often need elements like *it* and *there* to take over this grammatical function, calling them "dummy subjects" (*It's late/raining/a long way to Tipperary, There are many different kinds of butterflies, There's two boys waiting outside*). German behaves differently in this respect: neither does the subject obligatorily precede or the object obligatorily follow the verb (compare (7b-g)) nor does every sentence necessarily have a subject (8). The only element of the sentence which does not change its position in (7) and is also fixed in (8) is the finite verb.

SVO vs. V/2

(7)   a.   Mein Freund brachte mich gestern Abend nach Hause.
      b.   Gestern Abend brachte mich mein Freund nach Hause.
      c.   Gestern Abend brachte mein Freund mich nach Hause.
      d.   Nach Hause brachte mich gestern Abend mein Freund.
      e.   Nach Hause brachte mein Freund mich gestern Abend.

f. Mich brachte gestern Abend mein Freund nach Hause.
g. Mich brachte mein Freund gestern Abend nach Hause.

(8) a. Jetzt wird aber endlich geschlafen!
b. Mich fröstelt.
c. Ihm wurde geholfen.

discourse pragmatics:
theme/old – rheme/new

In German, as in all inflectional languages, the property of having a relatively free word order can be exploited for discourse-pragmatic purposes. The order of the constituents of a sentence is not subject to any grammatical requirements and can therefore be manipulated to fit the communicative needs of the speaker. In simple words: we can basically begin, continue and end a sentence as we please. If somebody asks *"Wer brachte dich gestern Abend nach Hause?"* ("Who brought you home last night?"), the answer may be (7'a) or (7'f).

(7') a. Mein Freund (brachte mich nach Hause).
f. Mich brachte mein Freund nach Hause.

The sentence in (7'a) starts with the new information whereas (7'f) starts with the information already known (i.e. established in the question), revealing the new information at the end of the sentence. The way the information is distributed in the latter example is usually considered to be the unmarked option in declarative sentences, progressing from old (or: given, known) information which is already known (e.g. as general world knowledge or shared knowledge of speaker and hearer) or can be deduced from the previous context to new information which can not be deduced from the context. This information structure is also known as theme-rheme or topic-comment structure. In a German sentence like (7'f), a topic-comment structure can be easily accomplished by changing the position of the subject and direct object, whereas this is not possible in English – or in any other predominantly isolating language. English uses a fixed basic word order for marking grammatical functions, and the information structure in English sentences is therefore subject to the limits of word order. To achieve the same effect as in (7'f), English has to use a passive construction (*I was brought home by my friend*). This is why inflectional languages are said to have a "pragmatic word order", while strongly analytical or isolating languages are said to have a highly fixed, grammaticalized word order.

Table V.1 Word order in English and German	
English	**German**
relatively fixed	relatively free
strongly grammaticalized	pragmatic
SVO (in main and subordinate clauses)	V/2 in main clauses; V-final in subordinate clauses

In English, the relatively strong fixing of a certain order of syntactic elements also shows in other domains. As can be seen from the sentences above (7a, d, f and g), German permits other positions and sequences of adverbials of time and place than English. In English, both of these adverbials can only occur at the periphery of a sentence (with the adverbial of time always first or last):

(9) a. Last year in Britain we met him for the first time.
        (not: In Britain last year ...)
    b. We met him for the first time in Britain last year.
        (not: ... last year in Britain.)

Let us take a last look at the basic word order in German, or more precisely at the position of the verb. Actually, not all linguists agree on German being, as argued here, a verb-second language. Quite a few German scholars and word order typologists insist on classifying it as an SOV-language, arguing that German has not suffered any fundamental change in word order. The arguments used to support the analysis of German as an SOV-language are quite complex. For the time being let us put it simple: all German subordinate clauses are SOV anyway, but SOV can also be claimed for simple declarative sentences if the focus is not on the position of the finite verb but on that of the main verb, be it finite or not. Some relevant examples are presented in (10a) and also in (10b and c) where the main verbs contain particles which can be separated from the stem (*zurückbringen*, *abholen*) – the German counterparts of English phrasal verbs:

German: V/2 or SOV?

(10) a. Mein Freund hat mich nach Hause <u>gebracht</u>.
      b. Mein Freund <u>brachte</u> mich nach Hause <u>zurück</u>.
      c. Ich <u>holte</u> den Brief von der Post <u>ab</u>.

What are the consequences of the fundamental word order differences between English and German – more precisely, what are the consequences of the strong restrictions on word order in English?

consequences of the word order differences

There are, basically, three major effects:

- First, English has developed a number of means to compensate for its fixed word order permitting a reconciliation of discourse-pragmatic needs with structural requirements (i.e. SVO order).
- Second, English sentence constituents may have lost their mobility within clause boundaries, but they have gained greater mobility across clauses. This results in what has been labelled "fused constructions" (*Konstruktionsverschmelzungen*) or "argument trespassing", which often makes it difficult to identify clause boundaries.
- And third: considering the two consequences above from a different perspective, one will notice a loosening of the relationship between form and meaning (or function) in several central domains of English grammar. The meanings and functions of constructions, constituents and words often vary more in English than they do in German and can only be derived from the immediate context.

compensation strategies

We will now outline the first two of these developments; more detail about the third will be added in section V.2.3.

The examples in (11) to (17) illustrate different strategies and information-structuring devices which English has developed in order to allow speakers to meet the word order requirements but still be able to structure the information in their utterances (the distribution of "old" and "new" information) according to their communicative goals. The first few sentences are examples of focussing construc-

clefts and pseudo-clefts

tions: cleft sentences (11a, b) and pseudo-cleft-sentences (11c, d), the use of which English has expanded considerably. These constructions make it possible to highlight (or focus on) single constituents of sentences like *John crashed my car*. In cleft sentences, the focus (and with it often the new information) is found in the superordinate clause, whereas in pseudo-cleft sentences the focus is on the complement of the *be*-form in the second part of the sentence. In each of the following sentences the focused constituent is underlined:

(11)	a.	It was <u>John</u> who crashed my car.	(question:	Who crashed your car?)
	b.	It was <u>my car</u> which John crashed.	(questions:	What did John crash?
				Whose car did John crash?)
	c.	What John crashed was <u>my car</u>.	(question:	What did John crash?)
	d.	What John did was <u>crash my car</u>.	(questions:	What did John do?)

Compared to German, English does not only use such constructions more often, but also has more clefting possibilities. The adver-

168

bial of an embedded clause, for example, can be the focus of a cleft sentence (12a,b). Besides, there is a variant of pseudo-cleft-sentences with an inverted information structure (12c):

(12) a. It was <u>yesterday</u> she said she would be coming ...
       b. It's <u>because he had stolen</u> that he was sacked ...
       c. Crash my car was what John did. (contrast with 11d)

Two further domains of grammar which are especially interesting from a contrastive point of view are the passive and the coding of grammatical functions. We have already mentioned the expansion of English passive constructions in this and previous chapters (also IV.3.2). Among other things, English uses the passive where German simply puts the object at the beginning of the sentence (compare 13a and b). In English, we can additionally use the indirect object of an active sentence (14a) and the object of a preposition (15a) as subjects, both of which is impossible in German. passive

(13) a. I was taken home by my friend.
       b. Mich brachte mein Freund nach Hause.

(14) a. He was offered a large amount of money.
       b. Ihm/*Er wurde ein großer Geldbetrag angeboten.

(15) a. This car has been meddled with.
       b. An diesem Auto/*Dieses Auto ist (an) herumgefummelt worden.

In all of the above cases, the use of the passive allows the subject of the sentence to be the topic, and thus to align the 'topic/old before comment/new' information structure with the obligatory word order. semantic roles of subjects

Exactly as in example (14a), and especially in (15a), there is a wide variety of unusual subjects in English. They are unusual because they are not prototypical subjects, i.e. subjects of active sentences which have the semantic role of an agent, or subjects of passive sentences which have the semantic (or: thematic) role of a patient (cf. chapter IV.2.3). Two things are crucial about the unusual subjects in (16): first, these constructions allow for a greater number of topicalization possibilities in English. And second: from a contrastive point of view, German has fewer possibilities in this respect, and also uses them less often.

(16) a. The fifth day saw our departure. (time)
b. The room seats 500 people. (place)
c. The stove has blown a fuse. (place, possessor)
d. The bucket was leaking water. (source)
e. A pound once bought two pints of beer. (instrument)
f. This ad will sell us a lot. (instrument)
g. John wounded his leg in the war. (experiencer/patient)
h. The latest edition of the book has added a chapter. (?)

semantic roles of objects

In a similar vein, English has many unusual objects, especially direct objects which do not fulfil the semantic role of a patient. Of the examples shown in (17), only (17a and b) are relevant for the topic-comment structure; they illustrate the emergence of a new rhematization device for objects. In each of these two sentences, the unusual object compensates for the loss of a construction consisting of a prepositional phrase with instrumental meaning (*with* + NP) immediately followed by a prepositional phrase with locative meaning (contrast (17a) with German *Sie strich mit ihren langen Fingern über den neuen Mantel*).

(17) a. She stroked her long fingers over the new coat. (instrument)
b. He wiped the wet cloth over the dishes. (instrument)
c. He swam the Channel in one day. (place)
d. They fled the capital. (source)
e. The albatross was riding the wind. (?)
f. He threatened violence. (?)
g. The march protested the invasion of Harikutu. (?)
h. The book sold two million copies. (?)

transitivity

The examples in (16) and (17) illustrate a general development of English: the functional expansion of subjects and objects. In more general terms, the functional range of transitive constructions has broadened considerably in English. This includes a development which was already mentioned as an example of word-class internal conversion (cf. chapters III.3.3 and chapter IV.3.2): some originally intransitive verbs have acquired an additional transitive use (e.g. *stand* in *stand the bank robbers against the wall*, or *run* in *run a horse in the Derby*), usually acquiring a causative meaning (e.g. 'make the bank robbers stand against the wall'). Conversely, there is also a great number of originally transitive verbs which can be used intransitively in mediopassive constructions (e. g. *This car won't sell* or *These shirts wash well*). This brings us back full circle (a) to the passive and to unusual subjects (since the subjects of mediopassives are subjects of active sentences which usually would be objects or typical subjects of passive sentences), and (b) to the possibilities English offers in terms of structuring information despite its relatively rigid word order. Yet another characteristic property of English is the possibility of fusing (or: blending) different constructions. In comparison to German, this results in strikingly blurred clause boundaries. For instance, an important type of clause fusion occurs when sentence constituents (especially verb arguments) move across clause boundaries (also known as "argument trespassing") . All examples in (18) result from an argument of the non-finite verb of the subordinate clause being converted into a (syntactic, not logical) argument of the finite verb of the main clause. These are so-called "raising constructions", of which we distinguish three main types:

fused constructions

argument trespassing across clause boundaries

(18) a. I believe <u>him</u> to be a nice person. (S_{sub} › O_{main})
     (vs. *I believe that <u>he</u> is a nice person*)
   b. <u>He</u> happened to know the answer. (S_{sub} › S_{main})
     (vs. *It (so) happened that <u>he</u> knew the answer*)
   c. <u>This book</u> is boring to read. (O_{sub} › S_{main})
     (vs. *It is boring to read <u>this book</u>*)

The raising of the object of a subordinate clause to the subject of a main clause (also known as *tough movement*) is yet another good example of unusual subjects in English. Raising constructions actually do occur in German (e. g. *Er scheint krank zu sein* (S_{sub} › S_{main}) or *Er ist schwer zu übersehen* (O_{sub} › S_{main})), but they are subject to much stricter constraints and are therefore not nearly as productive as in English. In English, even arguments of deeply embedded subordinate clauses can move to the main clause (e. g. *<u>This promise</u> will be hard to persuade her to keep*).

Further examples of clause fusion in infinitival subordinate clauses are shown in (19):

(19) a. He's a hard man to reach.
     (vs. *It is hard to reach this man*)
   b. That's a difficult book to translate.
     (vs. *It is difficult to translate this book*)
   c. That's a funny book to read on a train.
     (vs. *It is funny to read such a book on a train*)

In these examples, the adjectives *hard*, *difficult* and *funny* do not modify the nouns which immediately follow, (i.e. (19a) does not refer to a hard man, and (19b and c) do not refer to difficult or funny books), but rather characterize the overall situation (trying to contact a person, translating a book, reading a book on a train). Similar to the raising constructions in (18), there is a gap between the syntactic and the semantic structure. As a final example of the syntactic fuzziness of infinitival constructions, let us mention *for NP to* - constructions like the ones in (20). Again, there is no equivalent in German.

> **(20)** a. Bill wants for me to leave. (AmE)
> b. He did not want for you to get hurt. (AmE)
> c. She's waiting for her children to arrive.
> d. She's waiting for her children to finish school.

Where do we draw the line between the main and subordinate clauses in these examples? Is *for me* in (20a) a prepositional phrase of the main clause or is it a sequence of a subordinator (similar to *that*) and a subject which belongs to the non-finite subordinate clause? Do we bracket the sentence as [*Bill did not want for me*] [*to leave*] or as [*Bill did not want*] [*for me to leave*]? The latter is certainly to be preferred. In all four examples shown in (20), the *for NP to*-construction functions as a syntactic unit, for example when being moved to the beginning of the sentence *(For me to leave is what Bill wants)*. In (20c) and (20d), the problem is slightly different, because *wait for* (unlike *want for*) is a regular prepositional verb. What is interesting about these examples is their meaning. From a semantic perspective, it makes basically no difference what the woman in (20c) is waiting for exactly – her children or their arrival. The sentence in (20d), on the other hand, can semantically be analyzed in one way only: the woman is not waiting for her children but for her children to finish school.

Similar to the instances of argument trespassing in (18) to (20), where the boundary between the main and subordinate clause is blurred due to a verbal argument having 'crossed' it, there is syntactic fuzziness in the transitional areas between gerunds and participles. To start with, note that German – like all other Germanic languages – has no construction like the English gerund (see 21). The gerund has the special property of always qualifying as a noun phrase by virtue of its syntactic distribution (e.g. in subject or direct object function (21a and b)), yet having at the same time both verbal properties (e.g. having

gerunds

its own direct object (21c) or own negation, as in (21d)) and properties of a clause (own subject as in (21e)).

(21) a. Singing in public is fun.
  b. I hate singing in public.
  c. I hate singing Wagner in public.
  d. I hate not singing Wagner in public.
  e. I hate Domingo's/his singing Wagner in public.

The transition from a nominal to a verbal *ing*-form, that is the transition between gerund and present participle, is blurred in sentences like (22), however. The construction in (22a) still seems to be considered a gerund ("I hate (it) when ..."), whereas it is more of a participle in (22b) and a participle for sure in (22c) ("I listened to an exhausted Domingo when/ who ..."):

(22) a. I hate Domingo/him singing Wagner in public.
  b. I listened to Domingo singing Wagner in public.
  c. I listened to an exhausted Domingo singing Wagner in public.

The transition from gerund to participle poses, once again, the following problems: (a) whether *Domingo* is an argument of the finite verb or the *ing*-form, and therefore (b) where exactly the line runs between the main and the subordinate clause. In (22a), the speaker does not "hate" Domingo as a person, but the situation when Domingo sings Wagner in public. *Domingo* is therefore the subject of the *ing*-form, and the whole *ing*-construction is the direct object of the verb *hate*; in other words: (22a) is a simple sentence. In (22b), and even more clearly in (22c), *Domingo* is the object of the verb *listen to* and at the same time the logical subject (the agent) of the subsequent *ing*-form, which itself is the non-finite predicate of a shortened subordinate clause (more precisely of an adverbial clause or a restrictive relative clause).

2.3 Form-function mappings

In this section, we will reconsider some of the grammatical contrasts treated above from a different perspective, this time focusing on the relationship between form and meaning. Some of the most important morphological and syntactic differences between English and German boil down to the following tendency: in English, the fit between form

greater transparency in German

and meaning is much looser than in German, both with regard to individual words and syntactic constructions (cf. Hawkins 1986, 1992). This is another way of saying that in German the form of a word or syntactic construction more often indicates how it is to be interpreted; meanings and functions are coded in a more transparent way. In English, by contrast, meaning often cannot be inferred from the form of a word or construction alone but needs to be seen in context. English is a language which requires readers and hearers to invest more processing effort in what they read or hear because they have more inference work to do (i.e. work which is necessary when drawing conclusions). Therefore, Hawkins (1986) classifies English as a "loose-fit" language (since there is a relatively loose fit between form and meaning), whereas German is a "tight-fit" language. For Hawkins, the reason lies in the almost complete loss of inflectional morphology in English and its development towards an isolating language. Due to this historical process, the decreasing number of forms had to carry an increasing functional load, i.e. number of functions and meanings – which is why in less than a thousand years English developed from a "tight-fit" inflectional language into a "loose-fit", largely isolating language.

What follows will illustrate this relatively abstract parameter of "tightness/looseness of fit between form and meaning" with examples mostly familiar from earlier chapters. Let us turn to morphology first: due to the radical reduction of inflectional endings, any given English lexeme has fewer word forms than its German counterpart. Depending on the syntactic context, an English noun phrase like *the man* may correspond to German *der Mann* (nominative), *dem Mann* (dative) or *den Mann* (accusative). The German translations of a noun phrase like *the sheep* include not only the singular forms *das Schaf* (nominative, accusative) and *dem Schaf* (dative) but, additionally, different cases in the plural: *die Schafe* (nominative, accusative), *den Schafen* (dative). Thus here one English form corresponds to several different German forms, every single one of which has its own ending clearly indicating whether it functions as a subject, direct or indirect object in a given sentence. In English, however, we need to know the precise sentence in order to determine the grammatical function of such noun phrases. Case marking is also used for disambiguating polysemous expressions. Think of government: German prepositions such as *auf* ('on') or *hinter* ('behind') can, for example, specify a location or an endpoint of a movement in space. In the first sense, they govern the dative (23a, 24a), in the latter they govern the accusative (23b, 24b):

tight-fit vs. loose-fit

Old English
Old High German
Mod. German   Mod. Engl.
————————————→
inflecting   isolating
tight fit   loose fit

loss of case inflections

174

(23) a. Er stand auf dem Tisch.   b. Er sprang auf den Tisch.

(24) a. Er stand hinter dem Tisch.   b. Er lief hinter den Tisch.

In German, then, case marking alone sufficiently specifies the meaning of *auf* or *hinter* and which types of verbs they can combine with (a sentence like **Er stand auf den Tisch* is not possible). Needless to say, this is not possible in English, where both meanings are expressed by the same form: *on* or *behind the table*, as in (25); also note that *where* may refer to either a place or a direction: *He asked me where I was* vs. *He asked me where I went*:

(25) a. He stood/jumped on the table.
      b. He stood/ran behind the table.

Another example of the additional semantic and functional load that the largely invariable forms in English have to carry is the word *who* which is often used instead of *whom* as either interrogative or relative pronoun (*Who did you give the money to?*). Conversion, as an extremely productive word formation process in Present-Day English, is also a good example, of course.

In English syntax, the loosening of semantic from syntactic structure is superbly illustrated by predicate-argument structures as discussed in section V.2.2 above. Recall what was said about the considerable expansion of transitive constructions in English, which resulted in the frequent use of an amazing variety of unusual subjects and objects, especially when compared to German. This is not to deny, of course, that the prototypical subject (of an active sentence) in English is an agent, after all, and that the prototypical object is a patient. But English deviates much more frequently from these prototypes, whereas in German the prototypical relationship between grammatical function and semantic role is maintained to a much higher degree. Some of the unusual subjects and objects found in English are not permitted at all in German. In this context, we should also remember what was previously said concerning the conversion of intransitive verbs into transitive verbs and vice versa.

Predicate-argument structures are also at issue when addressing the ability of sentence constituents to move across clause boundaries, and the resulting clause fusion phenomena and the fuzziness of the border between syntax and semantics. Raising constructions are probably the best example for how loose the fit between syntax and semantics has become in English. In *I believe John to be a nice person,*

predicate-argument structures

John is the direct object of *believe*, but only syntactically; semantically, of course, the speaker does not believe John, but believes something concerning a certain property of John. The examples in (19), (20) and (22) are all quite similar in this respect: in English, the assignment of arguments (subjects and objects) to predicates is much more fuzzy than in German. Concerning this domain of contrastive grammar, in general, we can conclude that all the structural options German has are a proper subset of those English has. This also holds true, by the way, for movement operations of syntactic elements out of larger constituents. The best-known examples for such extractions are prepositional phrases where the nominal complement of the head is moved to a position earlier in the sentence, leaving the preposition isolated or "stranded" in its original position.

(26) a. The car <u>which</u> I saw you <u>in</u> looked quite expensive.
(alternatively: *The car in which I saw you looked quite expensive.*)
b. <u>Which</u> car did you see me <u>in</u>?
(alternatively: *In which car did you see me?*)

preposition stranding

Preposition stranding, as in (26a) and (26b), is possible in English, but not in German:

(27) a. Das Auto, in dem ich dich sah, …
(not: **Das Auto, dem ich dich sah in, …*)
b. In welchem Auto hast du mich gesehen?
(not: **Welchem Auto hast du mich gesehen in?*)

conclusion

There is more to the story behind the mobility of syntactic elements in English and German than just the (no doubt) crucial fact that English has a relatively fixed SVO word order and German has a relatively free word order. Both in terms of moving verb arguments across clause or sentence boundaries (e. g. raising constructions) and moving elements out of phrases (e. g. preposition stranding), English has more structural possibilities than German. In a nutshell: German has the tendency to keep together what (syntactically and semantically) belongs together. With some minor qualifications, this aversion to experiments can also be seen in the way German assigns semantic roles to subjects and objects. In all, this characterization of English-German contrasts in core domains of grammar corresponds to the judgement of historical linguists, according to which German is by far the more conservative language of the two whereas English qualifies as a highly innovative and progressive language.

One final typological remark is in order here: in those grammatical domains where we have characterized German to be "averse to experiments" and "rather conservative", other languages behave quite similarly (cf. Hawkins 1992). These languages, too, have highly developed case systems, subjects with the semantic role of an agent and direct objects with the semantic role of a patient, strong restrictions on raising constructions, and do not allow movement operations similar to preposition stranding. Interestingly, all of these languages share another property: they are SOV languages. Wouldn't this be another good reason for classifying German as a verb-final language – contrary to our earlier statement that, like all other modern Germanic languages, German is a verb-second language? It is too early to settle this issue, but one should keep in mind that exactly the same combination of properties also occurs in other SVO languages. However, SOV languages possess these properties far more consistently, while it is important to note that there are SVO languages, like English, which exhibit the directly opposite set of properties. At any rate, it is interesting to note that not a single of the other investigated SVO languages (Russian, Chinese, Indonesian, Hebrew) has the same combination of properties as English. This is yet another piece of evidence for English featuring many structural peculiarities which distinguish it from other languages, be they closely related genetically (e.g. German), typologically (e.g. SVO languages), or areally (other European languages).

German and English from a typological perspective

2.4 Further differences in the verb phrase

There is a whole catalogue of individual structural differences between English and German which cannot (or at least not easily) be subsumed under the sets of contrasts presented in sections V.2.1 to V.2.3. Among the most important of these, those in the verb phrase probably form the most coherent group. Many of these contrasts were mentioned in chapter IV already and will thus only be discussed briefly here.

auxiliaries and main verbs

German makes no strict distinction between auxiliaries and main verbs. Even modal verbs like *können* ('can'), *müssen* ('must'/'have to'), *wollen* ('want') or *sollen* ('should') have non-finite forms (e.g. *können – gekonnt, müssend – gemusst*). Further, auxiliaries in German have not lost their inflectional morphology (vs. *she cans, *she musts) and do not differ from main verbs syntactically in questions and negations. In English, by contrast, all full verbs need *do*-support in questions and negations (*Does he come? No, he doesn't* (*come*). This is an unusual property – not only from the perspective of German. The fact that English permits only this construction as a strategy for marking full verbs in negations and questions is unique among the European languages and even beyond. *Do*-support in questions, by the way, correlates with the canonical word order in English: it is a strategy which secures the correct order of subject, (main) verb and object, even in interrogatives.

Among the grammatical categories of the verb, tense and aspect are certainly the most salient. English has a strongly grammaticalized future tense, namely the construction *will/shall* + infinitive (in American English closely followed by the *going to* or *gonna* future). Of the different possibilities to express future situations and events in English, the *will/shall* construction is the most neutral one, i.e. the one which depends least on the context and is therefore also used most frequently. German, conversely, prefers the present tense for future time reference (*Nachher gehe ich einkaufen*), although the *werden* construction is available as well (*Nachher werde ich einkaufen gehen*). Unlike English – where *will* and *shall* have largely lost their modal meanings (*will* for 'wish' or 'want', *shall* for obligations) and become genuine future markers – the German constructions with *wollen* and *sollen* express modality only. To some extent, this also holds true for German *werden* (as in *Sie werden (wohl) essen gegangen sein* or *Du wirst mir doch (wohl) nicht widersprechen*). A second, even more striking difference between the tense systems of the two languages concerns the Simple Past and Present Perfect, on the one hand, and their German counterparts, i.e. the *Präteritum* and *Perfekt*, on the other hand. In German, mainly in the spoken standard, but also in standard written German the *Perfekt* has taken over the function of the *Präteritum*. It is now used as a narrative tense. In English, the situation is completely different, especially in Standard British English where there is a strict division of tasks between the Simple Past and Present Perfect. The Present Perfect must not be used with definite past time adverbials, i.e. adverbials of time identifying a situation clearly lying in the past (compare (28a) and (28b)). Additionally, the continuative perfect (28c) is obligatory in English in contexts where German often uses the present tense (often in combination with the adverb *schon*, as in (28d)):

future tense

Present Perfect vs. *Perfekt*

(28) a. Last year we visited Aunt Mary in hospital.
          (not: *Last year we've visited Aunt Mary in hospital.)
     b. Letztes Jahr haben wir Tante Marie im Krankenhaus
          besucht.
     c. We've known them for years.
     d. Wir kennen sie (schon) seit Jahren.

In German, a similar distinction between *Präteritum* and *Perfekt* is found only with the resultative perfect. Upon opening the window curtains in the morning and seeing that winter has arrived, a native speaker of German would rather say (29a) than (29b):

(29) a. Oh, es hat geschneit.   b. Oh, es schneite.

The third well-known contrast between English and German is that English is an aspect language while German is not. In English, the distinction between progressive and simple forms grammatically reflects the contrast between the internal view of a situation being in progress and the external, holistic view of a complete(d) situation, a grammatical distinction which has been continuously strengthened during the last few centuries. To express this aspectual contrast, German uses either adverbs (*Stör ihn nicht! Er liest gerade*) or constructions like *Er ist (gerade) am/beim Lesen*, but none of these is obligatory. Notice that this is another domain where German is the more 'normal' or 'mainstream' language, both among the Germanic and the European languages. It is, for example, hard to find another language with such strongly grammaticalized progressive and perfect constructions as English. In most languages which have a perfect, it has developed into a regular past tense, like in German. English, with its unusual tense and aspect system and its use of *do*-support, represents anything but a typical European language. A further generalization following from the properties of English discussed so far is this: all relevant constructions are periphrastic constructions which are firmly rooted in the grammar of English. This is further proof of the fact that English is clearly a more analytic language than German.

Non-finite forms, more exactly participles, are indispensable for forming the perfect and progressive constructions. It is worth noting that English makes use of non-finite verb forms much more frequently than German in other domains of grammar as well. One such domain where this is particularly noticeable was illustrated in examples (18) to (22): non-finite subordinate clauses which are mostly interlaced

progressive form

exceptional role of English in Europe

non-finite forms

with their main clause in such a way that a logical argument of the non-finite verb of the subordinate clause is at the same time an argument of the finite verb of the main clause (e. g. *I want him to go*). This is also typical of adverbial participles (e. g. *Walking along the river, he met an old friend*) where English again, as observed for raising constructions, does not only have more structural options than German (see example 30), but also makes much more use of these options than other Germanic languages:

(30) a. Being his mother, she had great power over him.
  (not: **Seine Mutter seiend, ...* but: *Als seine Mutter ...*)
 b. With profit margins getting ever smaller in traditional consumer banking, such
  economies are very welcome.
  (not: **Mit den Gewinnspannen ... immer kleiner werdend, ...*)

more verbal nuclei in English

Participles also figure prominently when it comes to so-called "restrictive (or: defining) relative clauses". English often prefers abbreviated relative clauses (*The man standing at the corner was my uncle*) to finite ones (*The man who stood at the corner was my uncle*). There is no structural equivalent to the former type among German relative clauses. In general, it can be stated for all types of subordinate clauses that English has more structural possibilities concerning the use of non-finite verb forms, and that the text frequency of such constructions is significantly higher than in German. It is, furthermore, remarkable that for many English non-finite constructions there exist no equivalent subordinate clauses in German. Some English non-finite verb forms appear redundant in German (31a) while others function rather like prepositions (31b-e) or conjunctions (31 f-h). As a matter of fact, several English prepositions actually developed from participles (e. g. *assuming, considering, providing, during, following* 'after').

(31) a. It cannot be achieved <u>without using</u> qualified professional people.
  (contrast <u>ohne</u> *qualifizierte Experten*)
 b. A map or plan <u>showing</u> the harbour limits ...
  (contrast ... <u>mit</u> *den Hafengrenz*en)
 c. Books <u>dealing with</u> sexual topics ...
  (contrast *Bücher <u>über</u> sexuelle Themen* ...)

d. The mystery <u>surrounding</u> the ship Marie-Celeste ...
(contrast *Das Geheimnis <u>um</u> das Schiff Marie-Celeste*)
e. <u>Following</u> growing unrest among their concerned friends
at the amount of time they spend apart, the Prince and
Princess of Wales ...
(contrast <u>*Nach*</u> *wachsender Unruhe* ...)
f. He wrote a letter <u>saying/to say</u> he could not come.
(*that, dass*)
g. I hate <u>to see</u> you waste your money like that. (*that, dass*)
h. Just <u>to let</u> you know. (*in order that, um ... zu*)

In sum, English clearly tends to distribute information on more
verbal nuclei than German does. This difference, which captures many
of the grammatical contrasts between English and German presented
in this chapter, should be kept in mind especially by very advanced
learners of English in order to counteract the tendency to avoid or
underrepresent certain English structures.

Finally, let us take a brief look at the major phonological differences
between English and German, starting with their consonant inventories. German lacks the (inter-) dental fricatives /θ, ð/, the bilabial
semi-vowel /w/ and the voiced post-alveolar affricate /ʤ/. English,
conversely, misses the two fricatives /ç/ and /x/, better known to
German students of linguistics as *ich-Laut* and *ach-Laut*. As for
affricates, the problem is that German phonologists are not in agreement whether /pf/, /ts/, /ks/ and /tʃ/ should be analyzed as one
phoneme each or as combinations of two phonemes. Still, the majority view appears to be that only /tʃ/ cannot be classified as one
phoneme. In terms of contrasting phoneme inventories, this means
that German additionally lacks the phoneme /tʃ/ and English has no
/pf/, /ts/ and /ks/ affricates.

Table V.2 Contrasting the consonant inventories of English and German

	English							German						
plosives	p	b	t	d		k	g	p	b	t	d		k	g
fricatives	f	v	θ ð				h	f	v		ç x			h
			s	z	ʃ	ʒ				s	z	ʃ	ʒ	
affricates				tʃ dʒ				pf	ts			ks		
nasals	m		n			ŋ		m		n			ŋ	
liquids & semi-vowels	w		l	r	j					l	r	j		

Some consonant phonemes which exist in both languages are realized differently, which means that English and German do not always use the same allophones. Liquids are a good example: in Received Pronunciation, the prototypical /r/ is post-alveolar, in General American it is retroflex and in German it is uvular (*Zäpfchen-r*) except when it is syllable-final. In addition, German does not distinguish between clear and dark /l/; the /l/ phoneme is always realized as clear /l/, even at the end of a word (compare contrasting pairs of English and German words like *ball – Ball, hell (N) – hell (A), still (Adv) – still (A), old – alt*, etc.). Furthermore, there is so-called final devoicing (*Auslautverhärtung*) in German: all obstruents at the end of syllables or words are voiceless, i.e. German words like *Stab, Rad* or *Tag* are pronounced /ʃtaːp/, /raːt/, and /taːk/ respectively. Due to final devoicing, many German learners of English make interference mistakes because the relevant English minimal pairs are lost, e.g. *dove–duff, rib–rip, ridge–rich, dog–dock* or *lose–loose*. The opposite case when voiced and voiceless obstruents are neutralized at the end of syllables and words usually presents no problem to English learners of German. In the domain of contrastive phonology English- German, final devoicing is thus one of the best-known pieces of evidence that there is a connection between typological markedness and the Contrastive Hypothesis (cf. section V.1). As this phenomenon can be observed in a relatively large number of languages, word-final devoicing can be considered a "natural" or "unmarked" rule, whereas the situation found in English is clearly less common (i.e. "marked"). In this case, the Contrastive Hypothesis is clearly unidirectional.

As far as the vowel inventories/systems of both languages are concerned, the most striking contrast is that English, as opposed to all other Germanic languages, has no rounded front vowels (which occur in German words like *Müll* /ʏ/, *Mühle* /y:/, *Hölle* /œ/ or *Höhle* /ø:/). Other German monophthongs which do not exist in RECEIVED PRONUNCI-ATION are /e:/, /ɛ:/ and /o:/ (cf. the German words *Ehren*, *Ähren* and *Ohren*). Gaps in the German vowel inventory can be found primarily among the diphthongs: of the eight diphthongs found in English, German only has the three closing diphthongs /aɪ/, /ɔɪ/ and /aʊ/. What at first glance might be identified as so-called centring diphthongs (e. g. *Tier* [tiːᴬ] or *leer* [leːᴬ]), are actually nothing more than monophthongs followed by an allophone of /r/. This allophone is used whenever the phoneme /r/ is not followed by a vowel (consider *Tier* [tiːᴬ] – *Tiere* ['tiːʀə], *ehrlich* ['eːᴬlɪç] vs. *Ehre* [eːʀə]). With regard to monophthongs, German lacks especially /æ/ *cat*, /ʌ/ *cut*, /ɔ:/ *caught* and /ɜ:/ *curt*. However, as can be seen from the contrastive vowel chart in Figure V.3 (note in particular the ellipses represented by solid lines), there are also differences in quality, i. e. in the position of the tongue, of vowel phonemes occurring in both languages. More often than not, English vowels are more open than German vowels, the position of the tongue being lower than in German. Most English vowels therefore take a lower position in the vowel chart. The three ellipses represented by dashed lines delineate pairs of vowels /e/ - /ɛ/, /ʌ/ - /a/, /ɒ/ - /ɔ/ which are phonetically similar but phonologically different in the two languages.

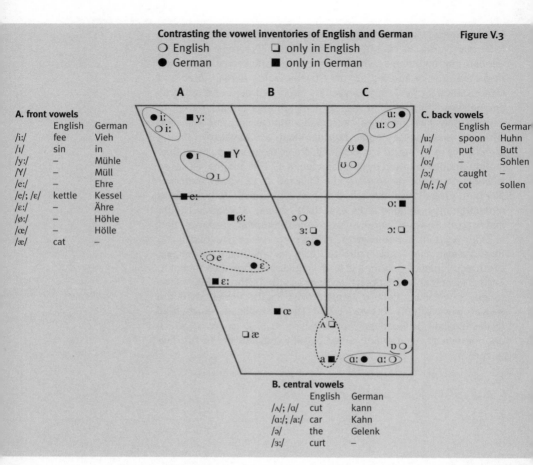

Contrasting the vowel inventories of English and German   **Figure V.3**

○ English   ❑ only in English
● German   ■ only in German

A   B   C

A. front vowels

	English	German
/iː/	fee	Vieh
/ɪ/	sin	in
/yː/	–	Mühle
/ʏ/	–	Müll
/eː/	–	Ehre
/e/; /ɛ/	kettle	Kessel
/ɛː/	–	Ähre
/øː/	–	Höhle
/œ/	–	Hölle
/æ/	cat	–

C. back vowels

	English	German
/uː/	spoon	Huhn
/ʊ/	put	Butt
/oː/	–	Sohlen
/ɔː/	caught	–
/ɒ/; /ɔ/	cot	sollen

B. central vowels

	English	German
/ʌ/; /ɑ/	cut	kann
/ɑː/; /aː/	car	Kahn
/ə/	the	Gelenk
/ɜː/	curt	–

There also are phonotactic differences (e. g. no /ps-, pn-, kn-/ at the beginning of words in English and no /st-, sp-/ at the beginning of words in German), just as there are differences in suprasegmental phonology. Concerning suprasegmental differences, it is much more difficult, however, to formulate generalizations than it is for phoneme inventories. With respect to word stress, one important contrast concerns compound nouns, especially those consisting of two components: in German, the main stress is usually placed on the first element, whereas in English it often happens that more than one element is stressed, and the main stress can even be on the second or third element of a compound (so-called "level stress" as in

word stress

184

'washing 'machine, 'front 'door, ‚apple 'pie and ‚waste 'paper). What is more, word stress is often phonemic in English, meaning that stress alone can be distinctive (in the sense of bringing about a change of meaning; cf. II.2.2). Another fundamental difference is the strong correlation between word stress and rhythm in English.

This takes us directly to differences in rhythm. Although, compared to other languages, English and German are both classified as stress-timed languages, syllable stress in English is much more isochronous, meaning that the intervals between stressed syllables are fairly regular (cf. II.2.2). It is the unstressed syllables and words which pay the price, as it were: very frequently, these are subject to vowel reduction, assimilation, or elision. As a result, function words have many weak forms in English while there are only few of them in German. Thus, many German speakers of English do not employ weak forms frequently enough.

rhythm

There are further phonological differences which, while not leading to errors, may contribute to a distinctly German accent. For one, there is the strong aspiration of voiceless plosives (/p/, /t/, /k/) in all positions, even where English does not aspirate or not even release plosives (apt [æpᵒt], worked [wɜːkᵒt]). Even more characteristic of native speakers of German is the so-called "glottal stop" before stressed syllables starting with a vowel. The glottal stop can be heard in conscious speech or, even more pronounced, when whispering an (admittedly somewhat constructed) sentence such as ʔAm ʔAbend ʔessen ʔer ʔund ʔich ʔErbsenʔeintopf ʔüber ʔalles gern. To a native speaker of English, a sentence like ʔAfter ʔall ʔI ʔeat ʔapples ʔin the ʔevening pronounced this way would sound very "clipped" and "staccato". This phenomenon is also the reason why German learners of English rarely use intrusive /r/ or linking /r/ (as in after all /ɑːftəˈrɔːl/) or other types of consonant-vowel liaison across word boundaries (as in fine arts /faɪˈnɑːts/ or at all /əˈtɔːl/. Last but not least, utterances by native speakers of English display a greater variation in the pitch range and pitch contour. Moreover, pitch is often lower in German than in English. But it should be added that English seems to be changing in this respect and that the relevant contrasts between English and German are becoming less and less noticeable.

Checklist Contrastive Linguistics – key terms and concepts

agreement ↔ government
analyticity
argument trespassing
blending of constructions
bundles of contrasts
case system
cleft (pseudo-)
compensation strategy
Contrastive Hypothesis
final devoicing
fused constructions
gerund
government
grammatical relation

grammaticalization
interference types (substitution; over-/underdifferentiation; over-/underrepresentation)
isochrony
language typology
loose-fit ↔ tight-fit language
markedness
Markedness Differential Hypothesis
passive construction
predicate-argument structures
preposition stranding

raising construction
rhythm
semantic roles of subjects and objects
theme ↔ rheme (topic ↔ comment)
transfer
transitive construction
transparency
typological distance
verb phrase contrasts
word order
word stress (accent)

1 a. Which typical mistakes of German learners of English are made in the following utterance: /tel miː vɒt ɪs zə pʀɒbləm vɪ'sɛt/ *Tell me, what is the problem with that?*
   b. The following pairs of examples often cease to be minimal pairs when uttered by German learners of English. Explain why and find two more examples of each neutralization of a minimal pair: *pat–pet, thin–sin, wine–vine, cherry–sherry, lag–lack, plays–place, jazz–chess.*

2 a. For which English vowels do German learners of English often employ one of the following German vowel sounds? Give examples. /ɛ/ /oː/ /ø/ /a/
   b. Which problems can German speakers of English be expected to have when pronouncing the underlined consonants in the following examples: *out*p*ut, ob*t*ain, go*t*, be*d*time, ra*g*, hol*d*, she li*ves*, an*d*, finge*r*, *s*o*

3 Sketch the major differences between English and German in the domain of relative clauses.

4 Consider the following examples of adverbial clauses in English and describe the major English-German contrasts in this domain of grammar.
   a. Looking out of the window, Mary saw a large truck approaching.
   b. With grandpa driving, I always have an awkward feeling.

5 Provide the most natural German translations of the English sentences in (17).

6 Identify for each of the following examples which syntactic contrast between English and German it illustrates.
   a. Das Paket gab der Mann der Frau und nicht dem Jungen.
   b. She photographs well.
   c. Jetzt wird aber gegessen!
   d. Did you see his face?
   e. Sie glaubt, dass er ein netter Kerl ist.
   f. This racket has never been played with.
   g. There's the guy (who(m)) I met at the disco last night.
   h. The ship tore a sail.
   i. What did he come in order to pick up?

7   There are many English-German contrasts in the tense and aspect system. Sketch the major contrasts by going one by one through the following examples.
    a. Gestern sind wir im Kino gewesen.
    b. Ich kenne ihn schon seit Jahren.
    c. Bis morgen mittag habe ich den Aufsatz geschrieben.
    d. Don't disturb Dad! He's watching telly.
    e. Morgen reist sie weiter.
    f. You must go. The train leaves at six.

8   Which of the following statements are true, which are false?
    a. Transfer is a special type of interference.
    b. The Contrastive Hypothesis has more prognostic than diagnostic value.
    c. Grammatical relations are marked by word order in English and by case marking in German.
    d. Different from English, German subjects are always agents and direct objects are always patients.
    e. Compared with German, English has a wider range of options in the domain of nonfinite clauses and makes greater use of them.
    f. The English Progressive and the use of *do*-support in questions are highly marked structures in the European languages.
    g. The Present Perfect in English is a true perfect while German *Perfekt* really is a tense.
    h. In the course of its history, English has undergone a major typological change which is responsible for many of the structural differences between Present-Day English and Present-Day German.
    i. The inventory of English diphthongs is a proper subset of the inventory of German diphthongs.

Exercises Advanced

9   Give a phonetic description of
    (i) all English sounds which lack an equivalent in the German sound system.
    (ii) all German sounds which lack an equivalent in the English sound system.

10 Sketch the major word order differences between English and German and draw up a list of all constraints and options these differences give rise to.

11 Discourse pragmatics is concerned with the distribution of old (or: given, presupposed) and new information in utterances. In neutral declarative sentences old information tends to precede new information. Sketch and illustrate the major differences between the way(s) in which English and German employ morphological and/or syntactic means for discourse-pragmatic purposes.

12 Try to find out which of the English-German contrasts described in this chapter are due to either English or German exhibiting a marked feature in the relevant domain of its phonological or grammatical structure compared with the majority of other languages (think of the Markedness Differential Hypothesis).

Sources and further reading

Eckman, Fred. 1977. "Markedness and the contrastive analysis hypothesis." *Language Learning* 27: 315-330.

Gass, Susan M./Larry Selinker, eds. 2001². *Language transfer in language learning*. Amsterdam/Philadelphia: Benjamins.

Gnutzmann, Claus, ed. 1990. *Kontrastive Linguistik*. Frankfurt: Lang.

Hawkins, John A. 1986. *A comparative typology of English and German: unifying the contrasts*. London: Croom Helm.

Hellinger, Marlis. 1977. *Kontrastive Grammatik Deutsch/Englisch*. Tübingen: Niemeyer.

König, Ekkehard/Johan van der Auwera, eds. 1994. *The Germanic languages*. London/New York: Routledge.

Kortmann, Bernd. 1998. "Kontrastive Linguistik und Fremdsprachenunterricht". In: W. Börner/K. Vogel, eds. *Kontrast und Äquivalenz. Beiträge zu Sprachvergleich und Übersetzung*. Tübingen: Narr.

Kufner, H. 1971. *Kontrastive Phonologie Deutsch-Englisch*. Stuttgart: Klett.

Legenhausen, Lienhard/Günter Rohdenburg. 1995. "Kontrastivierung ausgewählter Strukturen im Englischen und Deutschen." In: Rüdiger Ahrens/Wolf-Dietrich Bald/Werner Hüllen, eds. *Handbuch Englisch als Fremdsprache*. Berlin: Erich Schmidt. 133-139.

Mair, Christian. 1995. *Englisch für Anglisten*. Tübingen: Stauffenburg.

Mair, Christian/Manfred Markus, eds. 1992. *New departures in contrastive linguistics*. 2 vols . Innsbruck: Institut für Anglistik.

Odlin, Terence. 1989. *Language transfer. Cross-linguistic influence in language learning*. Cambridge: Cambridge University Press.

VI Semantics: Word and sentence meaning

Semantics (Greek *semainein* = to signify, mean) is the only branch of linguistics which is exclusively concerned with meaning. Semantics studies the meaning or meaning potential of various kinds of expressions: words, phrases, and sentences. This chapter is mainly confined to the study of word meaning (lexical semantics; lexicology). Research in lexical semantics addresses the following questions: (a) How to elucidate the concept of meaning, including the relation between meaning and external reality? (b) What are appropriate tools for analysing and describing meanings? (c) What kinds of semantic structures exist within the vocabulary (or: lexicon) of a language? These structures are uncovered by describing recurrent semantic relations between the words, more exactly lexemes, of a language (e.g. relations such as near-equivalence or contrasts in meaning). Lexical semantics proceeds from the assumption that words are symbols, i.e. signs expressing an arbitrary relation between a form

Introduction

lexicology

and its meaning(s). This relation is considered to be exclusively a matter of convention (cf. chapter I.2.1 on the model of the linguistic sign proposed by Ferdinand de Saussure).

VI.1 Branches and boundaries of semantics

semasiology
(form → meaning)
versus
onomasiology
(meaning → form)

Studies in semantics usually start out from a given form and ask for its meaning, i.e. move from signifier (*signifiant*) to signified (*signifié*). This direction of research is also most relevant to non-linguists: Whenever we consult a dictionary, we are looking for an answer to the question: What is the meaning of X? The branch of semantics which adopts this approach is called "semasiology" (science of meanings), a concept which originally covered all of semantics. It was only in the 20th century that the term "semantics" (introduced by Michel Bréal) replaced the term "semasiology".

The opposite way of studying meaning is called "onomasiology" (science of names; from Greek *onomazein* = to name). Onomasiology proceeds from a given meaning and asks for the kinds of forms that are used to express this meaning. Whenever we consult a dictionary of synonyms (thesaurus) such as *Roget's Thesaurus of English Words and Phrases*, we are adopting an onomasiological approach: We want to find out which word(s) can be used for expressing a given concept. Take, for example, the concept – or lexical field (cf. VI.3) – of "killing" (German *töten*): *kill, murder, slay, slaughter, butcher, massacre*, and *assassinate* are words which can be used to translate the concept expressed by *töten*.

paradigmatic versus
syntagmatic semantics

This lexical (or: semantic) field serves as a useful example for illustrating another crucial distinction, which ultimately derives from an important dichotomy proposed by Ferdinand de Saussure: The contrast between two distinct kinds of relations which every element in a language or, in fact, any kind of system enters into, viz. paradigmatic relations of choice and syntagmatic relations of combination. These relations are also relevant to semantics. Firstly, members of a particular lexical field can be replaced by other members of the field, especially if there are extensive similarities between the meanings of the relevant words (i.e. if these words are synonymous). The various semantic relations between lexical alternatives are the focus of paradigmatic semantics. Syntagmatic semantics, on the other hand, is concerned with questions such as the following: Which of the above-mentioned lexical alternatives is appropriate in a given sentence (e.g. *kill* as opposed to *murder* or *assassinate*)? *Kill* is the most general term; *murder* implies the intentional killing of a human being, *assas-*

selection restrictions

sinate relates to the killing of an important person (usually a politician). For this reason, only (1) is acceptable, while (2) is odd:

(1) President X was assassinated last night.

(2) ? Many innocent villagers were assassinated last night.

There is thus an increase in the number of semantic restrictions on the types of direct objects which can be combined with the relevant verbs: *kill* has fewer restrictions than *murder*, which in turn has fewer restrictions than *assassinate*. Such restrictions on possible combinations of meanings, so-called "selection restrictions", are sometimes very wide-ranging; in some cases, a given lexeme can only be combined with very few other lexemes. Extreme examples are provided by many words which are rarely used: It is often possible to predict which other lexemes such rare words occur with in a sentence. A popular example of such typical combinations of words, so-called "collocations", are the various expressions for groups of animals in (3): *collocations*

(3)

a	flock gaggle pack pride shoal	of	sheep/goats/birds geese wolves/hounds lions fish	

Syntagmatic semantics is not only concerned with possible combinations of particular words (such as those discussed for (1) to (3)), it also deals with the meaning of complex linguistic expressions (including sentences). The crucial principle that determines the structure of complex expressions is the principle of compositionality, which stipulates that the meaning of a complex expression in natural language depends on (and can be reconstructed from) the meaning of its parts and the syntactic relations holding between these parts. This important principle of sentence semantics is often called "Frege's Principle" or the "Fregean Principle", since it is commonly attributed to the German philosopher and mathematician Gottlob Frege (1848-1925). The principle of compositionality is held to ensure that we can understand the countless sentences we encounter every day, even though we have never heard them before. There are limits to compositionality, however. Consider, for example, idioms such as *to kick the bucket* or German *den Löffel abgeben*. Their meaning (here 'to die') cannot – or can only in part – be reconstructed from the *compositionality* meaning of their component parts; thus, for idioms the connection between form and meaning tends to be just as arbitrary and conventional as it is for most single words. But even where the principle of compositionality does apply, it does not guarantee that one really understands what the speaker or author means with a particular utterance, at least in those cases where the intended meaning goes beyond what is literally said (cf. chapter VII).

semantics versus pragmatics

This distinction between what is said and what is meant, i.e. between (literal) sentence meaning and (intended) utterance meaning, is closely linked to the distinction between semantics and pragmatics, even though the correlation is not perfect (cf. the detailed discussion in chapter VII). Pragmatics studies language use (*parole*), focusing on both the linguistic and the non-linguistic context of utterances, as well as speakers' utterance-related intentions. Thus, a central – for many *the* central – aspect of pragmatics is its concern with principles that allow us, in a particular context, to infer what is meant from what is said. At the heart of pragmatics as defined above are questions such as: What does the speaker mean by uttering X? and Why are hearers usually able to recognize speakers' intention(s) without greater difficulty?. In semantics, on the other hand, context is almost completely ignored, and speaker-intention is entirely left out of consideration. Thus, the division of tasks between semantics and pragmatics may roughly be characterized as follows: semantics deals with the meaning or the meaning potential of expressions out of context (with context-invariant, speaker-independent meaning), whereas pragmatics deals with the meaning of expressions (mainly utterances) in a particular context (with context-sensitive, speaker-dependent meaning).

VI.2
Types and facets of meaning

lexical versus grammatical meaning

What we typically have in mind when talking about word meanings are the meanings of lexemes that belong to one of the four lexical word classes (nouns, verbs, adjectives, adverbs). Lexical meaning contrasts with the grammatical meaning of function words (e.g. pronouns, prepositions, conjunctions; cf. chapter III.1 on auto- and synsemantic words). Grammatical meaning also includes the meaning of inflectional affixes and the semantic roles (e.g. agent, patient) associated with grammatical relations. The differences between grammatical and lexical meaning are only gradual. Grammatical meaning in general is abstract; just think of the meanings of case or tense morphemes, or of the marking of (in-) definiteness with the help of *a* and *the*. Lexical meaning, on the other hand, is frequently far more concrete. In this respect, grammatical meaning contrasts particularly strongly with the lexical meaning of those nouns that denote concrete countable entities. Note, however, that the (lexical) meanings of abstract nouns such as *condition*, *cause*, or *concession* are no less abstract than the (grammatical) meanings of adverbial subordinators such as *if*, *because*, or *although*. The above examples of grammatical and lexical meanings can thus be located at opposite ends of a continuum from abstract to concrete concepts. The meanings of personal pronouns and spatial prepositions tend to be located even further towards the middle of such a continuum (and thus towards the transitional area between grammatical and lexical meaning).

Another essential difference between lexical and grammatical meaning relates to the fact that the number of grammatical meanings expressed in languages is comparatively small and – even from a cross-linguistic point of view – probably also finite, whereas there is an infinite number of potential lexical meanings. It is therefore much easier to provide an overview of the domain of grammatical meanings. Not surprisingly, regular processes of meaning change – both within a single language and across languages – have been identified primarily in the domain of grammatical meanings. Meaning changes in lexical words, on the other hand, are clearly more idiosyncratic, and cannot be captured with the help of a relatively small number of general principles of the type discovered for function words. Issues of historical (or: diachronic) semantics, however, will not be discussed in this chapter (but cf. chapter I.3.2).

In what follows, we will largely focus on lexical meaning, more precisely on the descriptive (or: cognitive) meaning of lexical words. Thus, special emphasis will be placed on the representative function of language (cf. the various functions of language described in chapter I), i.e. on those aspects of meaning that allow us to describe the world. Expressive and social meanings will not be dealt with in greater detail. The following examples have to suffice: (a) the exclusively expressive meaning of *gosh!*, and the differences between *father* and *daddy*, *policeman* and *cop(per)*, or *very* and *jolly* with regard to their expressive meaning; (b) the exclusively social meaning of welcome and farewell words such as *hello* and *goodbye*, forms of address like *sir* and *madam* with their social meaning component, and the differences between forms of address like *pal*, *mate*, and *love* (as used in grocer's shops in England: "What can I do for you, love?") with regard to their (expressive and) social meaning. Generally speaking, the interpersonal function of language is relegated to the sidelines of

descriptive versus expressive versus social meaning

research in semantics: Semanticists rarely devote particular attention to those aspects of meaning that enable us to express feelings, points of view, and speaker judgments (i.e. expressive meaning), or which signal and establish social relationships (i.e. social meaning).

descriptive meaning

But what exactly is the descriptive meaning of a lexical word? To answer this question, we will turn to three central pairs of concepts used in semantics, which are more or less overlapping: *sense – reference, intension – extension*, and *connotation – denotation*. The first-mentioned terms in these three pairs (*sense, intension*, and *connotation*) relate to the conceptual side of meaning and to the problem how to provide a (language-internal) definition of meaning. By contrast, the three contrasting terms (*reference, extension, denotation*) relate to extra-linguistic reality, i.e. to the relation between language and the world. The term "reference", for example, designates the relation between entities in the external world and the words which are used to pick out these entities (e.g. persons, objects, events, places, points in time, etc.). The "referent" is the entity referred to (picked out) by an expression in a particular context.

reference

(4) a. Take the bottle and put it in the dustbin.
      b. He took a bottle and put it in a dustbin.
      c. A bottle is not a dustbin.

Both (4a) and (4b) deal with a particular bottle and a particular dustbin. The only difference between (4a) and (4b) is that in (4a) the referents of *the bottle* and *the dustbin* are accessible to the hearer. In both cases, the referents of *the/a bottle* and *the/a dustbin* vary from utterance to utterance. Matters are different in the case of (4c): here, *a bottle* does not refer to a particular bottle, nor does *a dustbin* refer to a particular dustbin; both noun phrases are thus used in a non-referring sense. But even though both noun phrases in (4c) lack a referent, they still have an "extension". The latter term designates the class of objects to which a linguistic expression can be applied, i.e. the class of its potential referents (in (4c) the class of all bottles and the class of all dustbins). A referent of a linguistic expression is always a member (or subset) of the class of objects that constitutes the word's extension. The term "denotation" is frequently used synonymously with "extension". Sometimes, however, "denotation" is understood in a broader sense which covers not only the relation between nouns or noun phrases and groups of individuals or objects, but also the relation between words belonging to other word classes and the

extension
denotation

196

extra-linguistic phenomena they relate to. Thus verbs denote situations, adjectives denote properties of individuals and objects, and adverbs denote properties of situations.

The sense of an expression is its descriptive meaning, which – in contrast to reference – is independent of a particular utterance and the situational context in which the utterance was made. The distinction between "sense" and "reference" was introduced by the philosopher Gottlob Frege. It is not difficult to see why such a distinction is useful. For one thing, linguistic expressions with different meanings (senses) may very well have the same referent(s). Just think of the noun phrases *the Leader of the Labour Party* and *the Prime Minister of Great Britain*, which differ in sense, but not necessarily in reference: The phrase *the Leader of the Labour Party* may refer to the same person as the phrase *the Prime Minister of Great Britain*. Similar observations apply to *the capital of Prussia, the capital of the Third Reich*, and the *capital of Germany*; all of these phrases refer to Berlin. This example also illustrates that the referent of a linguistic expression may change, while its meaning remains the same: in 1992 Bonn was still *the capital of Germany*, today the capital of Germany is Berlin. The relevance of the sense-reference distinction is also brought home by words which lack a referent, but do have a sense. Cases in point are *unicorn* and *dragon*. The sense of a linguistic expression essentially consists of characteristic features which determine the class of entities it may be used to refer to, i.e. its extension. This bundle of semantic features (e.g. [+HUMAN, -ADULT, +FEMALE] for *girl*) is called the "intension" of a linguistic expression (more on this in sections VI.3.1 and VI.4). Note that so-called "connotations" are not part of the intension. Connotations are typically secondary meanings which can vary according to culture, region, social class, etc. and which are often restricted to particular contexts. This does not mean, however, that connotations are completely subjective associations which different speakers connect with expressions on the basis of entirely different personal experiences. Connotations can be generalized to a certain extent, they are part of the encyclopaedic meaning of a lexeme (as opposed to its dictionary meaning, that is its descriptive meaning, the much more rigid definition we find in dictionaries).

The following sections deal with the two major approaches to the analysis of meaning: the first approach investigates recurrent semantic structures in the vocabulary (structural semantics: cf. section VI.3), the second examines the relations holding between word meanings and our conceptual system (cognitive semantics: cf. section VI.4).

sense (versus reference)

intension (versus extension)

connotation (versus denotation)

Even today, lexical semantics is still to a considerable extent committed to classical structuralist assumptions (cf. chapter I). One of the principles that has proved particularly influential is the idea of language as a complex system of relations: Every linguistic element is integrated in the system (*langue*) through a network of paradigmatic and syntagmatic relations; nothing happens outside of the system. Applied to semantics, this view implies that word meaning is to be treated as something relative, as a purely language-internal phenomenon. A word's meaning constitutes a node in a network of semantic relations. More precisely, the meaning of an expression is defined in part by what it has in common with other expressions, but above all by what distinguishes it from them (de Saussure speaks of the *signe différentiel*: the meaning of a word is what it is not). Thus, if we want to grasp the full meaning of a verb like *march*, we have to know how the manner of walking described by this expression differs from the manner of walking described by similar verbs like *pace* and *stride*. All of these terms are part of an extensive network of motion verbs. Some verbs that belong to this network, such as *amble*, *saunter*, and *stroll*, constitute a subclass of expressions which stand in a relation of oppositeness to *march*, *pace*, and *stride*. The latter verbs denote a quick, determined manner of walking, whereas the verbs in the former group denote a slow, aimless manner of walking. In sum, the principal goal of structural semantics is to show that the vocabulary of a language is a structured whole in which nothing happens in isolation and where various recurrent semantic structures can be identified. The two most important types of such structures (or: networks) are lexical fields and lexical (or: sense) relations.

signe différentiel

3.1 Lexical fields

Lexical (or: semantic) fields are groups of words which cover different or partly overlapping areas within the same extralinguistic domain. Above we already encountered three examples of lexical fields: verbs of asking (*ask, inquire, interrogate, question, wonder*, etc.), verbs of walking (*walk, march, pace, amble, stroll, prance, sneak, stagger, swagger*, etc.), and verbs of killing (*kill, murder, assassinate*, etc.). Further examples include colour adjectives, adjectives relating to mental abilities (*intelligent, clever, smart, bright, brilliant, brainy, stupid, dumb, silly, thick, dense*, etc.), different types of footwear (*shoe, moccasin, clog, slipper, sandal, trainer, boot*, etc.), legwear (*trousers, dungarees, socks, stockings, tights, leggings*, etc.), teaching and research staff at universities (*professor, reader, lecturer, fellow,* etc.), or temporal conjunctions (*when, as, while, after, since,* etc.); there is an infinite number of such lexical fields. The crucial idea motivating such groupings of lexemes by semantic similarities is the assumption that the meaning of a field member can only be fully determined and delimited with reference to its semantic neighbours. From a diachronic point of view, this means that any semantic change within a lexical field may affect all members of the lexical field as well as the intricate network of semantic relations holding between them. Such potential changes in lexical fields include the addition of a new word, the loss of a word, and a change in the meaning of one or more of their members.

In fact, the theory of lexical fields (*Wordfeldtheorie*), which was developed by the linguist Jost Trier in the 1930s, has its roots in the study of semantic change, and hence in diachronic (or: historical) semantics. However, it did not take long for the study of lexical fields to occupy a central place in synchronic word semantics, even if some aspects of Trier's account are in need of revision. Pertinent criticism has been leveled, for example, at his conception of lexical fields as mosaics, whose boundaries can be clearly delimited and which do not have any gaps or overlaps. This ideal hardly exists: (a) category boundaries are often fuzzy (cf. also section VI.4); as a result it may be difficult to determine which lexical field a word belongs to; (b) there are many examples of gaps in lexical fields (e.g. in English or German, adjectives are missing which – in analogy to *blind, deaf/taub,* or *mute/stumm* – denote the absence of the ability to smell or taste); (c) and, finally, in many cases there are more or less conspicuous meaning similarities (and thus overlaps) within a lexical field (e.g. *intelligent, clever, smart*). The suggestion to compare a lexical field to a piece of bread which is unevenly buttered (thicker in some places, thinner or not at all in other places) thus seems to be much more useful than the mosaic comparison. Much as the latter, however, this conception of lexical fields neglects the fact that field members are in most cases related to one another along more than merely two dimensions. For instance, *pace* may differ from *stroll* with regard to the dimensions 'speed' and 'purposefulness'; but these dimensions are no longer sufficient if we want to describe the difference between these two verbs and other members of the same lexical field (e.g. *stagger* or *trudge*). Here, we need further dimensions such as 'degree of body control' or 'degree of effort'. Componential analysis (or: feature analysis, semantic decomposition) has proved to be a very useful tool for describing semantic similarities and differences between

traditional versus modern conceptions of semantic fields

componential analysis

members of a lexical field. In analogy to the conception of phonemes as bundles of distinctive features (e.g. the phoneme /p/ as [+CONSONANT, -VOICED, -NASAL, +OCCLUSION, +PLOSIVE]; cf. chapter II.2.1), the meaning of a word is conceived of as a bundle of (ideally binary) semantic features or semes (e.g. *girl* [+HUMAN, -ADULT, +FEMALE] in contrast to *boy* [+HUMAN, -ADULT, -FEMALE], or *pace* [+QUICK, +PURPOSEFUL] in contrast to *stroll* [-QUICK, -PURPOSEFUL]. These features can roughly be equated with the dimensions that structure a lexical field, but wherever possible they should be chosen so as to allow a 'yes (+) / no (-)' characterization. The choice of relevant semantic features is to some extent arbitrary of course; singling out useful features is more difficult for some semantic areas than for others. In general, the method of semantic decomposition becomes more and more difficult to handle the more fine-grained the semantic analyses are supposed to be (just think of the lexical field of motion verbs). In addition, it is open to debate whether there really is a limited, universally valid inventory of semantic features relevant to the analysis of word meanings. It also remains unclear what role semantic features play in human categorization, i.e. whether semantic features are cognitively real (more on this in section VI.4).

structure of the mental lexicon

By contrast, the psychological reality of lexical fields is indisputable. It can be shown that they are more than simply a convenient theoretical construct, and that they do indeed fulfil an important function in structuring the information stored in our mental lexicon. Word association tests with ordinary people and especially with people suffering from aphasia have clearly shown that there is a much stronger psychological link between members of the same lexical field than between members of different lexical fields. This is hardly surprising: within a lexical field there is a much stronger network of lexical (or: sense) relations. Such relations represent another important principle structuring our mental lexicon. Of particular importance are the kinds of relations which hold between *red – blue – green – yellow*, or *Monday – Tuesday – Wednesday,* etc. (relations of semantic incompatibility), and those relations that hold between word pairs like *man – woman*, *husband – wife*, *hot – cold*, *buy – sell* (relations of oppositeness of meaning) (cf. section VI.3.2). Much as these paradigmatic lexical relations and lexical fields, *collocations* play an important role in processing, storing, and retrieving lexical information. Examples of collocations include syntagmatic lexical relations which exist, for example, between adjectives like *blond*, *auburn*, *curly*, *wavy*, or *unruly* on the one hand, and *hair* on the other (cf. also section VI.1).

3.2 Sense relations

Sense relations (or: lexical relations) are semantic relations between words. The five relations discussed in this section have in common that they systematically occur in an infinite number of word pairs or word groups (especially of course in lexical fields), and that they are all paradigmatic relations, thus representing possibilities of choice between lexical alternatives (e.g. *leggings* in contrast to *trousers, tights,* or *stockings*).

The concept of "synonymy" is used to describe semantic equivalence or rather extensive semantic similarity between two or more lexemes. The term is typically used in reference to the "descriptive" meaning of words (hence the term "descriptive" or "cognitive synonymy"). Synonyms thus have the same semantic features. However, most synonyms differ with regard to their conditions of use: Descriptive synonyms may be interchangeable in many, but not all, contexts. In (5a), for example, it is impossible to replace *deep* by its synonym *profound*; matters are different in (5b):

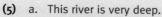

(5)   a.   This river is very deep.
        b.   The incident made a deep impression on me.

Descriptive synonyms may differ with regard to their connotations *(dog – mongrel, cock – rooster, worker – employee, baby – neonate)*, with regard to stylistic level or register *(begin – commence, buy – purchase, intoxicated – drunk – pissed)*, with regard to regional or social variety (e.g. differences between American and British English), or with regard to their collocations (e.g. *a big/large house,* but *Big/ ?Large Brother is watching you*). Cases of total synonymy, i.e. of interchangeability in all contexts (e.g. *Apfelsine – Orange* in German), are very rare. It is not difficult to see why. A linguistic system which has (many) total synonyms would be uneconomic. Why should a language have two (or more) lexemes with absolutely identical usage conditions? In fact, total synonymy between two words is always only temporary: either one of the synonymous lexemes is lost, or the two items will be semantically differentiated, developing different usage conditions.

Synonymy contrasts with antonymy, a term covering various types of semantic opposites (oppositeness). We speak of "complementary" or "binary antonyms" (or: "complementaries") if there is an either-or relationship between the two terms of a pair of semantic opposites, i.e. if the two antonyms exhaust all possible options in a particular

opposites

complementary antonymy

conceptual domain (e. g. *male – female, asleep – awake, dead – alive, live – die, pass – fail*). In these cases, the meaning of one lexeme is equivalent to the negation of the other lexeme. Complementary antonymy is commonly contrasted with gradable antonymy, where the two expressions involved merely constitute opposite poles of a continuum. Alternative terms for gradable antonyms include "contraries", or simply "antonyms". (Note, however, that the term "antonymy" can also be used in the wider sense of 'oppositeness'.) Examples of gradable antonyms are *hot – cold* (notice the various intermediate stages like *warm – tepid – cool*); *broad – narrow, large – small*, and *old – young* (cf. also pairs of nouns like *beginning – end, war – peace*). The great majority of gradable antonyms are pairs of adjectives. Some of these pairs display a certain asymmetry in the sense that one of the two contrasting lexemes can appear in more contexts than the other. Thus, if we want to know a person's age (*How ___ are you?*) or the length of an object (*How ___ is it?*), we use *old* or *long*, respectively, rather than *young* or *short*. The members of pairs like *old – young, long – short* differ in markedness: the term with the wider range of uses is called *unmarked (old, long)*, the one with a more limited range *marked (young, short)*. Relational opposites (or: converses) represent a further type of antonyms, which describe the same situation from different perspectives (e. g. *teacher – pupil* in sentences like *John is Mary's teacher* versus *Mary is John's pupil*). Further examples of relational opposites include pairs of deverbal nouns in *-er* and *-ee* (e. g. *employer – employee, examiner – examinee, interviewer – interviewee*), comparative forms of adjectives (*older – younger, longer – shorter*), pairs of verbs like *give – take, buy – sell, rent – let*, or pairs of prepositions like *above – below*. The fourth type of antonymy, directional oppositeness, does not involve different perspectives on the same situation, but rather a change of direction

(especially *motion* in different directions). Examples of directional opposites (or: reversives) include *open – shut, push – pull, rise – fall, come – go, leave – return, (turn) right – (turn) left, tie – untie*, and *button – unbutton*.

Let us now turn to sense relations which involve hierarchies in the vocabulary, i. e. super- and subordination. The term "hyponym" refers to words like *rose, tulip, daisy*, and *lily*, which stand in a relationship of subordination to a more general expression like *flower*. Conversely, the generic term *flower* is the superordinate or hyperonym (or: hypernym) of *rose, tulip, daisy*, and *lily*. Hyponyms have all semantic features of the hyperonym plus some additional ones, which distin-

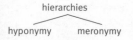

guish them from the hyperonym on the one hand, and from other hyponyms situated on the same hierarchical level on the other (consider, for example, the features distinguishing *rose* and *daisy*, or *daisy* and *lily*). Hyponyms relating to the same hierarchical level are called co-hyponyms or heteronyms. Interestingly, what is probably the oldest method of defining meanings is based on the concept of hyponymy: According to this approach we should first identify the superordinate category (the so-called *"genus proximum"*, i.e. the hyperonym), and then single out the specific properties (*differentia specifica*) which distinguish the lexeme to be defined from its hyperonym (e.g. *daisy* "a flower which is very common, small, and white with a yellow centre"). It follows from the relationship of inclusion between the intension of the hyponym and that of the hyperonym (i.e. the intension of the former including the intension of the latter), that there is a relationship of inclusion on the level of extension as well: the extension of the hyperonym includes the extension of the hyponym (the set of roses is a subset of the set of flowers.)

Alternative terms for "co-hyponymy", the relationship between hyponyms situated at the same hierarchical level, are "heteronymy" and "incompatibility". This captures the fact that in most cases co-hyponyms/heteronyms are semantically incompatible in a given context (either *This is a rose* is true in a particular context, or *This is a tulip is true*, but not both).

heteronymy (or: incompatibility)

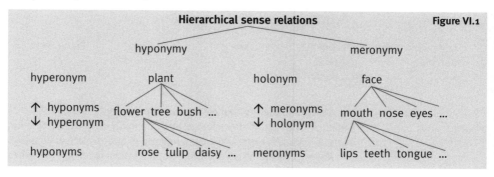

Hierarchical sense relations   **Figure VI.1**

Heteronyms are not always incompatible, however: e.g. *novel* and *paperback* are hyponyms of *book* and heteronyms of each other, but they are not incompatible (*This is a novel* and *This is a paperback* may both be true descriptions of the same object). Sometimes incompatibility is also described as a fifth type of antonymy.

Finally, *meronymy* refers to part-whole relationships (e.g. *finger – hand, toe – foot, mouth/nose/eye – face, door/window/roof – house*). Such meronymic relationships hold between words on different hierarchical levels. Thus, *door* is a meronym of house (the holonym), but the word also has its own meronyms (e.g. *handle* and *lock*). Meronymy, as opposed to hyponymy, is not necessarily a transitive relationship. Thus, if A is a hyponym of B, and B a hyponym of C, then A is always a hyponym of C (e.g. for A = *bobtail*, B = *dog*, and C = *animal*). By contrast, meronymic relations need not be transitive (e.g. for A = *hole*, B = *button*, and C = *shirt*), though there do exist examples of transitive meronymic relationships (e.g. A = *lips*, B = *mouth*, and C = *face*). Meronymy and hyponymy involve completely different types of hierarchies. Hyponymy involves a relationship of inclusion between classes: the extension of the hyponym is included in that of the hyperonym. The hierarchical relationships involved in meronymies are of a completely different type, relating to individual referents of meronymic terms (a finger is part of a hand, a hand part of an arm, etc.); this has nothing to do with a relationship between different classes.

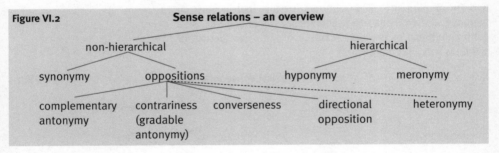

Figure VI.2 **Sense relations – an overview**

3.3 Lexical ambiguity: Polysemy and homonymy

polysemy versus homonymy

Lexemes with only one descriptive meaning are called "monosemous". Many lexemes, however, have several descriptive meanings and are thus (a) members of more than one lexical field, and (b) nodes in a network of sense relations that is even more complex than the network of semantic relations contracted by monosemous lexemes. Such ambiguous words can be divided into two major types: polysemous and homonymous items (homonyms). The different meanings of polysemous lexemes are commonly felt to be related. Typically, one of these senses has developed from the other sense via metaphorical or metonymical processes (e.g. *mouth* 'mouth (part of the body) / river mouth / cave entry', or *wing* 'wing of a bird / of a building / of a car / of an airplane / political party wing'). By contrast, with homonyms it is synchronically, and in many cases also diachronically, impossible to establish a connection between the different meanings (e.g. *race* 'a sports event / a human race', or mole 'animal / dark spot on a person's skin'). In the case of polysemy we can speak of a single lexeme having several meanings, whereas in the case of homonymy we speak of different lexemes that happen to have the same form. Dictionaries often reflect this distinction: a polysemous word has only one entry (with various meanings that are numbered consecutively), whereas a homonym has several entries (e.g. *mole[1], mole[2], mole[3]*).

types of homonymy

Homonyms can be differentiated more precisely with the help of two criteria: (a) medium-independent versus medium-dependent formal identity; (b) complete identity vs. differences in grammatical properties. In some cases, homonyms are identical in both spelling and pronunciation, and thus qualify as 'true' homonyms, or homonyms in the narrow sense. In many others, however, they are identical in spelling only, but differ in pronunciation, or vice versa. Homophones are lexemes which are identical in pronunciation, but differ in spelling (*see – sea, sight – site, flower – flour*), while homographs are identical in spelling, but differ in pronunciation (*lead* /led/ 'kind of metal' versus /li:d/ / 'piece of leather attached to dogs' collars', *bass* /beis/ in music versus /bæs/ 'type of fish'). The second criterion for distinguishing different types of homonyms applies equally to true homonyms, homophones, and homographs. It can be formulated as follows: Are the homonyms under consideration identical with regard to their grammatical properties (in particular their word-class and inflectional morphology)? If yes, we are dealing with total homonymy, total homophony, and total homography, respectively (cf. all examples above); if no, we are dealing with partial homonymy (*bear* N – *bear* V), partial homophony (*rite – write*), or partial homography (*tear* N – *tear* V).

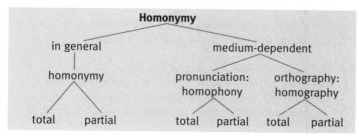

Figure VI.3

It is frequently impossible to give a clear answer to the question whether an ambiguous word is an example of polysemy or homonymy – which once again illustrates the fact that there are no sharp dividing lines in language. Even if we consult etymological information (e.g. with the help of the *Oxford English Dictionary*, short: *OED*), which should be avoided in synchronic analyses of meaning, it remains unclear how far back we should go in the history of a word, and of what use this method really is. Take, for example, the two senses of *pupil* ('student' and 'centre of the eye'). Even if we know that both meanings derive from the same Latin origin (*pupilla* = 'orphan, ward' and *pupula* = 'pupil, eye' are both derived from *pupa* = little girl, doll), which could count as evidence of polysemy, the two senses are so far apart in Present-Day English that we tend to classify *pupil* 'student'

"maximizing" polysemy

and *pupil* 'part of the eye' as homonyms. In general, however, polysemy is considerably more frequent than homonymy. This is not surprising from a psychological and economical perspective. Polysemy is a product of our metaphorical and metonymical creativity and allows us to describe – in a motivated way – something new with the help of something already known. In this way, polysemy adds to the flexibility and adaptability of the vocabulary of a language without increasing the number of lexemes. A language which makes extensive use of polysemy keeps the memory load to a minimum, because fewer words have to be stored in our minds than would be the case if we had to learn a separate word for every concept. Wherever possible, ambiguous words will be classified as cases of polysemy rather than homonymy. This tendency is particularly pronounced in cognitive semantics (cf. section VI.4).

ambiguity in puns

Polysemous and homonymous terms have one conspicuous feature in common: A given context usually forces us to select one particular meaning of these words. An exception to this rule are puns, which are based on the fact that two meanings of a word or word-form are activated at the same time. Examples include the newspaper heading *Wait watchers* (which alludes to the organisation *Weight Watchers*), the announcement in (6a) which informs us that a shoe shop will be opening soon, or the panda joke in (6b):

(6) a. Soon we'll take the wait off your feet.
  b. A panda walks into a bar, sits down and orders a sandwich. He eats the sandwich, pulls out a gun and shoots the waiter dead. As the panda stands up to go, the

206

bartender shouts, "Hey! Where are you going? You just shot my waiter and you didn't pay for your sandwich! Who do you think you are?"

The panda yells back at the bartender, "Hey man, I'm a PANDA! Look it up!"

The bartender opens his dictionary and sees the following definition for panda:

"A tree-dwelling marsupial of Asian origin, characterized by distinct black and white colouring. Eats shoots and leaves."

Usually, however, only one particular meaning of an ambiguous word fits a given context. Ambiguous words are disambiguated by contextual selection of one of their (descriptive) meanings. A common test for ambiguity are cases where two different contexts are relevant to the interpretation of a word; these contexts require the activation of different meanings of the word and therefore, when occuring in the same sentence, lead to a bizarre or unacceptable sentence meaning (in rhetoric, the term "zeugma" is used for cases such as (7a)). A second test, the so-called "identity test" in (7b), also shows very clearly that *expire* is ambiguous:

ambiguity versus vagueness

(7) a. ? John and his driving license expired last week.
      b. ? John expired last week; so did his driving license.

Such tests, then, allow us to determine whether a word is ambiguous or merely vague. Vague terms are unspecified for certain semantic features (e.g. *monarch* is unspecified for sex: *Her father / His mother was a monarch*). For this reason, they display a certain flexibility in their use. What is crucial, however, is that this flexibility does not lead to the assignment of more than one meaning. It is therefore characteristic of vagueness that we are not compelled by a particular context to decide between two or more meanings (thus there is no need for disambiguation by contextual selection). At most, a particular context leads to a more precise specification of the word's meaning (e.g. by emphasizing or suppressing a feature). This type of specification is called "contextual modulation" of meanings (cf. e.g. *window* in (8a–c):

(8) a. Joan opened/shut/repaired the window. (neutral)
  b. Joan painted the window. (frame)
  c. Joan cleaned/broke/looked through the window. (glass panel)
  d. While painting the window, Joan broke it.

As shown in (8d), such modulations can be combined in a sentence without leading to a zeugma. In sum, the distinction between vagueness and ambiguity is of great importance when it comes to determining whether a word has merely one meaning or whether it has several meanings: A word which is vague has one meaning only, while words that are ambiguous have several meanings.

VI.4 Cognitive semantics: Prototypes and metaphors

categorization

Cognitive semantics has developed in the 1980s on the basis of findings in cognitive psychology. Scholars working in this area of research have challenged many time-honoured assumptions familiar from structuralist semantics. The chief difference between the two approaches is that structural semantics defines and analyzes meaning from a purely language-internal perspective (i. e. on the basis of semantic networks connecting lexemes), whereas cognitive semantics explains meaning primarily in terms of categorization (i. e. the grouping of similar phenomena into one class). In cognitive semantics, meaning is considered to be inextricably linked to human cognition, to the way we perceive the world and group phenomena into conceptual categories. Language and cognition are taken to be inseparable: the structure of linguistic categories is held to reflect the structure of conceptual categories (e. g. in the sense that the meaning of a word is the cognitive category connected with it).

Categorization essentially involves the perception or construction of similarities between otherwise different entities. Prototypes and metaphors play a central role in this process: Prototypes are typically regarded as the reference points against which the entities to be categorized are compared. The concept of metaphor, on the other hand, is relevant to answering the following questions: What processes allow us to perceive or construct similarities? Are these similarities objectively given or subjectively created?

4.1 Prototypes

Before we categorize a given animal as a duck (rather than a goose), a given drinking vessel as a cup (rather than a mug), a given activity as running (rather than walking), and a given car as new (rather than used), we compare the entity or activity that needs to be categorized with what we know about poultry, cups, running, and the age of cars, respectively. This raises an important question: How is this knowledge organized? According to the traditional view, categorization is achieved by means of so-called "necessary and sufficient conditions": An object counts as an X just in case it possesses all the features which define an X. Necessary conditions (or: criteria) are features which are indispensable for an entity to qualify as a member of a given category. The term "sufficient conditions" is used when these features are jointly sufficient for assigning the entity to a certain category (i.e. when all of the various necessary criteria apply). This model of categorization implies that categories have clear-cut boundaries. The traditional account of categorization lies at the heart of feature (or: componential) semantics (cf. chapter VI.3.1), which is sometimes rather dismissively referred to as "checklist semantics". Componential semantics can be traced back as far as Aristotle's theory of concepts. Cognitive semantics, more precisely prototype semantics, rejects the classical view of categorization, at least for the majority of concepts: categorization in everyday life – less so in the domain of science – is much more flexible and fuzzy than is suggested by traditional componential semantics. Some ducks have no wings, others cannot quack, even though they have all other properties associated with ducks, and are therefore spontaneously categorized as ducks. Why? Because they do, after all, come very close to our idea of an 'ideal' (or: prototypical) duck, or at least correspond much more to the prototype of a duck than to the prototype of a rivalling category (e.g. a goose). Thus, we can assign an entity to a category if it shares at least some central features with the category prototype, and (in most cases) looks physically similar to it.

Prototype semantics assumes that all knowledge which is accessed in a particular situation is relevant to the process of categorization. For this reason, we cannot strictly separate 'dictionary' or expert knowledge (knowledge of what is essential, pertaining to what speakers know in virtue of their command of a language) from encyclopaedic knowledge (additional knowledge pertaining to what speakers know in virtue of their acquaintance with the world). For example, there may be situations in which what is crucial to cate-

prototype semantics versus feature semantics

prototypes as cognitive reference points

gorizing an animal as a duck is the encyclopaedic knowledge that during their search for food ducks hold their head under water and raise their tail in the air (cf. the German nursery rhyme *Alle meine Entchen*).

The above examples show that categories have an internal structure, which implies that they are not homogeneous: not all category members are equally good representatives of the category; rather there are different degrees of representativeness. Categories have a core consisting of the best representatives (the prototypes), which serve as reference points in the process of categorization, and which are surrounded by increasingly peripheral areas of members that are more and more different from the prototype(s). There is yet another important difference between the conception of categorization entertained in prototype semantics and the view adopted in traditional (including componential) semantics: Cognitive semantics emphasizes that category boundaries are often not clear-cut (fuzziness of category boundaries). Therefore, it is frequently not possible to give a clear answer to the question whether or not an entity belongs to a category. There are grey areas of transition between neighbouring categories where we are incapable of unambiguously assigning an entity to one category rather than another. Different speakers may thus assign the same entity to different categories; even individual speakers may classify the same entity differently on different occasions.

Many findings associated with the psychological theory of prototypes, which underlies prototype semantics, involve the notion of family resemblances. This concept was developed by the philosopher Ludwig Wittgenstein. Wittgenstein used the example of games to show that a category can be held together by nothing more than a complex web of overlapping and crisscrossing similarities among its members, comparable to the various similarities displayed by different members of a family. The analogy between categories and families is based on the fact that family members usually resemble each other with respect to various 'criss-crossing' similarities: Some members have a similar nose, others the same skin, yet others the same eyes, etc. Similar observations can be made with respect to the individual members of the category *game*. Some games are amusing; some involve winning and losing; yet others require particular skills, etc. In such cases, establishing necessary conditions is difficult if not impossible. There need not even be a single feature which is shared by all category members. As a consequence, prototype theory discards the

internal heterogeneity of categories

fuzziness of category boundaries

family resemblances

idea that category membership is determined by necessary conditions. It also rejects the assumption that categorization should be construed as a comparison between the entity to be categorized and the prototypes (cognitive reference points) of a category. This does not mean, however, that the concept "prototype" is given up; prototypes of a category are characterized by a high degree of family resemblances.

In cognitive psychology, the model of category structure based on family resemblances has superseded the 'standard model' of prototype theory dominant in the 1970s. By contrast, in cognitive (more exactly: prototype) semantics the family resemblance model has so far been largely neglected, presumably because of its implications for classical prototype theory (after all, taking family resemblances seriously would effectively force us to abolish the traditional model). Here, the classical prototype model of the 1970s is still widely used, and the concept of family resemblances is presented as being in harmony with the classical model. Some scholars suggest that the family resemblance model is particularly suitable for explaining superordinate categories, such as Wittgenstein's GAME, or ANIMAL, PLANT, FURNITURE, and CONTAINER, while the classical prototype model is particularly illuminating for those kinds of categories that are situated at the psychologically most basic level (so-called "basic-level categories" like DUCK, DOG, CAT, FLOWER, TABLE, BAG). These categories are psychologically basic in the sense that they contain the most information in relation to the cognitive cost of storing them. Their basicness is reflected in quite a number of facts: Basic-level categories are acquired very early by children, they are rapidly recognized and represent the default choice in spontaneous categorization ("Look, a … !"). The basic level is also the highest level of classification where a single image can represent the entire category.

basic-level categories

The connection between lexical semantics and what has been said above about categories should be obvious. According to prototype semantics, the meaning of a word like *duck* is the cognitive category that is associated with it. As a consequence, word meanings contain all of the above-mentioned properties of cognitive categories: we can distinguish central and more peripheral meanings of a lexeme; word meanings are not rigid, there are often gradual transitions between word meanings (recall the notion of contextual modulation discussed above; e.g. the different uses of *window* in *He painted the window* and *He smashed the window*). Prototype semantics is thus a 'more-or-less semantics', which – due to its integrative approach that rejects

significance of prototype semantics for lexical semantics

the traditional distinctions between dictionary and encyclopaedic knowledge, and between meaning and cognitive categories – is much closer to psychological reality than traditional feature semantics (or 'all-or-nothing' semantics) in structuralist lexicology. This does not, however, diminish the usefulness of feature semantics for the description and comparison of word meanings, especially for identifying semantic structures like lexical fields and sense relations. We do not even have to completely abandon the feature approach as a theory of how meanings are mentally represented: Neither the "standard version" of prototype theory nor the more recent family resemblance model can do without a feature-based classification. It is just that the features relevant for categorization are those belonging to the prototypes of a category; moreover, there is no list of necessary features that needs to be checked for successfully assigning entities to a particular category. Ultimately, prototype and feature semantics complement each other, in the sense that feature semantics receives a sounder psychological basis.

prototype and structural semantics complement each other

4.2 Metaphors

vehicle – tenor – *tertium comparationis*

The term "metaphor" (Greek *metaphora* = a transfer from *meta* = over, across + *pherein* = to carry, bear, with the noun *metaphora* already in its modern meaning) traditionally refers to a figure of speech which is based on a relationship of similarity or analogy between two terms from different cognitive domains. This similarity, which may be objectively given or merely subjective, is typically held to enable metaphors to 'transport' one or more properties of a (usually relatively concrete) source domain (or: vehicle) to a target domain (or: tenor), which is typically more abstract. The similarities involved in metaphorical mappings are often called the *"tertium comparationis"* (or: "ground"). Typical examples of metaphors are animal metaphors (*Smith is a pig / fox / rat / ass / stallion*), synaesthetic metaphors (extensions from one field of sensory perception to another, e.g. in *loud colours, soft / warm / sharp voice*), and so-called anthropomorphic metaphors (transfers from the human domain, especially human body parts, to all sorts of non-human domains, e.g. *leg of a table, arm of a river, face / hands of a clock, foot of a mountain, mouth of a river*).

Metaphors are traditionally neglected in lexical semantics, though they do play a role in historical semantics and in syntagmatic semantics. Historical semanticists view metaphor as an important cause of semantic change (cf. chapter IX). In syntagmatic semantics, metaphors have been explained in terms of selection restrictions. For example, in

different status in lexical and cognitive semantics

sentences like *Smith was a rat* or *He picked one hole after the other in my argument*, selection restrictions are violated (*semantic incongruence*): in the first example [+HUMAN] clashes with [-HUMAN], in the second [+CONCRETE] (*pick a hole*) with [-CONCRETE] (*into an argument*). In cognitive semantics, metaphors are seen in a completely different light: Metaphor is not considered a purely linguistic phenomenon, but a fundamental cognitive process which enables us to grasp the world and organize our knowledge. Metaphors pervade everyday language and are crucial to human thought processes; they are not simply dispensable ornamental accessories. Many metaphors are likely to go unnoticed by ordinary speakers. This is not surprising, however. We are often no longer aware of many metaphors simply because they are firmly anchored in human cognition and have become part and parcel of ordinary language.

How do cognitive semanticists arrive at this conception of metaphors? This question can be answered by having a closer look at the process of categorization, i.e. of comparing new things to already familiar ones. At the heart of this process lies the search for similarities or analogies. It is easier to understand and describe the world if we can grasp new concepts with the help of already existing categories. In some cases this may involve extending these categories. However, such a strategy of understanding unknown concepts in terms of familiar ones has the advantage that (a) the categories we need for grasping the world are not unnecessarily multiplied, and (b) that classifications are not arbitrary, but motivated by similarities between those entities that are new and those that are already familiar. Such similarities do not have to be objectively given; (some) similarities underlying (some) metaphors are predominantly constructed by speakers. It is language users who determine the ground of comparison (*tertium comparationis*). Some metaphors strike us as novel and original even after we have encountered them many times. Cases in point are 'poetic metaphors' found in classical rhetoric and literary works, e.g. *My life had stood – a loaded gun in corners* ... (Emily Dickinson). Cognitive semantics is not primarily concerned with this type of metaphor, focusing instead for the most part on 'everyday metaphors', i.e. conventional metaphors which are not isolated but rather part of entire systems of metaphors. It is commonly assumed that these metaphorical systems allow us to structure particular areas of experience. Let us take a look at some examples of relevant metaphors (9) and systems of metaphors (10). The arrows in the following examples represent the link between source and target domains,

metaphor as a basic cognitive process

highlighting one of the fundamental properties of metaphors, namely their asymmetry or unidirectionality (at the most general level: concrete → abstract, spatial → non-spatial). The above-noted emphasis on the conceptual nature of metaphors in cognitive linguistics is reflected in the distinction between metaphorical concepts and metaphorical expressions. According to cognitive linguists, metaphorical concepts such as ARGUMENT IS WAR take priority over concrete metaphorical expressions like *attack* (a claim) or *shoot down* (an argument). Every metaphorical expression can be subsumed under one or several metaphorical concepts. In fact, we can use such metaphorical expressions only because the corresponding metaphorical concepts are part of our conceptual system. Conceptual metaphors are usually indicated by capital letters.

(9) a. LIGHT → THOUGHT/KNOWLEDGE/INTELLECT
illuminating/obscure ideas, a murky discussion, a bright person, a clear argument, make ideas transparent; I see 'I understand'

b. WAR/PHYSICAL ARGUMENT → VERBAL ARGUMENT
his criticisms were right on target, shoot down an argument, attack a weak point in someone's argument

c. MONEY → LANGUAGE
coin new words, owe someone an answer, richness in expressions

(10) UP – DOWN → PERSONAL WELL-BEING (e.g. HAPPINESS, HEALTH, POWER, STATUS)

a. HAPPINESS/GOOD IS UP, BAD (LUCK) IS DOWN
feel up/down, be in high/low spirits, fall into a depression

b. HEALTH IS UP, ILLNESS/DEATH IS DOWN
be in top shape, be at the peak of health, fall ill, drop dead

c. CONTROL/INFLUENCE IS UP, LACK OF CONTROL/INFLUENCE IS DOWN
be in high command, at the height of power, on top of the situation, fall from power, be under control

d. HIGH STATUS IS UP, LOW STATUS IS DOWN
rise to the top, be at the peak of your career, be at the bottom of the social hierarchy, fall in status

It is a basic assumption in cognitive semantics that such metaphors are more or less constantly used for structuring abstract concepts in terms of concrete (especially spatial) ones.

Like metaphor, metonymy (Greek *metonymia* = a change of name) is a classical figure of speech which has been assigned a completely new status in cognitive semantics. Consider the examples in (11) and (12):

(11) a. PRODUCER FOR THE PRODUCT: He owns a Picasso and two Rembrandts.
 b. OBJECT/INSTRUMENT FOR OBJECT/USER OF INSTRUMENT: The buses are on strike.
 c. PLACE FOR INSTITUTION: The White House is planning to attack Iraq.
 d. INSTITUTION FOR THE PEOPLE IN CHARGE: The university will reject this proposal.
 e. PLACE FOR RESPONSIBLE PEOPLE: Table 10 want their bill.

(12) PART FOR THE WHOLE (*pars pro toto*)
 a. He's a good hand at gardening.
 b. There are not enough good heads in this company.
 c. I don't see any new faces – nothing seems to have changed.

Metonymy is also considered to be a central cognitive process which enables us to 'get a better grasp' on the world. The main difference between metaphor and metonymy is this: Metonymies do not involve a transfer from one cognitive domain to another; they are rather based on an objectively existing connection between two 'contiguous' phenomena, such that one phenomenon stands for the other. Thus, metonymies are not based on a relationship of similarity, but on contiguity; the phenomena or entities concerned are part of the same situation or, more generally, the same conceptual structure. Picasso does not resemble his pictures, buses do not resemble bus drivers, and table 10 does not resemble the restaurant guests that sit at that table. But there is certainly a direct connection between painters and their paintings, bus drivers and the buses they drive, or the plate and the dish that is served on it (just compare the standard encouragement for finishing off one's meal used in German especially when addressing children: *Jetzt iss schön den Teller auf!* lit. "Eat up the plate"). Various types of such connections are illustrated in (11) and (12); those in (12) form a separate group which in classical rhetoric is called *synecdoche*, a term which covers part-whole and whole-part relations (as in German *Zünd doch mal bitte den Weihnachtsbaum an!* lit. "Please light the Christmas tree").

The two central concepts of cognitive semantics – prototypes and metaphors – are both relevant to investigating polysemy at the level of word meaning. It is not difficult to see why prototypes are crucial to explaining polysemy: Polysemous expressions can be described as prototype categories in that they can have one or more central meanings (the prototypes), each of which can have increasingly peripheral sub-senses, and all of which are connected by different kinds of family resemblances. This can be illustrated with the help of prepositions, which are notoriously polysemous. For instance, there are countless ways in which *over* can be used as a preposition, but we can single out three central meanings: place ('above') in (13), place ('above') in connection with path ('across') in (14), and a covering sense in (15):

(13) a The lamp hangs over the table.
　　　b. The painting is over the mantelpiece.

(14) a. The plane flew over the house.
　　　b. John walked over the hill.
　　　c. John lives over the hill.

(15) a. The board is over the hole.
　　　b. The guards were posted all over the hill.
　　　c. There was a veil over her face.

Each of these three groups of central meanings has a prototypical core (the one in the (a)-examples) and other meanings that can be systematically derived from the central meaning (e. g. *over* in (15c), which involves a vertical rather than a horizontal axis). One of the above three (groups of) prototypical senses, notably the one in (14a), has a more central position than the others, and is thus even 'more prototypical' than the other two prototypes in (13) and (15). In many cases, the connections between the different meanings are established by metaphors. Metaphorical transfer both accounts for the synchronic relations between different senses of a word, and offers a diachronic explanation how one sense develops from another. There is thus a close connection between polysemy and metaphor as a central cognitive mechanism for grasping and classifying new entities with the help of familiar ones, and abstract things with the help of concrete ones. In this context, polysemy is deliberately construed in a wide sense, i.e. a polysemous word may have senses belonging to different word classes (e.g. *over* as a preposition, adverb, and part of a compound).

It is not only for ambiguous expressions, however, that cognitive semanticists have shown that the link between *signifié* and *signifiant* is more motivated than suggested by traditional structural semantics. The assumption that this link is far less arbitrary than is commonly conceded has led to further insights that put into perspective two central structuralist ideas: (a) linguistic categories provide speakers with the cognitive categories that enable them to grasp the world (extreme determinism); (b) therefore, the conceptual system of a language has to be analysed on its own terms. The second of these structuralist assumptions is inextricably linked to the hypothesis that languages are autonomous systems and cut up the same conceptual domain in different ways. For this reason, every language is held to create its own view of the world (extreme relativism). Cognitive semanticists challenge this position (also known as the linguistic relativity principle or the Sapir-Whorf hypothesis), arguing that the basic categorization and metaphorization processes are the same or at least very similar for all people – at least among the members of the same cultural community, but in many cases also across cultures. Consequently, the differences concerning the ways in which members of different speech communities categorize the world are limited. A well-known example illustrating this fact are colour terms. Comparative analyses of basic colour terms in different languages have shown that languages may indeed differ as to where they set the boundaries between neighbouring categories (here primary colours). Crucially, however, speakers of different languages agree on what constitutes the centre of the respective colour categories, i.e. on what constitutes the 'best' red, green, blue, etc. The perception and processing of reality is thus not primarily a matter of the native language one happens to speak. Linguistic categories do not determine our cognitive categories. Quite to the contrary, they reflect the structure of our conceptual system.

further differences between cognitive and structural semantics

Sapir-Whorf hypothesis

Checklist Semantics – key terms and concepts

ambiguity ↔ vagueness
antonymy (complementary
  antonymy; contrariness;
  converseness; directional
  opposition; heteronymy)
arbitrariness
asymmetry
basic-level category
categorization
cognitive semantics
collocations
componential analysis
conditions of use
connotation ↔ denotation
contextual modulation
contextual selection
conventionality
degrees of
  representativeness
descriptive / cognitive ↔
  expressive ↔ social
  meaning
disambiguation
encyclopaedic meaning ↔
  dictionary meaning
family resemblance

fuzziness of category
  boundaries
heterogeneity of categories
heteronymy / incompatibility /
  co-hyponymy
hierarchical sense relations
  (hyponymy; meronymy)
historical / diachronic
  semantics
holonym
homonymy (total ↔ partial;
  homography, homophony)
hyponymy ↔ hyperonymy
idiom
intension ↔ extension
lexical ↔ grammatical
  meaning
lexical/semantic fields
lexical semantics / lexicology
lexicology ↔ lexicography
markedness
mental lexicon
metaphor
metaphorical extension
motivation
necessary ↔ sufficient

condition
paradigmatic ↔ syntagmatic
  semantics
polysemy
prototype
prototype semantics ↔
  feature semantics
Sapir-Whorf-hypothesis /
  principle of linguistic
  relativity
selection restrictions
semantic feature
semantics ↔ pragmatics
semasiology ↔
  onomasiology
sense ↔ reference
sense/lexical relations
sentence meaning
sentence semantics
signe différentiel
source domain, vehicle ↔
  target domain, tenor
structural semantics
synonymy (descriptive /
  cognitive ↔ total)
utterance meaning

Exercises

1 Which of the following uses of *mean* are relevant in a discussion of what semantics is concerned with and how it differs from pragmatics?
  a. This face means trouble.
  b. What does *soliloquy* mean?
  c. If you're not there by six, I'll be gone. And I mean it.
  d. You're meant to take off your shoes in a mosque.
  e. Sorry, I don't quite understand. What exactly do you mean?
  f. Do you mean to say you can't come?
  g. His work means everything to him.

h. I never meant her to read this letter.

i. Smoke means fire.

2 Fill in the chart below with **+** or **−** as appropriate:

a. establishes a link between language and the world

b. independent of a particular utterance

c. involves a set of possible referents

d. to be found in a dictionary definition

e. lists defining properties

	sense	reference	intension	extension	denotation	connotation
a.						
b.						
c.						
d.						
e.						

3 a. Sketch the complex semantic network the verb *see* forms part of, using the following examples: *see – hear – feel, see – know – understand, see – look at – watch, see – visit – meet, see – imagine, see – sea*

b. Take the case of *see* as a starting point and sketch the conditions under which a lexeme can belong to more than one semantic field.

4 Identify the lexical relations holding between the following pairs of words: *frame – window, expand – contract, mole – spy, fill – empty, (go) in – (go) out, fail – succeed, hyponym – hypernym, picture – painting, zero – love, semantics – linguistics, freedom – liberty, after – before, book – index*

5 a. What is funny about the headline *Where's the party?* (Subtitle: *How to get young people to vote for their politicians*).

b. Explain the linguistic basis of the panda joke in (6b).

6 Explain the role of the context in drawing a distinction between (a) semantics and pragmatics, (b) vagueness and ambiguity, (c) total and cognitive synonymy.

7 a. What is structural about structural semantics?

b. What are the major differences between structural and cognitive semantics?

8   Which of the following statements are true, which are false?
    a. Compiling a semantic field and identifying the sense relations among the field members are both instances of adopting an onomasiological procedure.
    b. Semantic fields are two-dimensional and have neither gaps nor words with overlapping or identical senses.
    c. Polysemous lexemes cannot belong to more than one semantic field.
    d. Homonymy and semantic change are two sides of the same coin.
    e. Oppositeness plays an important role in the organization of our mental lexicon.
    f. Hyponymy involves the inclusion of semantic features of the higher categories.
    g. Semantics is exclusively concerned with the descriptive meaning of content words.
    h. Prototype categories (e.g. bird, dog, cup, toy) always have fuzzy boundaries.
    i. Componential analysis and prototype theory do not exclude each other.
    j. Categorization always involves metaphor.

Exercises
Advanced

9   Comment on the following excerpt from the language column by William Safire in the International Herald Tribune (5 January 1998):
    ... now, however, we must come to grips with the Adverb That Ate the Language last year. When the casino tycoon Donald Trump wanted to help defeat Governor Christie Whitman of New Jersey in her re-election bid, he announced, 'I was *totally* a good friend to her, and she showed *totally* no loyalty.'

    Last month, when the White House aide Lanny Davis announced he was quitting the job of scandal spinmeister, we recalled his pronouncement: The ads that both the Democrats and Republicans aired were *totally* legal.

    ...

    Here are a few variations for today's totalists. *Entirely* has a connotation equally sweeping but not as harsh; *fully* is not as emphatic; *perfectly* is somewhat defensive; *thoroughly* has a nonsense quality, but goes to depth rather than width; *wholly* is useful in print, but its homonym *holy* makes it confusing in oratory.
    Keep your eye on *utterly* in 1998."

10 Compare different dictionaries concerning their policies of (a) what they make the basis for ordering the senses of (polysemous) words, (b) drawing a distinction between polysemy and homonymy, and (c) making use of semantic fields.

11 a. Three of the following uses of *over* are metaphorical. Identify these three and associate them with the following tenor-vehicle relationships: LIFE IS A JOURNEY, AN ACTIVITY IS A CONTAINER, CONTROL IS UP.
   A. He rolled the log over.
   B. The power line stretches over the yard.
   C. The rebels overthrew the government.
   D. The city clouded over.
   E. Sam still hasn't got over his divorce.
   F. Don't overdo it.
   b. Find reasons why of the prototypical senses of *over* in (13) to (15) it is the 'above and across' sense that is typically regarded as the most basic one.

12 Path schemata typically allow a focus on the endpoint, as in (A2):
   A1. He walked across the street. (path)
   A2. He lives across the street. (endpoint)
   a. Illustrate this phenomenon for *over* and comment in the light of the sentences in (B) on the limits of meaning extension for *over* and the advantages of including crosslinguistic data in studies of polysemy.
   B1. He walked over the street.
   B2. *He lives over the street.
   B3. Er wohnt (gerade) über die Straße.
   b. Consider the use of *across* in (A2) and the use of *über* in (B3). Is it metaphorical or rather metonymic extension that is responsible for the development of these two senses?

Sources and further reading

Aitchison, Jean. 1994². *Words in the mind: An introduction to the mental lexicon*. Oxford: Blackwell.

Allan, Keith. 2001. *Natural language semantics*. Oxford: Blackwell.

Benson, Morton/Evelyn Benson/Robert Ilson. 1997². *The BBI dictionary of English word combinations*. Amsterdam/Philadelphia: Benjamins.

Cruse, David Alan et al., eds. 2002. *Lexikologie/Lexicology*. [HSK]. Berlin/New York: de Gruyter.

Cruse, David Alan. 2004². *Meaning in language: An introduction to semantics and pragmatics*. Oxford: Oxford University Press.

Cruse, David Alan. 1986. *Lexical semantics*. Cambridge: Cambridge University Press.

Davidson, George W./Roget, Peter Mark. 2004. *Roget's thesaurus of English words and phrases*. London: Penguin Books.

Davis, Steven et al., eds. 2004. *Semantics: A reader*. New York: Oxford University Press.

Geeraerts, Dirk/Hubert Cuyckens. forthcoming. *Handbook of cognitive linguistics*. Oxford: Oxford University Press.

Goatly, Andrew. 1997. *The language of metaphors*. London/New York: Routledge.

Lakoff, George. 1987. *Women, fire, and dangerous things: What categories reveal about the mind*. Chicago: University of Chicago Press.

Lakoff, George/Mark Johnson. 1980. *Metaphors we live by*. Chicago: University of Chicago Press.

Leisi, Ernst. 1985. *Praxis der englischen Semantik*. Heidelberg: Winter.

Löbner, Sebastian. 2002. *Understanding semantics*. London: Arnold.

Lyons, John. 1977. *Semantics*. 2 vols. Cambridge: Cambridge University Press.

Murray, James Augustus et al, eds. 1961². *The Oxford English Dictionary*. Oxford: Clarendon Press.

Oxford English Dictionary online: OED online. Oxford: Oxford: Oxford University Press.

Saeed, John. 2003². *Semantics*. Oxford: Blackwell.

Stechow, Arnim von/Dieter Wunderlich (Hrsg.). 1991. *Semantik*. Berlin: de Gruyter.

Taylor, John R. 1995². *Linguistic categorization. Prototypes in linguistic theory*. Oxford: Clarendon Press.

Traugott, Elizabeth Closs/Richard B. Dasher. 2002. *Regularity in semantic change*. Cambridge: Cambridge University Press.

Ungerer, Friedrich/Hans-Jörg Schmid. 2003. *An introduction to cognitive linguistics*. London: Longman.

VII Pragmatics:
The study of meaning in context

Pragmatics (from Greek *pragma* = deed, act) is the newcomer among the major branches of linguistics. Its precise definition and status within linguistic theory is still being debated, however: Is it a linguistic subdiscipline like, for example, phonology, morphology and syntax, or is it a new, interdisciplinary approach which is concerned with all kinds of linguistic structures?

Introduction

We can roughly distinguish between a broad and a narrow definition of pragmatics. In semiotics, pragmatics is traditionally defined as a subdiscipline of semiotics which is concerned with the relationship between signs and their users (cf. chapter I). The roots of pragmatics as the study of language use or linguistic performance lie in this (primarily) European tradition of research in semiotics. The pragmatic approach is usually contrasted with the structuralist approach, which is solely concerned with language systems in a vacuum, as it were (i.e. with the *langue* or the linguistic competence of a member of a certain

**VII.1
Competing
definitions:
Perspective or
component?**

broad definition

speech community), independent of concrete communicative situations. The 1970s saw an upsurge of interest in pragmatics (the so-called "pragmatic turn"), as a reaction to the neglect of language users and functions in Chomsky's generative grammar, which was influenced by structuralism. The new pragmatic approach focused on the process of communication which results from the interaction between speakers and hearers in actual linguistic contexts. Its major goal was to investigate the prerequisites for successful communication. If we define pragmatics this way, it can hardly be regarded as just another branch of linguistics (along with phonology, syntax or semantics). Rather, pragmatics provides a new perspective on the various aspects of linguistic structure. The fact that, under this broad conception, virtually all aspects of language can be the object of research in pragmatics (although the focus has always been on language use) has naturally led to dismissive characterizations of pragmatics as the "wastebasket" of linguistics or "a useless catch-all term".

narrow definition   In the past few years, a more narrow definition of pragmatics has emerged, which is adopted by most linguists working in an Anglo-American tradition. According to this definition, pragmatics represents a linguistic subdiscipline which complements semantics. This line of research focuses on concepts such as utterance meaning, intention and inference. Communication is primarily seen as the negotiation of meaning between interlocutors (or between authors and readers). Since in everyday communication many things remain implicit, the hearer's central goal is to recognize the speaker's communicative intention. Hearers achieve this aim with the help of inferences based on what has been literally said, knowledge about the utterance context, and general background knowledge shared by speakers and hearers. In many cases, such inferences are necessary for establishing coherence (i.e. an underlying link) between different utterances in a conversation. In the brief dialogue in (1), for example, much more is going on than a mere exchange of statements about the world:

(1)   The telephone is ringing.
       A: That's the telephone. // B: I'm in the bath. // A: OK.

Speaker A does not simply tell B that the phone is ringing, and B does not simply mention that he/she is in the bath. A's statement obviously functions as a request directed at B to pick up the phone; B's response indicates that (or why) he/she cannot comply with this request. A clearly grasps the actual message conveyed by B's utterance and acknowledges it by saying "OK"; so A is likely to pick up the phone himself/herself. The main focus of such a pragmatic approach, sometimes also called "conversational pragmatics" or "micropragmatics", is on principles which allow us to bridge the gap between the descriptive meaning of a sentence, i.e. its proposition or what is said, and the meaning it has in a specific context (i.e. what is meant, the so-called "utterance meaning)". ("What is) said" and ("what is) meant" are two technical terms introduced by the philosopher Herbert Paul Grice (cf. section VII.4 below). In general, micropragmatics is concerned with all aspects of meaning anchored in actual conversational contexts, especially with utterance meaning (cf. sections VII.3 and VII.4), but also with word meaning (cf. section VII.2). This view of pragmatics lies at the heart of an over-simplified definition of the term, as encountered in the familiar equation "Pragmatics = meaning minus semantics". The following list of differences between semantics and pragmatics offers a somewhat more fine-grained and accurate picture, which will be further elaborated in the following sections (cf. especially section VII.4.2):

micropragmatics

semantics	pragmatics
context-invariant, speaker-independent meaning	context-sensitive, speaker-dependent meaning
meaning potential	concrete meaning in a given context
What does X mean? (conventional meaning, what is said)	What does the speaker mean by uttering X? (non-conventional meaning, what is meant)
principles for describing meaning, meaning relations and meaning combinations	principles for bridging the gap between what is said and what is meant

In some publications the notion of "context" is defined in a narrow sense, relating exclusively to the situational context, which covers aspects such as time and place of the utterance, the interlocutors' social and cultural background, the level of formality, topic and overall aim of the conversation. Thus defined, context is opposed to "cotext", the purely linguistic or textual context of an utterance. In this book, "context" will be used in a broader sense, referring to both the linguistic and the non-linguistic (situational) context of an utterance.

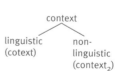

context
linguistic (cotext)   non-linguistic (context$_2$)

The main focus of pragmatics as the study of meaning in context are utterances rather than single words. Thus, the two most influential pragmatic theories, speech act theory (cf. section VII.3) and the theory of conversational implicatures (cf. section VII.4), investigate language on the utterance level. Nevertheless, we shouldn't overlook the importance of context as far as word meaning is concerned. After all, it is on the word level that the necessity of drawing a boundary between semantics and pragmatics is particularly prominent. There are, in fact, numerous expressions (primarily personal, possessive and demonstrative pronouns, and adverbs of time and place) which have a context-independent, invariant meaning as well as a context-dependent meaning which varies with the circumstances in which they are used. From a semiotic point of view, such terms are hybrids, combining aspects of two different types of signs (cf. chapter I): symbols (which express arbitrary and conventional relationships between *signifiant* and *signifié*) and indexes (which typically indicate physical and causal relationships between signs and what they refer to).

semiotic hybrids:
symbol and index

Let us imagine that we are on a train and find a note containing the following request:

(2)   Meet me here same time tomorrow with a book about this size.

It would not be difficult for us to understand this sentence – but only up to a certain point. We know that "me" refers to the writer, but who is that person? We know that "here" refers either to the place where the note was written or (less likely) to the place where the note is being read, but only the latter place is known to us. We will encounter similar difficulties with all other expressions underlined above: What point in time is referred to by means of the phrase "same time", what date is referred to by means of "tomorrow", and how big is "this size"? Therefore, the proposition in (2) is underspecified. A complete understanding of (2) is possible only if we know the context-dependent meaning of the underlined expressions. Pointer words like *here* or *this* are called "deictic (or: indexical) expressions" or "deictics" (from Greek *deiknynai* = to prove, point out), because they point to a certain entity or aspect of the utterance context.

The speaker and certain features of the utterance context (primarily time and place) represent the central point of reference (*origo* or deictic centre) for context-dependent meaning. The deictic centre naturally shifts as soon as another speaker starts talking, but it can also be deliberately projected onto the hearer/reader, resulting among

deictic centre

other things in a shift in the time and place coordinates. Take the following example:

(3) a. When you read these lines <u>today</u>, I'll be no longer in the country.
     b. This programme was recorded <u>last December</u> to be relayed <u>today</u>. (delayed radio broadcast)

It is therefore no coincidence that in indirect (or: reported) speech the deictic expressions used in the original utterance have to be replaced:

(4) a. <u>I</u> won't be <u>here</u> <u>next Monday</u>.
     b. He said <u>he</u> wouldn't be <u>there</u> <u>the next/following Monday</u>.

The three major deictic dimensions (i. e. reference dimensions in a certain context) are person, place, and time. Person deixis encodes the different persons involved in a communicative event. In English, personal and possessive pronouns are used for this purpose (e. g. *I/we* – speaker(s), *you* - addressee(s), *he/she/it/they* – persons not involved in the communicative event). Examples of place and time deixis are given in (5) and (6):

deictic dimensions

(5) Place deixis
     a. here – there, hither – thither, near – far, left – right, this – that (in the sense of 'this here – that there')
     b. come – go, bring – take, borrow – lend

(6) Time deixis
     a. now, soon, then, ago, today, yesterday, tomorrow
     b. present, actual, current, former, future, next, last

In the pairs of opposites illustrating place deixis (5), the relevant expressions differ with regard to the parameter "near vs. far from the speaker" (proximal vs. distal) in (5a), and "movement towards or away from the speaker" in (5b). The usual reference point for time deixis is the moment of utterance (or: coding time; the examples in (3) are therefore exceptions). For this reason, absolute tenses (i. e. present, past and future; cf. chapter IV.3.1) are also considered to be deictic categories. Deixis, then, is not only found in the lexicon, but also in grammar.

There are further types of deictic expressions, the most important being social deictics. This deictic dimension relates to the (absolute or relative) social status of the persons directly or indirectly involved in a communicative event (directly involved: speaker, addressee; indirectly involved: the persons talked about and bystanders. In English, expressions like *Sir, Madam, Your Honour, Mr President* or titles (*Doctor, Professor*) are used to indicate social status; in German and French the distinction between *Du – Sie* and *tu – vous* is highly important. In certain languages (like Japanese and Korean), such honorifics are far more grammaticalized. These languages indicate social differences and varying degrees of intimacy between the interlocutors by different types of personal pronouns and inflectional morphemes on verbs. Social deixis is clearly more important in these linguistic communities than e.g. in European societies.

Two further deictic dimensions, which are usually considered much less important than those mentioned above, are discourse deixis and manner and degree deixis. The latter is always accompanied by gestures:

(7) a. The book was this thick.
    b. The fish was so big.
    c. Why don't you do it like so/this.
    d. Du sollst den Deckel nicht so rum drehen, sondern so rum.

Discourse deictics provide a means of increasing text coherence by explicitly referring to specific parts of the discourse which follow or precede the deictic expression:

(8) a. I bet you haven't heard this story.
    b. in the last chapter, in the next paragraph, as mentioned above, in what follows
    c. in conclusion, all in all, anyway, however, besides, therefore, so, etc.

Figure VII.1

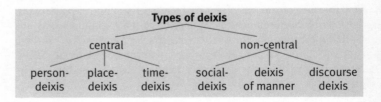

Types of deixis

central — person-deixis, place-deixis, time-deixis

non-central — social-deixis, deixis of manner, discourse deixis

It is important to draw a distinction between discourse deixis and the non-deictic, more exactly (ana)phoric use of deictic expressions, i.e. the use of deictics (especially pronouns) to refer to an entity which has already been introduced (9a,b) or which will be introduced later in the conversation or text (9c):

(ana)phoric meaning

(9)   a. In 1998 Fiona worked as a part-time teacher. <u>She</u> was married <u>then</u> and had three children. <u>They</u> were two, four and eight years old.
      b. Mandy wants to go to the theatre, but doesn't know how to get <u>there</u>.
      c. <u>He</u> is a kind man who gives a million dollars to the poor.

The concept of "coreferentiality" is crucial to explaining how anaphoric terms work. The expressions underlined in (9) do not directly refer to extra-linguistic entities; they rather refer to them indirectly by referring to linguistic expressions which follow or precede. If a deictic expression is coreferential with an expression introduced in the preceding context (or better: cotext), the so-called "antecedent", it is used anaphorically (*anaphora*). Much less frequently, deictics are coreferential with expressions introduced later in the text, in which case we speak of a cataphoric use (*cataphora*). The term "anaphora" (or "phoric word") often serves as a cover term for both cataphoric and anaphoric uses (in the narrow sense of anaphora) which deictic expressions may have in a text. But there are also cases where deictics are used neither deictically nor phorically, as illustrated in (10):

(10) a. <u>There</u> we go. Well done, lad!
       b. <u>There</u> is a story I'd like to tell you.
       c. These days <u>you</u> can never be sure what sex they are.
       d. What I did yesterday? Oh, I did <u>this</u> and <u>that</u>.
       e. Mary lives <u>opposite</u> Bill. (versus Mary lives opposite.)

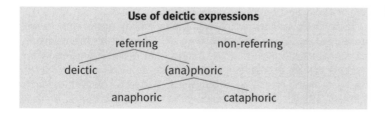

Use of deictic expressions

Figure VII.2

What is particularly fascinating about deictics is that they straddle the fence, as it were, between semantics and pragmatics, with one foot in semantics (their invariant or symbolic meaning), and the other in pragmatics (their context-dependent or indexical meaning). Both meaning components are necessary to turn a deictic into a referential expression – which may either have its own, direct referent (when used deictically) or an indirect (co-)referent (when used phorically) – thus completing the proposition expressed by a certain utterance. It is therefore hardly surprising that deictic expressions are investigated both in pragmatics and in semantics (especially referential semantics).

VII.3
Speech acts
origin of pragmatics

Pragmatics was not put on the agenda of linguistics by linguists. Defined as the study of meaning in context, it has developed from a branch of philosophy which offers a critical perspective on attempts at applying principles of formal logic to the analysis of natural language. Concepts that are crucial to logic include truth conditions and truth values (i. e. true or false). Truth conditions relate to the conditions that have to be fulfilled for a statement to be true in a certain context. Truth values are assigned to sentences by determining, among other things, the referent(s) of the deictic expressions they contain (cf. the last paragraph in VII.2). The fact that the meanings of some expressions are at least to some extent context-dependent was not ignored in truth-conditional semantics.

ordinary language
philosophy

But the true origins of pragmatics lie in ordinary language philosophy, as represented in the writings of the late Ludwig Wittgenstein and the work of John L. Austin, John R. Searle and Herbert Paul Grice. This school of thought saw itself as a countermovement to traditional logic, which due to its focus on truth conditions ignored central aspects of natural language and ordinary communication. Ordinary language philosophers developed the two most important pragmatic theories: speech act theory (Austin and Searle) and the theory of conversational implicatures (Grice). These approaches will be explained below and in section VII.4.

speech act theory

Speech act theory, which was pioneered by Austin and further developed by Searle, proceeds from the observation that everyday communication is more than just an exchange of statements about the world which are assessed in terms of truth or falsity. For one reason, there are many utterances which are not used for describing some state of affairs, and hence cannot be assessed in terms of truth conditions (see 11a-c); for another, truth conditions are often not very useful if we want to understand the speaker's intention, i.e. what is really meant by an utterance (11d):

> **(11)** a. Happy birthday!
> b. Merry Christmas!
> c. I hereby declare the meeting closed.
> d. A: Will you come to my party tonight?
>   B: I'm still fighting this flu.

Examples (11a-c) cannot be assessed in terms of truth-conditions. What is relevant is rather whether the respective utterances are appropriate and therefore successful in conveying the intended message: is it really the addressee's birthday at the time of utterance (11a), is it really Christmas (11b), and does the speaker in (11c) really have the authority to close the meeting? In (11d), B's utterance can be assigned a truth value, but this is not crucial. The relevant information is not that B is still fighting the flu, but that B intends to give a negative answer to the question asked by A. B does so indirectly by mentioning the fact that he or she has the flu, which is a good reason for not going to a party. The actual message contained in this answer is not explicit but must be inferred by A. Therefore, those aspects of meaning which are relevant to truth-conditional semantics underspecify the message conveyed (11d).

The examples above enable us to illustrate some further basic tenets and concepts associated with speech act theory: Communication is a dynamic process, to communicate is to act, and communication is successful if the hearer grasps the speaker's intention(s). The basic unit of verbal interaction is defined as a speech act. A speech act is an utterance made by a certain speaker/author to a hearer/reader in a certain context. It is not their structural (phonological/syntactic) or semantic properties (proposition) which are crucial to speech acts, nor their possible effect on the addressee (perlocution). The most important aspect of speech acts is rather the speaker's/author's communicative intention (the illocution). For example, is the utterance in (12) intended as a simple statement (made by tourists: "Look! I've never seen a bobby before."), as a request (made by a foreigner: "Go and ask him for directions."), as a warning (uttered by criminals: "Watch out, be careful.") or even as a threat (in a heated argument: "If you don't stop I'll scream.")?

key assumptions and concepts

speech act

illocution

> **(12)** There is a policeman at the corner.

Since the illocution or illocutionary force (role, point) of a speech act is its most important aspect, the term "speech act" is often used in a narrow sense referring to illocutionary acts. Speech act theory in general has become a theory of illocutionary forces focusing on the following questions: What kinds of communicative intentions can be expressed by utterances? What kinds of devices are used to signal these intentions? What kinds of conditions have to be met in order to successfully convey these communicative intentions, i.e. in order to successfully perform a request, warning, threat or promise?

3.1 Classification of illocutionary acts

Searle distinguishes five basic types of speech acts, i.e. communicative intentions expressed in utterances. These types are held to be universal:

- **Assertives** or **representatives** are used to describe the world (e.g. state, express, claim, tell, describe, assert, admit something).
- **Directives** are attempts to get people to do things, to change the world in the way specified by the speaker (e.g. give an order, ask something or ask somebody to do something).
- By means of **commissives** speakers commit themselves to a future action which will change the world in some way (e.g. by promising, threatening or committing oneself to something).
- We use **expressives** to express our feelings and opinions; expressives offer a glimpse of the hearer's psychological state (e.g. thank, greet, congratulate, apologize, complain).
- **Declarations** essentially serve to bring about a new external situation; they show that the world can indeed be changed by language (e.g. baptisms, marriages, divorces, declarations of war). This type of speech acts is clearly different from the other four types in that it requires specific extra-linguistic institutions or legal settings.

speech act verbs

As can be gleaned from the above examples of different types of speech acts, there are certain verbs (so-called "speech act verbs") which can be used to render illocutionary roles explicit. Speech act verbs are used, for example, in indirect speech to express someone's communicative intention:

(13) a. Read my paper, please.
  b. He <u>urged</u> his professor to read his paper.

(14) a. What a great performance!
  b. He <u>congratulated</u> her on her great performance.

(15) a. There is a policeman at the corner.
    b. He <u>warned</u> his friend that there was a policeman at the corner.

Of course, the speech act verbs in the (b) examples are not used to perform the speech acts they name. These verbs merely spell out what types of speech acts have been performed. They thus differ from utterances such as *Thank you, I promise, I forgive you,* or *I warn you,* where the speaker performs the relevant illocutionary act by using a speech act verb. The latter types of utterances are called "performative utterances". Such utterances can fulfil their function only if they display a certain form, the so-called "performative formula". Performative utterances have the form of declarative sentences in the first person singular, present tense, indicative and active; they may also contain an adverb such as *hereby*. However, the mere fact that a certain utterance follows this pattern does not guarantee that the primary communicative intention motivating the utterance is made explicit. (16a), for example, primarily functions as a directive rather than as an expressive (it does not really express gratitude, but rather represents a request); the commissive speech act in (16b) is obviously not a promise but a threat:

performative utterances

(16) a. Thank you for not smoking.   b. I'll kill you, I promise.

In addition to speech act verbs there are further devices indicating illocutionary force, for example particles such as *please* ("Will you leave, please?" – which functions as a request rather than as a question), the three major sentence types (declarative, interrogative, imperative), and intonation. In general, such devices do not determine illocutionary force, however; the (primary) illocution of an utterance may well be at odds with the illocution indicated by the relevant devices (cf. also VII.3.3 below).

illocutionary force indicating devices

3.2 Felicity conditions

Speech acts have to meet certain conditions to be successful (as has already been illustrated above for (11a)). These so-called "felicity conditions" provide a grid for analyzing particular speech acts and comparing them with others. Searle proposes the following four types of felicity conditions:

- propositional content conditions represent restrictions on what can be said about the world by means of a certain speech act. For example, we cannot promise something or warn against something that has already happened.

- preparatory conditions specify real-world prerequisites for the successful performance of a speech act. For example, is the speaker able to keep his or her promise? And does the hearer wish for the promise to be kept?
- sincerity conditions are restrictions on the speaker's psychological state, on his attitude towards the propositional content expressed. Does the speaker, for example, really intend to keep his or her promise?
- the essential condition is constitutive of speech acts; it provides the most important criterion for classifying speech acts. For example, the use of a speech act verb can count as the performance of a particular speech act (the utterance *I promise* counts as a promise, the utterance *I warn you* counts as a warning).

From these types of felicity conditions follow the rules for the appropriate use of speech acts. Of course, speech acts may be successful even if the relevant preparatory or sincerity conditions are not fulfilled. In this case, speakers simply violate the rules. Violating such rules is comparable to violating traffic regulations: A driver may 'successfully' overtake the car ahead of him, even if he violates traffic regulations in doing so. All rules for the appropriate use of speech acts, except for those based on the essential condition, are merely regulative, i. e. they are rules for pre-existing activities which can also take place without these rules. The rule based on the essential condition is different. It is a constitutive rule, i. e. utterances which do not follow the constitutive rule associated with a particular speech act cannot in principle be used to perform that speech act. The essential condition determines all other felicity conditions for a given speech act, and thus the rules for its felicitous use.

regulative versus constitutive rules

3.3 Indirect speech acts

speech act

```
       speech act
       /        \
  direct       indirect
  (explicit,   (implicit,
  secondary)   primary)
```

As illustrated in (11d), (12) and (16), the primary communicative intention of an utterance is often – maybe even in most cases – different from what it may seem to be at first sight. Some sentences which look like neutral statements ("It's freezing in here.") can be used as requests ("Please shut the window."), others which look like announcements ("Soon I'll come and get you.") may function as warnings or threats. Such examples are cases of indirect speech acts. In indirect speech acts, speakers perform a speech act (the primary speech act) via another (secondary) speech act. In some cases, then, two speech acts are realized at once, one of them being explicit, the other implicit. As far as the speaker's communicative intention is concerned, the implicit speech act is the more important one.

Indirect speech acts are standardized to varying degrees. Some of them are strongly conventionalized. For example, the appropriate response to a yes-no question like *Could you tell me the time?* is to tell the time, rather than to mumble *yes* and walk away. But many indirect speech acts require the hearer to infer the speaker's real intention (what he or she wants to communicate) by means of a more or less complex reasoning process. The hearer can infer the speaker's intention only if he/she takes into consideration both the literal meaning of the utterance and various other factors, including his/her knowledge about the speaker/hearer, the knowledge shared by speaker and hearer about the utterance context, as well as their shared world knowledge (including their knowledge of the importance of politeness in the respective culture; cf. also section VII.4.2). Even more essential to the inferential process required to arrive at the speaker's intended meaning is knowledge of general principles of cooperative behaviour. When investigating the inferential processes necessary to identify indirect speech acts, speech act theory thus ties in with, and indeed needs to draw upon, another pragmatic approach, the so-called theory of conversational implicatures.

degrees of standardization

4.1 The original theory by Grice

Conversational implicatures are the most important link between sentence meaning and utterance meaning, between what is said and what is actually meant. They are a special type of pragmatic inferences and must be distinguished from semantic inferences.

Semantic (or: logical) inferences are inferences which are exclusively based on the conventional meaning of words, phrases and sentences. Two typical examples are semantic implications (or: entailments) and presuppositions. A proposition X entails a proposition Y if the truth of Y follows necessarily from the truth of X, i.e. if, every time sentence X is true (*There is a bobtail*), sentence Y is also true (*There is a dog*). In cases of entailment, it is impossible to claim X and deny Y. The concept of entailment is very useful for defining sense relations such as hyponymy. Presuppositions (also known as "conventional implicatures") are predications that are taken for granted when a sentence is uttered, i.e. expectations which are naturally associated

VII.4
Conversational implicatures

semantic inferences

presuppositions
conventional implicatures

with particular linguistic expressions (including sentences). Verbs such as *manage* or *fail* in (17a), for example, presuppose an attempt (17b); the sentence in (18a) presupposes (18b):

(17) a. John managed/failed to repair his computer.
b. presupposition 1: John tried to repair his computer.
c. presupposition 2: John has a computer.

(18) a. Christine has the noisiest children one can imagine.
b. Christine has children.

Unlike semantic entailments, presuppositions hold under negation, i.e. the presuppositions (17b,c) and (18b) remain valid if we negate (17a) and (18a).

pragmatic inferences
Pragmatic inferences are different from the semantic inferences encountered above: they are not merely based on the conventional meaning of utterances, but additionally require some contextual knowledge, i.e. the type of knowledge outlined at the end of chapter VII.3. In different contexts, the very same utterance may lead to completely different pragmatic inferences. By contrast, the semantic inferences associated with utterances are context-independent. In (19), B's remark is a valid answer to A's question – B of course assumes that both A and B have some background knowledge concerning the time when the evening news usually starts. In (20), B's answer is exactly the same, but here it is supposed to indicate that B wants to watch the evening news first (and maybe go for a walk at a later time). B does not reject A's suggestion directly but his/her utterance allows A to draw the inference *Not now*, [but maybe] *after the evening news*:

(19) A: What's the time?
B: The evening news just started.

(20) A: Let's go for a walk.
B: The evening news just started.

pragmatic principles
Usually, interlocutors tacitly adopt certain basic principles of human interaction. Different types of pragmatic inferences are distinguished according to the kind of principle they are based on. Politeness is one of these principles (cf. VII.4.2). Another one is the pragmatic principle of cooperative behaviour. This principle lies at the heart of Herbert Paul Grice's theory of conversational implicatures.

The basic idea which underlies Grice's Cooperative Principle is that communicating is cooperative behaviour, and that therefore every communicative event proceeds on the assumption that speaker and hearer (or author and reader) want to cooperate – even if at first sight this might not seem to be the case. For example, B's remark in (19) does not specify the time, but A will nevertheless regard it as a valid answer. If the context was the same but the question was asked by a different person, e. g. a tourist who does not know what time the evening news starts in, say, England, B's answer would be uncooperative. As far as the hearer or reader is concerned, cooperative communication primarily consists in asking oneself: What does the speaker/ author mean? What is the intention behind his/her utterance? (How) is his/her utterance connected to what has been said earlier in the discourse? In other words, we generally assume that the speaker/author wants to communicate something, which may either be obvious or which needs to be inferred from his or her utterance. There seems to be no other possibility: we always look for the (deeper) meaning of utterances (effort after meaning).

the Cooperative Principle with its conversational maxims

Now, in what sense precisely do we cooperate in communication? Grice distinguishes four different types of cooperative behavior, three of which relate to the content and one of which relates to the form of utterances. These four types of cooperative behaviour are captured by the four maxims given in Table VII.3. The Cooperative Principle itself Grice formulates as follows: "Make your conversational contribution such as is required, at the stage at which it occurs, by the accepted purpose or direction of the talk exchange in which you are engaged."

levels of cooperation

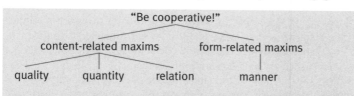

Figure VII.3
Grice's Cooperative Principle

Quality: Make your contribution one that is true. Do not say what you believe to be false (Quality$_1$). Do not say that for which you lack adequate evidence (Quality$_2$).
Quantity: Make your contribution as informative as is required for the current purposes of the exchange (Quantity$_1$) and not more informative as required (Quantity$_2$).
Relation: Be relevant. Do not change the topic.
Manner: Be perspicuous: Avoid obscurity of expression (Manner$_1$), avoid ambiguity (Manner$_2$), be brief (Manner$_3$) and orderly (Manner$_4$).

One might be inclined to think that these principles are merely a convenient theoretical construct unrelated to the real world, no more than wishful thinking of a philosopher. However, quite a few facts argue in favour of Grice's theory. First, there are a great number of meta-linguistic expressions, so-called "hedges", which we use to pre-assess what we are going to say in terms of the maxims of conversation, especially when risking to violate one or even several of them. Just think of remarks like *I'm not sure whether it's true but ...* (Quality$_1$), *as far as I know* (Quality$_2$), *to make a long story short* (Quantity$_2$, Manner), *by the way* (Relation) or *this may be irrelevant but ...* (Relation). Even more important are the following facts:

- The maxims of the Cooperative Principle are neither arbitrary conventions nor do they constitute norms or rules of conduct. They simply reflect our everyday behaviour in a purely descriptive way. Grice's maxims represent the basis for negotiating all kinds of human interaction, including not only linguistic communication, but also actions such as helping someone to change a tyre or to park his or her car.
- Grice was aware of the fact that expectations concerning whether the maxims will be obeyed depend on the type of verbal interaction involved. A police officer will hardly expect a suspect to tell the (whole) truth, and persons at a party are unlikely to regard the umpteenth remark on the weather (or the delicious food) as highly informative. This emerges clearly from the way the Cooperative Principle has been formulated: "Make your conversational contribution such as is required, at the stage at which it occurs, by the accepted purpose or direction of the talk exchange in which you are engaged." According to Grice, cooperation is therefore a relative concept which has to be adapted to each individual context; cooperative behaviour is the kind of behaviour which is appropriate in a particular communicative situation.
- Possibly the most remarkable property of conversational maxims is their robustness. The assumption that the maxims apply is not easily given up, not even when an utterance seems to violate them in form, content, or both. This aspect has been mentioned above (effort after meaning): we always assume that the person we are talking to is cooperative and observes the maxims, at least to a certain extent. The central maxim in this context is certainly the maxim of Relation: as long as we consider an utterance to be relevant in a given context, we will try to understand it.

- The Cooperative Principle has never been considered the only pragmatic principle. Other principles (such as politeness or face saving) can also motivate pragmatic inferences (cf. section VII.4.2). Such inferences are not examples of conversational implicatures, however; this technical term is exclusively used for pragmatic inferences based on the Cooperative Principle.

Conversational implicatures can be classified according to two different criteria: (a) whether they are based on the fact that speakers follow the maxims or whether they are based on the fact that speakers violate them – at least at first sight; (b) whether or not they are confined to a certain context. As far as the first aspect is concerned, we distinguish standard and non-standard implicatures. Examples of non-standard implicatures are presented in (21), where the maxims of Quantity$_1$ and Relation seem to be violated, and (22), where the maxim of Manner seems to be violated.

types of conversational implicatures

> **(21)** A: Would you like some dessert?
> B: Do they eat rice in Japan?
> (conversational implicature: "Yes, of course")
>
> **(22)** A: Let's get the kids something.　B: But no I-C-E-C-R-E-A-M.
> (conversational implicature: "Don't mention *ice cream*. As soon as the kids hear the word, they will ask for it")

In these two examples, the speakers violate the maxims deliberately and ostentatiously, which qualifies as what Grice called *flouting* the maxims. However, non-standard implicatures can also result from a maxim clash. In the brief dialogue in (23), for example, B has to violate Quantity$_1$ in order to obey Quality$_2$. B simply does not know where exactly John spends his holidays.

> **(23)** A: Where does John spend his holidays?
> B: Somewhere in Germany.

The prototypical conversational implicatures are dependent on a particular context and called "particularized implicatures". Most non-standard implicatures belong to this group, but we have also encountered some standard implicatures of this type (19 and 20). Particularized implicatures are commonly contrasted with generalized implicatures, which are not restricted to a particular context. Generalized implicatures are especially relevant to the division of tasks between semantics and pragmatics. Of particular interest are a subgroup of generalized implicatures, the so-called "scalar implicatures", which are based on the first maxim of Quantity. Scalar implicatures can be characterized as follows: the hearer assumes that a given utterance presents the strongest possible statement which can be made in a given context, so that there is no need to read 'more' into it. Scalar implicatures are thus essentially negative inferences from the statement of one position to the negation of a stronger one. They always involve lexical items that are gradable or can be arranged on a scale; these items must be of roughly the same length, and lexicalized to the same degree:

(24) a. ‹all, most, many, some›   c. ‹excellent, good›
     b. ‹always, often, sometimes›   d. ‹love, like›

If one of the expressions on such a scale is used in a given utterance, hearers will typically derive the scalar implicature that none of the stronger expressions on the same scale could have been used in the context at issue. Consider the examples of scalar implicatures illustrated in (25). The first maxim of Quantity ("Make your contribution as informative as is required") allows us to draw the negative inference in (25a) that the biscuits were not eaten by all children. In a similar vein, this maxim explains why (25b) implies that John does not always lie.

(25) a. Many kids ate biscuits.   b. John often lies.

The different expressions on such scales are characterized by a pragmatic inferential relationship from right to left (scalar implicature: no stronger interpretation possible) and a semantic inferential relationship from left to right (entailment: if it is true that many kids ate biscuits, it is also true that some kids ate biscuits). Scalar implicatures enable us keep the number of senses of a word down to a minimum.

Consider, for example, the coordinating conjunction *or* and corresponding expressions in other languages. These conjunctions can be used in two different ways (exclusive *or* and inclusive *or*). If only one of the two alternatives conjoined by *or* applies, the term exclusive *or* is used (as in *On the $5 lunch you may take a soup or a salad* [... but not both]). On the other hand, we speak of inclusive *or* if both alternatives may apply: for example, *or* in *We will listen to the tape today or tomorrow* is used in an inclusive sense: the sentence is true if either *We will listen to the tape today* is true or if *We will listen to the tape* *tomorrow* is true, or if both are true. The sentence is false only if none of these possibilities apply. Despite these different uses of *or*, we do not have to posit different *senses* of the word (an exclusive versus an inclusive sense). The different uses can rather be explained by scalar implicatures: There is a scale ‹*and, or*› such that if a speaker says "p *or* q", he or she implies that he or she is not in a position to make the stronger claim "p *and* q". In this way, the exclusive interpretation "p or q, but not both" can be derived by means of the scalar implicature that "p *and* q" does not apply. Thus, the only sense of *or* which has to be posited in a semantic account is the inclusive interpretation, the exclusive use can be attributed to scalar implicatures. In this way, pragmatics simplifies semantic analysis.

(26) I need someone who speaks Russian or Polish.

One might be tempted to argue that due to the scalar implicature discussed above, the speaker in (26) must be looking for someone who speaks either Russian or Polish, but not both. Such an interpretation is absurd; it ignores what is probably the most important property of conversational implicatures, viz. their cancellability: Conversational implicatures may be cancelled without a sense of contradiction. In (26), for example, the speaker could add "Of course, anyone speaking both languages will be most welcome". This would not be a contradiction. The fact that conversational implicatures can be cancelled makes them even more attractive; it is always possible to add "... but I didn't mean to say/suggest that ...". Further important characteristics of conversational implicatures include calculability and non-conventionality. Conversational implicatures are calculable in the sense that it is generally possible to reconstruct the inferential process which leads to a conversational implicature. Of course, no complex inferential process is involved in the highly standardized indirect speech acts mentioned above (e.g. *Could you tell me the time?*) (cf. VII.3.3). Non-conventionality relates to the fact that conversational implicatures are not part of the conventional meaning of particular words or utterances, and that knowing the conventional meaning of expressions is not sufficient for grasping such implicatures. As already noted, scalar implicatures, for example, can only be inferred on the basis of the first maxim of Quality.

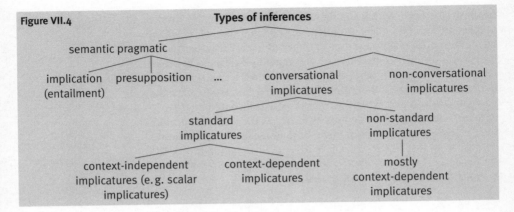

Figure VII.4 — Types of inferences

4.2 Post-Gricean models

During the 1980s, several models of implicature were developed, which will only be sketched in outline here. In general, two types of approaches can be distinguished: reductionist models that contain fewer maxims or principles than Grice's original theory, and expansionist models which add further maxims to those posited by Grice. Despite the various modifications of Grice's account suggested in these models, there is only one model that criticizes the basic ideas of Grice's theory of conversational implicatures and has explicitly been developed as an alternative to it (see the remarks on Sperber & Wilson below). All other models still subscribe to Grice's model and the basic assumptions underlying it, but simply offer attempts at improving or complementing it.

Horn: Quantity principle versus Relevance principle

Almost all recent approaches are reductionist. The two most interesting reductionist models have been proposed by Horn and Sperber & Wilson. Horn, who developed the concept of scalar implicatures, does not so much reduce as rearrange Grice's conversational maxims. His model includes a maxim of Quality (essentially the same as Grice's), a Quantity principle (which covers Grice's first maxim of Quantity as well as the first two maxims of Manner), and an R(elation)-Principle (which covers Grice's second maxim of Quantity, his maxim of Relation and the third maxim of Manner). Horn's rearrangement of the maxims explains an important fact about Grice's conversational maxims: They give rise to two entirely distinct types of conversational implicatures. On the one hand, there are implicatures leading to enriched, stronger, interpretations (e.g. indirect speech acts which seem to be based on the following principle: "Hearer, read as much into the utterance as is compatible with your world knowledge and the situational context".) On the other hand, there are "negative" implicatures which do not allow for a "stronger" interpretation (e.g. scalar implicatures which seem to be based on the following principle: "Hearer, the speaker said everything he could. Don't try to read more into his utterance.") The examples in (27) clearly illustrate this paradox:

(27) a. I broke a finger last night.
   b. I slept on a boat last night.

(27a) carries the implicature "it was my finger", i.e. invites a stronger interpretation, whereas (27b) conveys the implicature "it was not my boat", i.e. a negative inference. Horn offers a solution to this paradox (which Grice had noticed but did not explain): The R-Principle motivates conversational implicatures that lead to stronger interpretations (so-called "R-based implicatures"), and the Q-Principle motivates "negative" implicatures. According to Horn, these two pragmatic principles as well as the Gricean maxims can ultimately be traced to a more general principle of linguistic economy, the Principle of Least Effort (or simply human laziness). The R-Principle follows from speaker economy (minimization of linguistic output: "Say no more than you must"; "Hearer, infer as much as possible."), whereas the Q-Principle follows from hearer economy (maximization of informational content: "Speaker, say as much as you can and say it as clearly as possible.").

language economy

Unlike Horn, Sperber & Wilson ([1986] 1996²) heavily criticize Grice's model. In their view, the set of maxims put forward by Grice can be replaced by a single principle, the Principle of Relevance. However, the notion of relevance has a different status in Sperber & Wilson's theory than it has in Grice's and Horn's models. According to Sperber & Wilson, relevance is a psychological principle that involves a kind of cost-benefit analysis. Relevance is a function of an utterance's contextual effects (to be understood in psychological terms, i.e. as cognitive effects) and the processing effort involved in achieving these effects: The greater the contextual effects, the greater the relevance; and the smaller the processing effort required to obtain these effects, the greater the relevance. Thus:

Sperber & Wilson: Relevance Theory

relevance = contextual effects : processing effort

According to the Principle of Relevance, utterances create the expectation that they are optimally relevant. Hearers/readers may thus assume that everything speakers/authors say is optimally relevant,

i. e. that their utterances yield the greatest possible contextual effects in return for the smallest possible processing effort.

contextual effects

There are different types of "contextual effects". The term covers cases where new assumptions (contextual implications) are derived in a specific context, cases where the hearer's assumptions are eliminated or revised (e. g. because new evidence contradicts or weakens the original assumptions), and cases where existing assumptions are strengthened due to further evidence in favour of them. Language users have to invest processing effort in deriving such contextual effects and accessing that context which, according to the Principle of Relevance, is the optimal one for processing a certain utterance.

> **(28)** A: Bet no one's understood today's pragmatics lecture.
> B_1: Well, there are several students of philosophy in the class.
> B_2: Well, there are several mountaineers in the class. (???)

If A is to infer from B's reply that there are indeed students who understood the pragmatics lecture, the first of the two possible remarks made by B (B_1) is certainly more relevant than the second (B_2). To derive the same conclusion from the second answer, A would have to make a much greater processing effort, and try to construct a context in which mountaineering can in some way be related to understanding a pragmatics lecture. Much as the notion of relevance, the term *context* has a different meaning in Relevance Theory than in other accounts: it is primarily a psychological concept which refers to the world and to the interlocutors' background knowledge. In many cases, the context is not there right from the beginning but has to be constructed during the inferential process.

> **(29)** Mary: Have you read *The Revenge of the Black Forest*?
> Peter: I never read books that win awards.

In this brief dialogue, for example, it is absolutely possible for Mary to correctly infer that Peter has not read the book without knowing beforehand that it won an award. She would have to construct the necessary context before being able to make the inference, which inevitably means that Mary has to make a greater processing effort. Nevertheless, this would not diminish the relevance of Peter's answer, because his utterance enables Mary to gain new information. Peter's answer thus yields an additional contextual effect, redressing the balance between cost and benefit. Of course, Mary could also respond to Peter's remark by saying: "But *The Revenge of the Black Forest* has never won an award". In this case, Mary would also have to construct an appropriate context for Peter's answer, for example that Peter obviously believes (i.e. presupposes) that the book has won an award. In this scenario, however, Peter's answer would be clearly less relevant than in the former one: Mary would have to make a greater processing effort (asking herself (a) whether the book might have won an award despite her assumptions to the contrary, and especially (b) how Peter's answer relates to her question); nevertheless, she would be able to derive fewer contextual effects from Peter's answer.

Sperber & Wilson's Relevance Theory, which they consider a cognitive and psychological theory rather than a pragmatic one, is certainly the most widely discussed model among those presented in this chapter. It is also the most controversial of these theories, far more controversial than, e.g. Grice's 'standard theory'. Relevance Theory has been criticized, for example, for failing to explain how processing effort is to be calculated. As a result, it remains unclear how relevant a certain utterance really is. Also, the Relevance Principle cannot do without at least some Gricean maxims. The Cooperative Principle is more plausible and offers a more fine-grained analysis of the mechanisms underlying the processing of utterances in ordinary communication. But in one respect Relevance Theory has managed to spell out and show more clearly what Grice had already recognized but not further elaborated in his theory: Sperber & Wilson give a convincing account of why Grice's distinction between what is said and what is meant cannot be equated with the distinction between semantics and pragmatics. Pragmatics (the context of an utterance or pragmatic inferences) is crucial not only to what is meant, but also to what is said (i.e. we need pragmatic inferences and the context to complete the proposition conveyed by a certain utterance; such pragmatic inferences which complete a proposition are called *explicatures* by Sperber & Wilson). Semantics on its own underspecifies what is said. Thus, as already noted, it is often impossible to assign reference to referential expressions in the absence of information about the situational context (e.g. *the boy* in (30)). Contextual information is also required for disambiguating ambiguous expressions (e.g. are the boy's *trainers* in (30) persons or shoes?).

(30) The boy was looking for his trainers.

[margin note: what is said ≠ semantics]

[margin note: explicatures]

Such examples demonstrate that familiar accounts of the distinction between semantics and pragmatics (including the division of tasks sketched at the end of chapter VII.1) are simplified and have to be revised: pragmatic processes already play a role in establishing what is said. Again, pragmatics is claiming part of the territory formerly occupied by semantics.

Leech: Politeness Principle

Having discussed two reductionist models, we will now take a brief look at a well-known expansionist account. Leech (1983) adds another pragmatic principle to Grice's framework, the Politeness Principle ("Be polite, make the addressee feel good."). Its most important maxim – especially in English-speaking countries – is the tact maxim ("Minimize the hearer's processing effort and maximize the hearer's benefit."). This principle is not designed to explain how we can infer the communicative intention of speakers/authors; it rather helps us understand why we use indirect speech acts so frequently. The key idea underlying this principle is the assumption that many speech acts are spontaneously felt to be either polite (e.g. offers, promises) or impolite (requests, orders). Depending on such factors as, for example, how much authority the speaker has over the hearer (or vice versa) or how close the relationship between the speaker and the hearer is, the speaker has to choose the appropriate speech act. For Leech, the Politeness Principle is ultimately more crucial than the Cooperative Principle, because it is only by observing the Politeness Principle that a good and friendly social relationship between interlocutors can be established and maintained, which in turn is a precondition for their willingness to cooperate.

macro-pragmatics

Leech's socio-pragmatic theory represents a transition from micro-pragmatics to macro-pragmatics, i.e. from an approach which focuses on the meaning conveyed by utterances to a much broader approach which places particular emphasis on the social and cultural factors affecting the way we use language. Macro-pragmatics includes the study of politeness (especially Leech and Brown & Levinson 2002), and both conversation and discourse analysis (e.g. Schiffrin 1994). Another branch of macro-pragmatics is cross-cultural pragmatics. Scholars working in this field have alerted linguists to the danger of basing theoretical considerations in linguistics largely on a single language and culture, and have warned especially against an anglocentrism in pragmatic theory (e.g. Wierzbicka 2003). It is, for example, not possible to make unrestricted generalizations about the importance of politeness in communication or about the evaluation of speech acts as inherently polite or impolite on the basis of our knowledge of Anglo-American culture and Western societies. Macro-pragmatics is no longer close to philosophy and semantics. It rather borders and draws upon the concepts, methods and insights in text linguistics, on the one hand, and sociology and anthropology, on the other hand.

Checklist Pragmatics – key terms and concepts

(ana)phoric use (anaphora ↔ cataphora)
antecedent
coherence
context ↔ cotext
contextual effect
conversational implicatures
conversational maxim (quality; quantity; relation; manner)
Cooperative Principle
coreference
deictic dimensions
deixis (person, place, time, social, discourse, manner and degree)
explicature
felicity conditions
hedges
honorifics
illocution

illocutionary force
implicature (standard ↔ non-standard; scalar; generalized ↔ particularized)
index (ical expression)
inference (semantic ↔ pragmatic)
intention
linguistic economy
micro-pragmatics ↔ macro-pragmatics
ordinary language philosophy
origo
performative formula
performative utterance
Politeness Principle
presupposition (conventional implicature)
Principle of Relevance

properties of conversational implicatures (cancellability; calculability; non-conventionality)
proposition
Q- and R-Principle
robustness of maxims
rules (regulative ↔ constitutive)
semantic implication
speech act (direct ↔ indirect)
speech act theory
speech act verb
symbol
truth condition
truth-conditional semantics
types of illocutionary speech acts (assertive / representative; directive; commissive; expressive; declarative speech acts)
utterance meaning

Exercises

1   Fill in the blanks:
    Pragmatics can be defined as the study of ... in ..., with the speakers
    and their ...s at the centre. Its two most important theories oper-
    ate on the ... level. Speech act theory was developed by ... and his
    pupil ..., and the theory of ... implicatures by ... All of them are ...
    belonging to the movement of ... language ... Grice's theory
    helps us account for the frequently observable fact that we ...
    more into an utterance than what is ... said. In this respect it links
    up with the study of ... within speech act theory. Different from
    Grice's theory, the ... theory developed by Sperber and Wilson is
    not a pragmatic, but rather a ... theory. What stands at the heart
    of this theory is the calculation of contextual ... against ...

2   Identify the deictic expressions in the following examples and
    specify
    a   whether they are used deictically or anaphorically
    b   the relevant deictic dimension.
        a. There she was, sitting right next to my mother.
        b. Listen, mate, there is only one solution to your problem:
           you finish your essay and submit it next Monday.
        c. There you go.
        d. The hotel was just terrible. So the next Monday we left this
           hotel for good.
        e. Two days ago I met Mary. She looked tired and said she
           wasn't looking forward to her sister's birthday party a week
           from today.

3   a. Spell out the symbolic and indexical meanings of *today* and
       this morning respectively. Make use of the term *coding time*.
    b. What is understood by *deictic projection*? Apply this notion to
       the following conversational exchange:
       Fred: It's the one on the right.
       Mary: My right or yours?
       What can we assume concerning the locations of Fred and
       Mary relative to each other?

4   Which of the following utterances qualify as performatives?
    Identify the relevant speech acts.
    a. I promised never to do it again.
    b. I promise I'll never do it again.
    c. Don't worry, be happy!
    d. She declared the meeting closed.

e. I hereby fulfil my promise and paint the fence.

f. Don't you dare look at my daughter again!

5 Identify both the direct and the indirect speech act for each of the following examples:
   a. Could you get me a cup of coffee?
   b. I could do with a cup of coffee.
   c. I would not do this, if I were you.
   d. Would you like to come to my party?
   e. I wish I knew when the boss is coming back.
   f. Didn't I tell you to be careful?

6 Try to identify for each of the following exchanges (a) the shared background assumptions of A and B, (b) the conversational implicature B wants A to draw, and (c) the relevant maxim(s) of the Cooperative Principle:
   a. A: Did you bring the baby?
      B: Do you see a pram or a bag full of nappies?
   b. A: Have you cleaned the kitchen and done the shopping?
      B: Well, I've done the shopping.
   c. A: Have you seen George recently?
      B: I saw him sometime last spring.
   d. A: Does your dog like bones?
      B: Do cats chase mice?
   e. A: There's a good movie on BBC 2 tonight.
      B: Good for you. I still have to finish this essay.

7 a. Name and illustrate three central properties that Grice identified for conversational implicatures.
   b. What is understood by scalar implicatures? In what way can they be characterized as "negative" inferences?

8 Which of the following statements are true, which are false?
   a. Modern pragmatics was born in philosophy.
   b. Deictic expressions make the illocutionary point of an utterance explicit.
   c. Politeness is perhaps the most important motivation for being indirect.
   d. For each individual speech act the essential condition determines the other felicity conditions.
   e. Most felicity conditions represent regulative rules.
   f. The Cooperative Principle is a normative pragmatic principle explaining all language use.

g. Cultural differences play no role in inferencing.
h. Particularized implicatures are the prototypical conversational implicatures.
i. Relation-based conversational implicatures generally yield enriched readings.
j. Relevance Theory cannot do without Grice's Quality maxim.

9 What are the major differences between speech act theory and the theory of conversational implicatures, and what do the two theories have in common?

10 a. Describe the central role that the maxim of Relation plays in the Cooperative Principle.
b. Why is it misleading to assume that Relevance Theory is a reductionist pragmatic model compared with the one developed by Grice?

11 Grice tried to account for our understanding of figures of speech (notably metaphor and irony) in terms of the Cooperative Principle and his theory of implicature.
a. Why is Grice's approach unsatisfactory?
b. What is the contribution that Relevance Theory makes in this respect?

12 Compare with each other the Gricean and the various post-Gricean theories of implicature. Which role do (a) considerations of economy and the balance between cost and benefit, and (b) the often diverging interests of speaker and hearer play in them?

Sources and further reading

Austin, John L. 1962. *How to do things with words*. Oxford:
  Clarendon Press.
Blakemore, Diane. 1992. *Understanding utterances: an introduction
  to pragmatics*. Oxford: Blackwell.
Brown, Penelope/Stephen Levinson. 2002. *Politeness: some
  universals of language use*. Cambridge: Cambridge University
  Press.
Bublitz, Wolfram. 2001. *Englische Pragmatik: Eine Einführung*.
  Berlin: Schmidt.
Cruse, Alan. 2004. *Meaning in language: an introduction to
  semantics and pragmatics*. 2. ed. Oxford: Oxford University Press.
Cutting, Joan. 2002. *Pragmatics and discourse: a resource book for
  students*. London: Routledge.
Davis, Stephen, ed. 1991. *Pragmatics: a reader*. Oxford: Oxford
  University Press.
Green, Georgia M. 1996[2]. *Pragmatics and natural language under-
  standing*. Hillsdale: Erlbaum.
Grice, Paul. 1989. *Studies in the way of words*. Cambridge, Mass.:
  Harvard University Press.
Horn, Laurence R. 1988. "Pragmatic theory". In: F.J. Newmeyer, ed.
  Linguistics: The Cambridge survey, vol. I. Cambridge: Cambridge
  University Press. 113-145.
Horn, Laurence R. and Gregory Ward, eds. 2004. *The handbook of
  pragmatics*. Malden, MA : Blackwell.
Huang, Yan. 2004. *Pragmatics*. Oxford: Oxford University Press.
Jaszczolt, K. M. 2002. *Semantics and pragmatics: meaning in
  language and discourse*. London/Munich: Longman.
Kasper, Gabriele. 1990. "Linguistic politeness: current research
  issues". *Journal of Pragmatics* 14. 193-218.
Leech, Geoffrey N. 1983. *Principles of pragmatics*. London:
  Longman.
Levinson, Stephen C. 1983. *Pragmatics*. Cambridge: Cambridge
  University Press.
Levinson, Stephen C. 2001. *Presumptive meanings: the theory of
  generalized conversational implicature*. Cambridge, Mass.: MIT
  Press.
Mey, Jacob L. 2001[2]. *Pragmatics. An introduction*. Oxford: Blackwell.
Schiffrin, Deborah. 1994. *Approaches to discourse*. Oxford:
  Blackwell.

Searle, John R. 1969. *Speech acts. An essay in the philosophy of language.* Cambridge: Cambridge University Press.

Sperber, Dan/Deidre Wilson. 1996². *Relevance: communication and cognition.* Oxford: Blackwell.

Thomas, Jenny. 1995. *Meaning in interaction: an introduction to pragmatics.* London/New York: Longman.

Verschueren, Jef. 2003. *Understanding pragmatics.* London: Arnold.

Wierzbicka, Anna. 2003². *Cross-cultural pragmatics. The semantics of human interaction.* Berlin/New York: Mouton de Gruyter.

Yule, George. 1996. *Pragmatics.* Oxford: Oxford University Press.

VIII Sociolinguistics: Regional and social varieties of English

Introduction

language as a social phenomenon

Similar to pragmatics, sociolinguistics studies language use in real life. It is an illusion to think that language communities are homogeneous; instead heterogeneity determines everyday language use. Linguistic heterogeneity has many different facets. Besides differences in linguistic competence and expressive ability among the members of any language community, each speaker uses certain linguistic features which distinguish him or her from the other members of their language community. Each individual has his or her specific idiolect. In everyday language use, heterogeneity also means that, depending on the communicative situation, each member of a language community chooses between different language forms, so-called varieties (see section VIII.1). This can happen either consciously or subconsciously. Sociolinguistics studies the effects social factors have on language use and language structures. Acknowledging that human beings are "social beings", sociolinguistics is aware of the fact that language use and language structures cannot be separated from,

idiolect

varieties

and indeed depend on, the speaker's social self, i.e. the diversity of (coexisting) group identities and social networks every one of us is a part of (a given female speaker, for example, can at the same time be a woman, somebody's partner, daughter, mother or friend, a student, a catholic, a villager, a member of a political party, a member of a choir or team, etc). The group identity of a speaker is largely formed by his or her geographic, social and/or ethnic background (cf. sections VIII.2 to VIII.4), but other factors may also play a role, such as the speaker's age, profession, level of education and sex (the latter especially brought to the fore in feminist linguistics; cf. section VIII.5).

language and identity

Language plays an important role in identity formation, although we are not aware of it most of the time. Quite often, a few utterances or words are all we need for drawing conclusions on a speaker's sociological background (origin, level of education, etc.), while the speakers themselves are not aware of the fact that the language they use serves as a window on their social reality. But speakers can also use language deliberately to signal that they belong (or want to belong) to a certain group. They can consciously or unconsciously adapt their language or language style to that of their interlocutors, thus improving the social relationship with them and creating a basis for a more successful communication. How 'successful' this verbal interaction is, primarily depends on whether the speaker accomplishes his or her communicative goals (for more details see VIII.5).

sociolinguistics versus sociology of language

Two scientific disciplines constitute the interface between linguistics and sociology: sociolinguistics and the sociology of language. The focus of sociolinguistics is on the relationship between language and society. Its aim is to study the use of different forms or varieties of language and the social factors which determine them. The research interest of the sociology of language is the exact opposite: its main motivation for investigating language is to increase the ability to understand social structures. Thus the distinction between sociolinguistics and the sociology of language is mainly motivated by a difference in perspective. What is common to both disciplines is that they are strictly empirical and exhibit a high degree of methodological rigour, as known from sociology.

When speaking of the relationship between sociolinguistics and the sociology of language, and characterizing sociolinguistics as a relatively young branch of linguistics which only started to flourish in the political climate of the late 1960s, we are adopting a narrow definition of sociolinguistics, namely sociological (or: variationist) sociolinguistics. But we should not forget that there are two other,

sociolinguistics

geo-graphical (since 19th c.)	socio-logical (since 1960s)

anthropological
(since 1920s)

considerably older branches of sociolinguistics: anthropological sociolinguistics, which is concerned with the relationship between language, culture and thought (just recall the Sapir-Whorf hypothesis according to which language determines thought), and, above all, geographical sociolinguistics, better known as dialectology, which was already popular in the 19th century. Of these three branches of sociolinguistics, only geographical and sociological sociolinguistics will be addressed in this chapter. Its primary aim will be to present the basic structural properties of different regional and social (standard as well as non-standard) varieties of English used in the British Isles and the United States. But let us first have a look at the range and nature of varieties we encounter in language.

dialectology

Sociolinguistics is most easily defined as variationist linguistics, that branch of linguistics which is concerned with the different forms of (a) language and the factors that determine their structure and use. Variation is possible on all structural levels. The individual varieties of a given language may differ phonetically, phonologically, pragmatically, with regard to their lexicon and – to a smaller extent – their morphology and syntax. These differences are not necessarily reflected in the presence or absence of certain structural properties; they can simply manifest themselves in terms of preference and, as a consequence, frequency of use.

We can distinguish three main types of varieties (or: lects), depending on the extralinguistic factors that motivate their use: dialects, sociolects and registers. The most widely known of these three types is "dialects", which can be given a narrow and a broad definition. Traditionally in linguistics (and also in everyday language use), dialects are defined as regionally restricted varieties. Under a broad conception, dialect is synonymous with the neutral hypernym "variety", as in terms like "standard dialect"(s) or "social dialects". The latter, better known as "sociolects", are motivated by the socio-economic status, level of education, profession, age, ethnicity or sex of the speaker. Two examples of sociolects are genderlect and (professional) jargon (special vocabulary of a particular profession). Both, dialects (in a narrow sense) and sociolects, are intimately linked to the speaker's sociological background. By contrast, register and style refer to varieties which are primarily determined by the relevant communicative situation. It is not easy to distinguish between register and style. The term "register" often refers to the vocabulary chosen (and even expected)

VIII.1
Different types of varieties

varieties

regional social functional

genderlect
jargon

register/style

in a certain communicative situation. "Style" also includes variation in grammatical structures and is, in general, less predictable and somehow more tied to individual preferences than register. The central question informing research on registers and styles is the following: Under which circumstances, for which purpose, and interacting with which person(s) does a speaker use a certain variety? The choice of a certain register is strongly influenced by such factors as the discourse topic (*field of discourse*, e. g. professional vs. private), the relationship between the speakers involved in the conversation (tenor of discourse, e. g. friendship vs. authority relationship) and the medium of communication (mode of discourse: spoken vs. written language).

standard - variety - dialect

Among the most interesting issues, to linguists and nonlinguists alike, concerning the terms "variety" and "dialect" is the question how they relate to the terms "standard" and "language". Let us consider the former relationship first. In modern linguistics, neither the neutral term "variety" nor the term "dialect" – which often has a negative ring in everyday language – imply inferiority or that, where differences compared with the standard are observable, these are to be interpreted as deficiencies. Rather the contrary is true: for example, Standard English and Standard German are seen as the standard varieties or standard dialects of the English and German language communities respectively. As far as their structural properties are concerned, standard varieties are of no higher value or quality than other varieties. For obvious reasons, they do of course enjoy a higher prestige. Standard English, for example, is used

- in written language, especially literature and print media.
- in television and radio broadcasts.
- as official language in politics, administration, court, etc.
- as language of instruction in schools and universities of all English-speaking countries.
- as teaching target of learners of English in schools and universities all over the world.
- by the educated middle and upper classes.

This characterization of the standard is exclusively based on social and functional considerations. In German this is reflected in the fact that expressions like *Hochsprache* and *Schriftsprache* may be used as synonyms of the more neutral term *Standard(sprache)*. The standard variety represents something like the common structural core of all varieties (especially the national varieties) of a language. Accordingly, Standard English represents the common core of the different

Englishes – the "old" Englishes, especially British and American English, as well as the so-called "New Englishes" (e. g. Australian, New Zealand, Indian, Caribbean and African English). This common core is relatively homogeneous, i.e. there are relatively few differences between the national standard varieties of English, especially as far as grammar is concerned. Where there are differences in grammar, these concern for the most part different degrees of preference for individual forms and constructions, measurable in terms of high(er) or low(er) frequencies of use (cf. section VIII.2 on British and American English).

Due to its special structural and functional status, the standard can be seen as the fourth main type of variety (see Figure VIII.2), although its classification as a primarily social dialect would be adequate, too. In all language communities, the standard variety is only used by a relatively small minority of speakers (in Great Britain by an estimated 12-15 per cent of the population) who, in addition, belong to the educated middle and upper classes (having enjoyed a higher education at school or college and often university). Accordingly, the standard variety is usually perceived and accepted as the prestigious linguistic norm by all members of a given language community (including non-standard speakers), especially in class-conscious societies like the one in England.

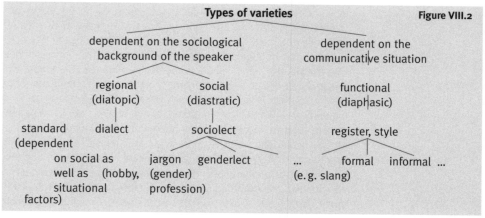

Types of varieties   **Figure VIII.2**

In accounts of the standard variety, regional considerations typically only play a role when turning to the standard accent. Accent only refers to the pronunciation and the phonological system of a given variety, whereas dialect also includes lexical and grammatical

dialect versus accent

properties of a (regional) variety. This distinction is especially important in Britain for example, where according to some estimates only about a third of those who use Standard English have a marked Received Pronunciation accent. Standard dialect and regional accent thus do not exclude each other. However, speaking a regional or even local dialect with the standard accent is not possible.

Table VIII.1	standard dialect can be spoken with	non-standard dialect can be spoken with
standard accent	+	-
non-standard accent	+	+

standard – dialect – language

All books on the grammar of a given language describe the standard dialect; it is also usually the standard dialect upon which any kind of comparative (e. g. contrastive or typological) studies are based. But one point must be stressed over and over again: whether a certain dialect is attributed the status of the standard variety and, consequently, seen as an independent language does not depend on its inherent structural properties. No dialect is inherently superior or better suited for serving as the standard than other dialects. The development of a standard depends on a number of political, historical, social and psychological factors. Discussions on the status of a dialect as the standard variety or even as a language of its own are generally politically and emotionally charged. Linguistic identity plays a crucial part in defining the degree of independence and autonomy of a people, the self-conception and self-confidence of a nation, and this includes the acknowledgement of its dialect as a language of its own or, at least, as an independent national variety, on an equal footing with other established national standards. The word "language" (as opposed to "dialect") seems to have a primarily political connotation – especially when discussed by non-linguists. According to an often-quoted 'definition' (by Vriel Weinreich), a language is basically no more than "a dialect with its own army and navy" (and especially with its own constitution). There are many examples: The North Germanic languages spoken on the Scandinavian mainland (Danish, Norwegian and Swedish) are structurally closely related dialects; Afrikaans, spoken in South Africa, was considered a Dutch dialect as late as the beginning of the 20th century; and, considering the present situation, not treating Croatian and Serbian as independent languages would definitely be a political issue – even though they were regarded as closely related dialects until the beginning of the 1990s, Serbo-Croatian having been the national language of former Yugoslavia.

In the past and contemporary history of the United Kingdom we find further evidence of the crucial political, historical and social dimensions once it comes to decisions on whether a certain variety can claim the status of a language or (only) a dialect. Scots lost its status as the official national language of Scotland at the beginning of the 17th century, directly after the Scottish and English crowns were united and the royal court moved to London (1603). Just about 400 years later, approximately in the late 1980s, English varieties spoken in the former colonies of the British Empire started experiencing a very different, positive change. In these parts of the world, the sense of national identity has started to grow, and their political, economic and cultural independence is now to bring them linguistic sovereignty, i. e. acknowledgment of the respective varieties as independent stand-ards, comparable to Standard British and American English. Claims for linguistic sovereignty are increasingly respected and accepted (at least in present-day English language and literature studies) and have become manifest in new terms and scholarly fields of studies like "(New) Englishes" and "Standard Englishes" (the latter having been formed in analogy to the term (postcolonial) "English literatures"). Besides the traditional countries of the Anglophone world (including Australia, New Zealand and South Africa) where English is a native language, there are about sixty countries where English is either the only official language (e. g. Ghana, Nigeria, Simbabwe and Jamaica) or at least one of two official languages (e. g. in India, Singapore, the Philippines and Cameroon). "Official" means that it is the language used by the authorities, in education and the media. English is there-fore clearly a pluricentric language. Its different centres have started to develop and will certainly continue to develop new linguistic norms independent of one another and, what is more, independent of the British and American models. Nevertheless, there is no doubt that, among the different standard varieties of English, British and American English are still used as the target models for teaching English to foreign-language learners.

The standard varieties of British and American English differ primarily with regard to their accents (i. e. RECEIVED PRONUNCIATION as opposed to GENERAL AMERICAN), followed by differences in their vocabularies. There are even fewer differences in orthography and, especially, in grammar. Before moving on to a survey of the major generalizations concerning structural differences between British and American English, three points are worth noting:

- It is surprising how little these two standard varieties differ from each other.
- Most of these differences, especially those in the domain of grammar, are not categorical but rather tendencies concerning the (dis)preference and frequency of use of certain constructions.
- Several of the differences which can currently be observed may well disappear during the next few decades. The two varieties seem to converge, especially in the lexicon but also with regard to some grammatical differences. In most cases the direction of this convergence is towards the American norm. Already a number of relevant differences are no longer observable for today's younger speakers, one main reason being the overwhelming media presence of American English.

phonology: RP versus GA

Concerning their status, note that both standard accents, RP and GA, are somewhat idealized – each in its own way. RP is a social, supranational prestige accent. Despite the fact that it is known to the whole world as the British (or more precisely English English) standard accent and used as a reference accent in school and university education, at least the marked and more traditional version of RP is spoken by a small (3 to 5%) and continuously shrinking minority of standard speakers of the upper and upper middle classes. The term RECEIVED PRONUNCIATION itself reflects the importance of social norms: in Victorian times, "received" meant "generally accepted in polite society". If we compare the number of people actually using the two standards, GA can be said to be much more "anchored in the real world" than RP, even than the unmarked or mainstream RP version spoken by the majority of younger native speakers of Standard British English (also labelled "Broadcast RP"). In the US, an estimated two thirds of the population speak GA. It should be noted, though, that it is not a single homogeneous accent. Primarily, GA is defined negatively: It stands for a number of very similar accents which all have the property of sharing neither the characteristics of the accents of the southern US (Southern) nor of New England (Eastern). According to another negative definition, the standard accent of American English is the result of what is left over if its speakers (typically educated speakers in formal settings) suppress all salient and notoriously regional and social features. Due to its extensive use, especially by the large American TV and radio stations, it is also called "Network English" or "Broadcast English".

If we compare prototypical English speakers with prototypical American speakers, the most prominent and (even among non-linguists) most notorious difference is a phonotactic one. There are many cases where American speakers pronounce /r/ (i.e. realize an orthographic ‹r› phonetically) but British English speakers do not. What is at issue here is called rhoticity: like the majority of regional English rhoticity accents and all national standard varieties which follow the British English model, RP phonetically realizes /r/ only before vowels; there is neither a /r/ at the end of words (*car* [kɑː], *her* [hɜː]), nor between vowels and consonants (*card* [kɑːd], *herd* [hɜːd]). Therefore, RP qualifies as a non-rhotic accent. It has pre-vocalic /r/, but no pre-consonantal /r/ (which can alternatively be described as postvocalic or coda /r/ because the unpronounced /r/ belongs to the same syllable as the preceding vowel; compare *hair* [heə] and *hairy* ['heəri]). By contrast, GA is a rhotic accent, unlike RP (and also unlike the Eastern and Southern US accents, although increasingly less so) but like other standard accents such as those of, for example, Canadian, Irish and Scottish English. In GA, /r/ is pronounced in all positions. Other striking differences between GA and RP are the following:

- different phonetic realizations of certain phonemes (partly only in consonants certain positions):
  /r/ post-alveolar in RP [ɹ], retroflex in GA [ɻ]
  /l/ more velar in GA [ɫ], especially between vowels (e. g. *jelly*)
  /t, d/ in GA the opposition between this pair of phonemes is neutralized between vowels, resulting in the tap sound [ɾ]: *latter* and *ladder* are both pronounced ['læɾər]
- phonotactics: in GA no realization of /t, d/ between /n/ and a vowel if the main stress is on the next but one syllable: *international* [ɪnər'næʃənəl], *understand* [ʌnər'stænd]; in GA no /j/ following /d, t, n, θ, z, s/ in the same syllable: *due* [duː], *tune* [tuːn], *new* [nuː], *enthusiasm* [ɪn'θuːzɪæzəm], *presume* [prɪ'zuːm]
- in GA [æ] is used before voiceless fricatives /s, f, θ/ or nasals /n, m/ vowels followed by a voiceless consonant, instead of southern British RP [ɑː] or northern British RP [a]; this affects about 150 words, e. g. *fast, after, path, dance, sample*;

- neutralization of phonemic oppositions:
  neutralization of the opposition /ɑ:/ – /ɒ/ in /ɑ/, thus *father* and *cot* are pronounced: /fɑðər/ – /kɑt/ respectively;
  in some GA varieties neutralization of the opposition /ɒ/ – /ɔ:/ *cot* – *caught* in /ɑ/: /kɑt/ (sometimes in addition to the neutralization of /ɑ:/ – /ɒ/ in /ɑ/, e. g. in California). This neutralization is characteristic of the Northern accents and Canadian English.
- in GA, rhoticity results in:
  an r-coloured central vowel [ɝ] (e.g. in *bird, word, hurt*); the absence of centring diphthongs: [ɪr, er, ʊr] instead of RP [ɪə, eə, ʊə]

Table VIII.2 Vowel differences between RP and GA

	sample	psalm	cot	caught	bird	go	beer	bare	poor
RP	ɑː	ɑː	ɒ	ɔː	ɜː	əʊ	ɪə	eə	ʊə
GA	æ	ɑ	ɑ	ɔː/ɑ	ɝ	oʊ	(ɪr)	(er)	(ʊr)

word stress

Of course, there are many other, less systematic pronunciation differences affecting individual words. Some of the best-known examples are shown in (1) and (2), the latter of which result from differences in word stress:

(1)	tomato	clerk	(n)either	vase	anti-	‹ z ›
RP	/təˈmɑːtəʊ/	/klɑːk/	/(n)ɑɪðə/	/vɑːz/	/ænti/	[zed]
GA	/təˈmeɪtoʊ/	/klɝk/	/(n)iːðər/	/veɪz/	/æntaɪ/	[ziː]

(2) RP 'ballet – GA ba'llet, RP ciga'rette – GA 'cigarette, RP con'troversy – GA 'controversy, RP a'ddress – GA 'address, RP maga'zine – GA 'magazine, RP in'quiry /ɪnˈkwaɪəri/ – GA 'inquiry /ɪŋkwəri/, RP trans'late – GA 'translate

Word stress differences, however, appear to diminish as American accent patterns are spreading among British speakers, especially among the younger generation. This is a domain where the influence of American English on British English is particularly noticeable.

intonation

The probably most salient intonation difference between British and American English concerns yes/no questions, which are usually *high rise* in American English (*Are you going a^way?*) and *low rise* (less often *low fall* or *high fall*) in British English. In informal American English, and especially among younger speakers, one can often hear a rising intonation curve at the end of declarative sentences, especially when somebody is telling something in an emotional way. This phenomenon, known as *high rise terminal* (compare chapter II), is also increasingly frequent in the Southeast of England (and in many other regional and national varieties of English), once again predominantly among the younger generation. Thus, this intonation difference might soon cease to be perceived as such.

The most important orthographic differences are shown in (3). In general, American English orthography tends to be shorter.

orthography

(3)		**BrE**	**AmE**	
	colour	⟨-our⟩	⟨-or⟩	color
	theatre	⟨-re⟩	⟨-er⟩	theater
	emphasise, -ize	⟨-ise, -ize⟩	⟨-ize⟩	emphasize
	analyse	⟨-lyse, -lyze⟩	⟨-lyze⟩	analyze
	amoeba	⟨oe⟩	⟨e, oe⟩	am(o)eba
	encyclopaedia	⟨ae⟩	⟨e, ae⟩	encyclopedia
	fulfil	⟨-l⟩	⟨-ll⟩	fulfill
	catalogue	⟨-gue⟩	⟨-g⟩	catalog

In grammar, there are only relatively few and rather minor differences between American English and British English. The probably most interesting of these can be observed in the verb phrase. Consider especially the past participle of *get*, for which American English has two forms: *got* and *gotten*. This difference in form reflects a semantic distinction: while *gotten* is used for situations that are dynamic or in progress (4), *got* is rather used to describe static situations and resultative states (5):

grammar: VP

(4)   a.   They've gotten a new car. ('have received')
     b.   They've gotten interested. ('have developed interest in ...')
     c.   I've gotten to know a lot of songs from jazz records. ('that's how I learnt about them')

(5)   a.   They've got a new car. ('possess')
     b.   They've got interested. ('are interested')
     c.   I've got to know a lot of songs from jazz records. ('that's how I have to learn them')

Unlike in British English, *have got* in American English is rather rare in sentences like (5a), where *have* is clearly preferred (*They have a new car*). Further characteristic differences will be given below. It should be borne in mind, however, that these represent only tendencies, not categorical differences:

- irregular verb forms: AmE tends to regularize verb forms (e.g. *burned, learned*)
- perfect: (a) BrE uses the so-called *experiential perfect* (or: *indefinite past*) whereas AmE prefers the Simple Past: *Did you ever go to Rome?* (vs. *Have you ever been to Rome?*), *Did you eat (yet)?* (vs. *Have you eaten yet?*) AmE allows the Simple Past with adverbs like *just*, *recently*, *already*: *She just finished her essay.* (vs. *She has just finished her essay.*) *They left already.* (vs. *They have left already.*)
- mood: of the three alternative constructions which can be used to express the so-called *mandative subjunctive*, AmE clearly prefers (6a) over the constructions in (6b) and especially in (6c), which are both characteristic of BrE:

(6) a. We demanded that the manager resign.
      b. We demanded that the manager should resign.
      c. We demanded that the manager resigns.

- auxiliary verbs: (a) BrE tends to use modal verbs more frequently; (b) *shall/should/ought to* are even less frequent in AmE than in BrE; (c) AmE increasingly allows *must not* as negation of epistemic ('concluding') must in contexts where BrE uses *cannot* or *can't* (AmE *My mistake must not have been noticed*); (d) BrE also allows *usen't to* for *used not to*.

Besides differences in the verb phrase, there are only a couple of other grammatical differences worth mentioning. On the one hand, there exist (hardly systematisable) differences concerning the use of prepositions (e.g. BrE *different from/to* vs. AmE *different than*). On the other hand, AmE and BrE differ in the domain of subject-verb agreement with collective nouns (i.e. nouns like *family*, *orchestra*, *government*). In AmE, the verb is generally singular while in BrE the verb can be either singular or plural (*The government is/are divided about this question*), depending on whether the homogeneity or the heterogeneity of the group is to be emphasized.

3.1 Traditional and modern dialectology

Traditional dialectology (or: dialect geography), as practiced since the middle of the 19th century, focusses on regional varieties, more precisely on the observable variation in the phonological systems (hence, in the regional accents) and in the lexicon of predominantly elderly male speakers in rural areas, known as NORMS (non-mobile old rural male speakers) in British dialectology. NORMS

The traditional dialectological method has been, and still is, the use of questionnaires, although tape-recorded interviews obviously constitute a further invaluable data source and have been in use now for several decades. Originally, informants had to pronounce single words so that phonological variation could be detected. To determine lexical variation, informants had to name the expressions they used in their respective dialect for certain objects, actions and properties, mostly taken from everyday rural life. This method yields the geographical area where a certain expression is used to denote a certain concept, and where it gives way to a different expression. The aim of such investigations is to draw boundaries, so-called "isoglosses", isoglosses which indicate the geographical spread of a certain expression on a language map. A language map of England and Scotland would, for example, reveal the isoglosses for the different expressions used to denote 'autumn' (*autumn, fall, backend*) or 'female cat' (*betty cat, ewe (cat), queen (cat), tib (cat), she, she cat, sheeder (cat)*).

The two phonological isoglosses that are probably best-known among the population in England largely run along the same route. They define a dividing line between the North and the South (see Figure VIII.3, see inside back cover): (a) *pub* is pronounced /pʌb/ in the South and /pʊb/ in the North (analogous to other words such as *cut, love, some* or *fun*); (b) *path* is pronounced /pɑːθ/ in the South and /paθ/ in the North (analogous to words like *pass, past, laugh, daft, dance* or *sample*). In other words, the accents of the Midlands and the North use /ʊ/ where RP uses /ʌ/, and, in front of voiceless fricatives as well as before a nasal /n/ or /m/ followed by a consonant, a short, 'flat' /a/ where (southern) RP uses /ɑː/.

A third well-known isogloss in England separates rhotic from non-rhotic accents. Rhotic accents are characteristic of the Southwest of England, although they are rapidly receding (see Figure VIII.3; in the British Isles, they are of course also characteristic of Irish English and Scottish English). Wherever several such (phonological and lexical) isoglosses coincide, we can postulate a dialect boundary. Collections of linguistic maps from different geographical areas are called linguistic atlases or dialect atlases.

We should keep in mind, though, that dialect boundaries can never be more than rough approximations. The transition between different dialect areas is fluid, which is why we also speak of dialect dialect continua continua. These continua do not follow political borders or politically motivated language borders (as shown above). Usually, speakers from neighbouring dialect areas have little problems understanding each other, but the larger the distance between two dialect areas is, the greater these problems become. In extreme cases, complete mutual incomprehensibility is possible. Still, we cannot conclude that dialects which are mutually incomprehensible automatically belong to different languages. The best-known dialect continua in northern and western Europe are the Scandinavian dialect continuum (Danish, Swedish, Norwegian), the West Germanic dialect continuum (running from Flanders and the Netherlands in the West to Austria in the East, via Germany and Switzerland) and the West Romance dialect continuum (reaching from Wallonia in northern France to the Iberian Peninsula in the South-West and Italy and Sicily in the South-East).

But let us return to the situation in Great Britain and Ireland. It is in these countries where we find the by far greatest dialect diversity in the English-speaking world (compare chapter VIII.3.2). This holds true although these differences, similar to differences in other countries, are gradually disappearing due to increasing mobility, increasing urbanization and the overwhelming influence of the media and educational institutions. Especially in big conurbations such as London, Birmingham or Manchester, we can currently observe the assimilation of dialects, a process known as dialect levelling. Moreover, it is interesting to note that there are numerous dialect features in the British Isles which are so commonly found that it is hard, if not impossible, to identify any regional restrictions. With regard to these features, which do not only occur in individual (regional or urban) dialects, Standard English, especially Standard BrE, almost appears to be the odd one out among the English dialects. Among the grammatical phenomena with the widest geographical reach in Britain are the following. Some of these can even claim a 'near-universal' status in the anglophone world, in general:

dialect levelling

- **pronouns**
  us instead of me
  me instead of my
  all reflexive pronouns formed
    by using possessive pronouns
  them instead of those

  Give us a kiss
  he knew me name; where me sister live
  he saved hisself with this; they just work
  the farm theirselves
  if you had them sixty pound

- **verb paradigms**
  regularization of irregular verb paradigms:
  - reduced to 2 forms (instead of 3)   *They (have) done a lot of damage. I (have)*
    (*past vs non-past*)   *seen one the other day. I gived eighty pound*
       for the two. I catched her enough for the
       three garments.

  - *was/were* without singular-plural   *he were nineteen then; she were laughing*
    distinction, not even in *there*-   *There was two houses here. There was*
    sentences   *three days in the week that ...*

  general reduction of modal verb paradigms (e.g. *ought to* and *shall* are practically non-
  existent in many dialects)

- **tense & aspect**
  the progressive form is used more   *I'm liking this; So what are you wanting*
  frequently and possible in more contexts   *from me?*
  (e.g. verbs describing states)
  less strict in several respects:
  - *would* in subjunctive clauses   *If they wouldn't have made a scrap of slate*
  - sequence of tenses less fixed   *I noticed the van I came in (instead of had*
       come in) was not really a painter's van.

- **negation**
  double or multiple negation   *I ain't never seen it. I couldn't say nothing*
     about them.

  ain't as universal negation of *be* and   *He's so cuddly ain't he? You ain't got no*
     have forms (*amn't, aren't, isn't, wasn't,*   *alibi. I was so busy ain't I?*
     weren't, hasn't, haven't)
  don't as negation for all persons   *He don't eat. Well she don't own him.*
  innit as universal tag   *But they make dustbins big enough now*
     in't it? Doesn't he look spastic with that
     pencil behind his ear. Innit?
  never (= StE *didn't*) as negation in   *But this fellow never stopped until he got me.*
     past-tense contexts (including   A: *Did you do that?*   B: *No, I never.*
     one-time events)

- **subordination**
  different inventory of relative pronouns   *as; what; which* [+ ANIMATE] (*The girl as/*
     what/which ...)
  more constructions possible (e.g.   *Sell that to any dealer' Ø d buy it. But there*
     zero relative clauses (*gapping*)   *was no more Ø went till the States.*
     also used for subject relative pronouns)   *There's a lot more children Ø go these days.*

- **other**
  no marking of plural subjects,   *two mile_; thirteen year_*
     especially after numerals
  no *-ly* used to mark adverbs derived   *hope we get it organized as quick_ as we can*
     from adjectives

The rural dialects, as recorded in the *Survey of English Dialects* (*SED*, 1946-61), form the basis for all dialect atlases and dialect dictionaries, and for most studies on the dialects of England conducted over the past few decades. But some of these rural dialects have died out and others have been subject to levelling, while at the same time the varieties spoken in larger cities are becoming more and more important. As a result, modern dialectology is increasingly occupied with studying urban dialects, in close connection with social variation. An early finding of such studies was the correlation of regional and social variation: the lower the socio-economic status of a speaker, the higher the probability that he or she speaks a regional dialect. In the 1970s, dialectology cross-fertilized with the burgeoning field of sociolinguistics, and thus modern dialectology as a whole is more in touch, and has indeed contributed to, current linguistic theorizing. There are two further important innovations in modern dialectology, which are closely related: the systematic investigation of regional variation in grammar (cf. section VIII.3.2), and the use of corpus-linguistic methods for the compilation, investigation and statistic analysis of large corpora, which have been an essential tool of English linguistics for the last two decades at least. Analyses of syntactic phenomena require large quantities of data. In modern dialectological studies, especially those including syntax, it has become more and more important to base linguistic analyses on databases that are as large as possible and adequately represent different dialect regions (e.g. *FRED*, the *Freiburg English Dialect* corpus). In addition, the questionnaire method is now also used to investigate grammatical phenomena (see, for example, the *Survey of British Dialect Grammar* (1986-1989) and the *Survey of Regional English* (*SuRE*) at the Universities of Leeds and Sheffield).

traditional dialectology	modern dialectology
rural areas	urban areas
regional variation	social variation
accent and lexicon	also grammar
questionnaires, interviews	also corpora, modern statistical methods

The distinction between traditional and modern dialects – which is not clear-cut anyway – is not crucial for the distinction between traditional and modern dialectology. The *Survey of English Dialects*, based on language material by informants born in the late 19th century, is considered clearly traditional, whereas dialect speakers born after World War I usually represent a transitional stage between traditional and modern (non-standard) dialects (except perhaps in some remote rural areas). In any case, it is important to note that modern dialectology does not exclusively deal with modern dialects, but also studies traditional dialect material.

3.2 Syntactic variation in the British Isles

Morphological and syntactic variation is less salient and more difficult to detect (and to elicit) than lexical and especially phonological variation. This is probably the reason why this domain has been rather neglected in traditional dialectology. This section is therefore meant to serve as an appetizer, showing how many fascinating grammatical phenomena can be observed in regional varieties (beyond those mentioned earlier), and why these are interesting from a typological perspective. Those who are interested in varieties of English outside the British Isles will, by the way, notice that a large number of structures observed in the New Englishes spoken in former British colonies were 'imported' or transplanted from England, Scotland or Ireland. These features were shipped over to the new homeland together with numerous immigrants from these countries and developed a life of their own in the new environment. A look at American English may suffice to get an impression of some such phenomena.

Most of the examples described below are self-explanatory. Only two of them require a short explanation: pronoun exchange and gender diffusion, two phenomena characteristic of the South-West of England. The term "pronoun exchange" refers to subject forms being used in object position (*Don't talk to she about grub; You did get he out of bed in middle of the night; Never mind about I*) and, vice versa, object forms being used in subject position, as in *Her don't like it*, especially when the relevant forms are heavily stressed (*That was through THEY not ME*). At least in the first person singular and plural, object forms in subject position are also known from other non-standard varieties (*Us women are not to blame for this AIDS, So us haven't managed to get a drink*).

Gender diffusion is an unusual semantic principle of gender assignment whereby the choice of a personal pronoun (*he, she* or *it*) or possessive pronoun (*his, her* or *its*) for anaphoric reference to a certain noun depends on whether it is a count or a mass noun. *It* and *its* are used for mass (or non-count) nouns (e.g. *bread, water, sand*), *he* and *his* as well as *she* and *her* are used to refer to count nouns – *she/her* only referring to female referents, *he/his* to male referents and

pronoun exchange

gender diffusion

inanimate objects (e.g. *When the pond was empty you wait for him to fill up again*). Thus there are contrasting pairs like the one in (7):

(7) a. Pass the <u>bread</u> – <u>it's</u> over there.
     b. Pass the <u>loaf</u> – <u>he's</u> over there.

	he/his	she/her	it/its
count noun	+	+	-
animate	+	+	-
male	+	-	-
female	-	+	-
inanimate	+	-	-
mass noun	-	-	+

This gender assignment principle, exceptional also among non-European languages, was exported from the South-West of England and introduced into Newfoundland (Canada), where today the choice between *he/his* and *she/her* seems to follow even more complex rules.

Here are some more examples of morphological and syntactic variation in Great Britain and Ireland, together with the region(s) in which they characteristically occur:

- **pronouns**

South-East	3rd person singular *that* instead of *it*	*That's raining!*
Ireland/Scotland	distinction 2nd person singular and plural	*you had a good week's pay bemong the both of youse*
North	*us* instead of *our*	*We like us town.*
Midlands	possessive pronouns ending in *-n*	*mine/yourn/hisn/hern/theirn …*
	reflexive pronouns ending in *-sen(s)*	*mysen/yoursen/hissen/hersen*
Scotland/Ireland	*myself* instead of *me/I*	*This is myself with a cow.*

- **tense & aspect**

Ireland	different uses of the perfect	*I know her all my life; he hasn't a penny invested; you were only after going over*
	grammaticalization of habitual *be* and *do*	*he be's at home; I never be in the pub; They do come home at night … when we do feed them.*
South-West	grammaticalization of habitual *do*	*I tell you about what else we did do; in fall when the nuts do fall*

- **modal verbs**

| Scotland/ North-East | double/multiple modals | *And you might could try a thousand; I might could have done that.* |
| | epistemic *mustn't* (meaning *can't*) | *This mustn't be the place; The lift mustn't be working.* |

- **negation**

Scotland/Ireland	negation particle *-nae*	*They cannae sell it now. It hadnae been for that. That wasnae bad.*
	non-clitic *no*	*She's no leaving. This'll no do.*
Midlands	negation particle *-na*	*I shouldna like to be up there. I donna suppose it matters.*

- **subordination**

Ireland/Scotland/ Wales	complementation with 'unsplit' *for to*	*just for to get over this drought we did mix it up. For to get a temperature of about 60 degrees ...*
Ireland	subordinating *and*	*He seen a boat passin' along and him cuttin' oats.*
	verb + infinitive without *to*	*She allowed him stay out late.*

While geographical sociolinguistics is concerned with the regional, i. e. horizontal, differentiation of language, sociological sociolinguistics (for many people identical to sociolinguistics in general) focusses on the social differentiation of language. It studies the effects which the (actual or envisaged) group identity of a speaker has on variation in language use, be it language use among the members of a group or the situation-specific language use of individuals. The central assumption of sociological sociolinguistics is that variation in language communities or for individual speakers in the choice between structural alternatives is not random but correlates with the social (would-be) group membership of the speaker(s). This has also been called "orderly heterogeneity". Relevant instances of variation in this context are, for example, rhoticity in some words like *car, farm, beer*, but not in other words (New York); or the realization of the suffix in *singing* or *walking* as /ɪŋ/ in some cases, but as /ən/ or /ɪn/ in others (Norwich and Sydney respectively). The most important factors for the classification of social groups are social class (more precisely socio-economic status), ethnicity, sex and age; of these factors, studies on the correlation between language use and social group identity still consider

**VIII.4
Social varieties**
social differentiation of language

social class to be the one which is by far the most relevant. Therefore, the social differentiation of a language is often equated with its vertical differentiation or social stratification.

social and regional variation correlate

Of course, the horizontal and vertical differentiation of language, i.e. regional and social variation, often correlate. The older a speaker and the lower his or her social class, the more likely he or she will be to use a regional dialect and the stronger his or her regional dialect will be. Besides, the use (and most interestingly the deliberate use) of regional dialects and accents is closely linked to informal spoken language. The characterization of the standard variety (section VIII.1; middle and upper class, written language, formal style) is determined by both social and functional aspects, and the same holds true for non-standard varieties (lower social class, spoken language, informal style).

William Labov

William Labov, the pioneer of sociological (more exactly: variationist) sociolinguistics whose work and ideas are still leading the way today, is the founder of what is sometimes known as Labovian Sociolinguistics or the Labovian Paradigm (as opposed to the Chomskyan Paradigm). Labov's early work of the 1960s features the whole range of different topics, theories, methods and explanations of (sociological) sociolinguistics. Labov coined two key concepts: the linguistic variable and the linguistic variant. The former refers to variation phenomena (e.g. rhoticity, -ing), the latter to possible realizations of such phenomena (e.g. /ɪŋ/ or /ən/ for -ing). Needless to say, linguistic variables may also be morphological, syntactic, or lexical in nature (e.g. whether multiple negation is used or not). Investigations of linguistic variables aim at determining how often, by whom and in which social (but also regional) context or contexts each variant is used. To determine the frequency of different linguistic variants and their significance, sophisticated quantitative methods are employed, which is why the Labovian approach is also often referred to as quantitative sociolinguistics. Other basic ingredients of this approach are the development of new methods for selecting informants and for compiling corpora, the investigation of dialects – especially urban dialects – on a micro- and macro-sociological level (e.g. language use correlating with social status or ethnicity, but also language use in youth gangs) and Labov's primary interest in language change: its documentation and the elucidation of the social conditions under which it takes place (for more details see section VIII.6). Two of Labov's best-known studies, both conducted in the 1960s, are still exemplary of sociological sociolinguistics today. They investigate the

linguistic variable
linguistic variant

correlation between language or language use and (a) ethnicity (African-American English) and (b) socio-economic status (rhoticity in New York).

African-American Vernacular English (AAVE) is not a completely homogeneous sociolect but a cover term for a group of closely related sociolects spoken by the vast majority of African Americans, especially among the working class and those with a relatively low level of education. Most of the relevant linguistic studies are based on AAVE spoken in the urban 'ghettos' of the Northern US, but in informal settings AAVE is also used by African Americans with a higher socio-economic status and higher educational level. In less politically correct times, this group of dialects was known as "Negro English", or in linguistics as "Black English" (Vernacular). A relatively recent and publicly very effective alternative term emerging from the reawakened positive identification of the Afro-American population with its own language is "Ebonics" (a blend of "ebony" and "phonics"). Labov demonstrated that AAVE is a complex and rule-governed variety and thus invalidated the deficit hypothesis postulated by the British linguist Bernstein. The deficit hypothesis, which was rather popular during the 1960s, said that, compared to middle and upper-class children, working-class children had linguistic deficiencies: a smaller and less differentiated lexicon, lack of explicitness, grammatical deficits (e. g. in complex sentences), and deficits in their logical and argumentative structures. Consequently, working-class children were alleged to also have cognitive deficiencies – an inference which nicely dovetailed with the fact that their scholarly achievements did not match those of middle-class children. In 1960s America, the deficit hypothesis was applied to African Americans in particular and to their dialect or sociolect. One outcome of this attitude were different special-needs programmes designed to boost linguistic proficiency and bring African American pupils closer to the elaborate linguistic code normally used by the middle classes. None of these programmes was particularly successful. Labov propagated a different view, i. e the so-called "difference hypothesis", arguing that AAVE was structurally different from middle class English but no less well-structured and well-suited for all communicative purposes (sometimes even more differentiated) than the latter. Labov's findings and arguments are very much up to date. As recently as 1996, a decision by the Oakland (California) school board to admit Ebonics (i. e. AAVE) as a tool of instruction (co-equal with Standard English) provoked a public outcry. Due to massive public pressure, this resolution, the original motiv-

African-American Vernacular English (AAVE)

deficit versus difference hypothesis

ation of which were the poor academic achievements of African American children (constituting, after all, almost half of the pupils in Oakland), was repealed shortly after being enacted.

structural characteristics of AAVE

In the following, some of the most important phonological and grammatical properties of AAVE will be listed. These properties will not be commented on in detail, but it is important to note that AAVE shares a number of properties with other American (and British) dialects, even with the informal spoken standard. We will also refrain from a detailed account of the central debate surrounding the genesis of AAVE in the 17th and 18th century. Suffice it to mention that monocausal theories are insufficient since a number of factors contributed to the emergence of AAVE (primarily an African substrate, English dialects, and deficient acquisition of the respective southern dialects).

Phonological properties:
- non-rhotic accent
- often no /l/ at the end of words or before consonants at the end of words (*fool* /fuː/, *help* /hep/), especially after back vowels
- consonant cluster reduction by dropping of the last consonant at the end of words (e.g. /ks/ > /k/: *six* /sɪk/), especially in consonant combinations like /-st, -ft, -nt, -nd, -ld, -zd, -md/: *past* /pæs/, *rift* /rɪf/
- weakening (i.e. loss of voicing or glottal stop) or dropping of /t, d/, less often of /k, g/, at the end of words, e.g. *boot* /buː/, *seat = seed = see* /siː/
- use of /f, v/ instead of /θ, ð/ (similar to Cockney): *Ruth* /ruːf/, *brother* /brʌvə/
- monophthongization of diphthongs: /aɪ/ and /aʊ/ > /ɑː/, e.g. *find = found = fond* /fɑːn/, *time = Tom* /tɑːm/.

Grammatical properties:
- homophones such as *he'll = he, kicks = kicked = kick* /kɪk/, *past = passed = pass* /pæs/, primarily due to phonological properties such as the omission of word-final /l/, /t/ or /d/ and the simplification of word-final consonant clusters
- multiple negation, e.g. *We ain't never had no trouble about none of us pullin' out no knife*, which sometimes also allows constructions known from only very few other English nonstandard varieties, e.g. *Nobody can't step on her foot 'nobody can step on her foot'*, where the auxiliary is negated, too
- no 3rd person singular present indicative -s: *he kick, she kiss, she see*
- omission of *be* (copula deletion, in questions as well as declarative sentences) where Standard English permits contractions (e.g. *I'm, you're, she's*): *I gonna do it, you real silly, she mine, she the first one started us off, he fast in everything he do*
- uninflected *be* used to mark habituality: *my father be the last one to open his presents*

274

- perfective *been* for events or actions still relevant at the moment of utterance: *I been know your name*
- *done* used as perfect marker (*he done talk to you*); also instead of *will have*: *We be done washed all those cars soon*
- *it* instead of dummy *there*: *It a boy in my class name Mike.*

Labov's analysis of variable rhoticity in New York has served as a model for a large number of sociolinguistic studies. Traditionally, the accent spoken in New York is non-rhotic (as in New England, in general), but it seems to be becoming more and more rhotic. Along these lines, Labov observed the following variation in the early 1960s: (a) only a small number of New Yorkers used post-vocalic (or: pre-consonantal) /r/ (as in *fourth floor*) as consistently as General American speakers, but some New Yorkers used it generally more often than others; (b) all informants used post-vocalic /r/ more often when consciously trying to pronounce words accurately. Labov showed that both of these tendencies correlated with the informants' socio-economic status: the higher their status, the more often they would use post-vocalic /r/; the harder they tried to 'belong' to a highly prestigious group (think of *upward mobility*), the more often and the more consistently they chose the prestigious variant (sometimes even more often among lower middle-class than among upper middle-class speakers). We may add that it is certainly no coincidence that the prestigious variant corresponds to the standard accent of the US and is, at the same time, clearly different from both the non-rhotic accent used among African American 'ghetto' speakers and the highly stigmatized New York "toidy-toid" (33rd street) accent, which is a white accent.

social stratification in New York City

Therefore, it is not surprising that Labov's analyses of the social stratification of the linguistic variable /r/ were fully supported by studies carried out in the mid 1980s, with the difference being that the overall proportion of /r/-speakers had increased by 10%. New York seems to be following the American mainstream and is developing into a city with a rhotic accent.

Another field of study, which did not reach its heyday until the late 1970s and which is orthogonal, as it were, to the classic studies conducted in modern sociolinguistics, explores social networks. Unlike early mainstream sociolinguistics, the study of social networks (which is closely associated with research by Lesley and James Milroy in Belfast) is not concerned with correlations between language use and established macro-sociological variables such as socio-economic

social networks

status, age or sex. Rather, it investigates correlations between language use and the self-perception, the values and attitudes of a specific social group on the micro-sociological level. What is at issue is language use in social networks, i.e. in the diverse and manifold constellations of family members, friends and acquaintances from school, work, leisure, the same residential area, etc. of which, eventually, every one of us is part. The level of integration into such a network is basically determined by two factors: network density (the quantity or number of relationships) and multiplexity of the network (quality or type of the relationships). Additionally, so-called "sociometric studies" can determine which persons are central and which are peripheral to the relevant network. The level of network integration, in turn, determines the amount of possible communicative events inside the network.

network density

One of the most important findings of network studies is that group identity becomes manifest in language. Analyses of the communication taking place in various vastly different social networks (especially in working-class districts and youth gangs in schools and ghettos) have shown that variation in language use and in the language system is indeed directly linked to the level of integration into some social network. On the one hand, the degree of integration correlates with the frequency with which a certain regional or urban dialect is used: the more integrated a speaker is, the more frequently he or she uses the dialect. On the other hand, conscious or subconscious peer pressure to follow the norms of the network increases as network density intensifies. Sociologists think of the fact that individuals are required to observe these norms as a crucial social function of such networks. As for language, this behaviour manifests itself in the tendency to maintain certain language structures and speech habits. To a large extent, communication takes place within the network only, leaving little space for the language to change (for more details see sections VIII.5 and VIII.6). The tendency to use language to define one's group identity and one's level of identification with a certain group is particularly pronounced among the upper and lower social classes, where speakers are pressured to orient themselves towards either the standard dialect (upper class) or a certain regional/urban dialect (lower class). Besides that, network density and the level of network integration also interact with other social variables such as age and sex (cf. section VIII.5).

integration in a network – norms – language use

One means of being integrated into a certain group is adapting one's language or language style to that used in the group. Besides

accommodation

276

its use among group members, accommodation of dialect (especially accent) and/or register (e.g. slang in youth gangs), i.e. linguistic convergence of the speakers involved in a communicative event, is a general means of achieving social acceptance and making communication more efficient. It is particularly often used in intercultural communication. But this is only the linguistic aspect of a much wider adaptation process which, in social psychology, is described as follows: the individual's social acceptance increases as the individual reduces differences. Of course, language can also be used to dissociate yourself from the person you are talking to. Linguistic divergence is one of the strategies investigated within the framework of accommodation theory. By including social context (more precisely the relationship, whether truly existing or just aspired to, between people engaged in a communicative event), accommodation theory offers an explanatory framework for functional variation, i.e. the context-dependent language use of the individual.

The origins of feminist linguistics date back to the feminist movement of the 1960s and 1970s in the United States. The central topic of feminist linguistics is "language and gender", where gender is neither a biological nor a grammatical concept (i.e. neither sex, distinguishing between male and female, nor grammatical gender, distinguishing between feminine and masculine, although the latter distinction is quite important in a large number of languages, and in European languages in particular). In feminist linguistics, gender is a sociological or socio-cultural concept: the socio-cultural construction of gender roles in ("patriarchal") societies dominated by men. Therefore, two of the basic assumptions of feminist linguistics are:

- Women and the language they use are the product of male-dominated society. Social gender is activated in any kind of interaction between human beings, naturally including verbal interaction. Social gender manifests itself, for example, in prototypical or stereotypical notions of gender roles, which most people spontaneously associate with particular occupations or professions (professions such as *secretary, nurse, cleaner* or *primary school teacher*, for example, are usually associated with female referents, while professions such as *President of the Unites States, engineer, pilot* or *doctor* tend to be associated with male referents). This is why, if the referent does not have the stereotypical gender, certain expressions describing the referent's gender are sometimes added, as in

VIII.5
Feminist Linguistics

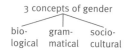

3 concepts of gender

bio-   gram-   socio-
logical matical cultural

social gender

woman doctor or *lady doctor* (two expressions which are nowadays stigmatized) or in *male nurse* (which is not stigmatized).

- Language structure and language use do not only reflect male dominance, but are also used to perpetuate this dominance.

language criticism and language therapy

In its early phase, feminist linguistics was highly politicized. It was strongly influenced by the goals of the feminist movement, and its primary concern was the documentation of sexist language use (more precisely: language used to discriminate against women) and making people aware of this so it could be remedied. In that phase, feminist linguistics meant two things: on the one hand, and primarily, feminist linguistic criticism and, on the other hand, feminist language politics aiming at 'therapies' for patriarchal language(s) – not only taking on male-dominated, male-centred language use, but also the corresponding language system(s). The immediate goal of the linguistic therapies suggested by feminist linguists was, and still is, to make women visible in language, or at least to make men invisible (e. g. *humankind* instead of *man(kind)*, *chair(person)* instead of *chairman*). But its ultimate goal is to use controlled language change as a means to alter people's attitudes towards women (thus pushing back stereotypical views of gender and gender roles) and to initiate societal change (especially by abolishing the existing gender hierarchy). The proposed strategies to avoid (a) sexist language use and (b) the linguistic manifestation of outdated gender-role stereotypes have been compiled in official guides and regulations for the equal treatment of women and men. By now, in North America and many European countries at least, these are being complied with by all levels of government, and are increasingly observed by other strata of society as well. Among the most important measures adopted to avoid sexist language use in English are the following:

avoidance of sexist language use

- avoiding generic *he/him(self)/his*, as in *Ask <u>anyone</u> and <u>he'll</u> tell you*, *In communication <u>the speaker's</u> primary aim is to get <u>his</u> message across*. Most expressions including both alternatives are only used in written language (*he/she, he* or *she, s/he, (s)he*). Another expression which is being generally accepted is *they/their* as a neutral singular pronoun (as in *In communication <u>the speaker's</u> primary aim is to get <u>their</u> message across*), which is exactly the function *they* and *their* had after indefinite forms like *anyone* or *everyone* up to the 18th century (compare *God send <u>every one</u> <u>their</u> heart's desire* in *Much Ado About Nothing* by Shakespeare).

- avoiding the expression *man* for "human race" or "human being" or "person" (as in *Museum of Man*, the song lyrics *now it's been 10,000 years, man has cried a billion tears* or in set phrases like *the man in the street*); instead, use of neutral forms like *humankind* or *person*.
- doing away with the asymmetry between *Mr* (unmarked for the features married vs. unmarried) and *Mrs/Miss* by introducing the term *Ms* /mɪz/.
- gender-neutral job titles, e.g. *flight attendant* instead of *steward/ stewardess*, *server* instead of *waiter/waitress*, *head teacher* instead of *headmaster/headmistress*; use of neutral terms like *person*: *chair(person)* instead of *chairman*, *anchor(person)* instead of *anchorman*; *salesperson* or *layperson*, plus the corresponding neutral plural forms *sales people* and *lay people*; *parent* instead of *mother/ father*.
- no adding of *lady* or *woman* to describe jobs done by women (e.g. *lady doctor* or *woman doctor*), because such expressions support stereotypical views of sex roles associated with a great number of occupations and professions.
- avoiding lexical asymmetry (use of the morphologically unmarked noun for male referents evoking no or a positive connotation, while the noun derived from it to refer to female referents has a rather negative connotation): *governor – governess, master – mistress*.
- compliance with the so-called "Titanic-Principle": "Women and children first!", which means that in listings, feminine forms or forms with female referents are to precede masculine forms or forms with male referents (e.g. *girls and boys, women and men, she or he*).

As far as the 'curing' of sexist language use is concerned, there is an interesting difference between English and German. English has the tendency to abstract from gender, i.e. neutralize gender differences by introducing neutral terms not marked for gender (lexical solution), whereas German feminist linguistics tends to specify gender, i.e. make women visible in language by introducing parallel expressions, e.g. by the consistent use of the suffix *-in* (*Frisörin* instead of *Friseuse* 'hairdresser'), *-innen* (plural referents, female only) or *-Innen* (preceded by glottal stop /ˈɪnən/, plural referents, female and/or male, as in *FrisörInnen, BürgerInnen, StudentInnen*, 'female hairdressers/citizens/students'), or by using feminine articles and demonstrative pronouns (*die/diese/eine Studierende* vs. *der/dieser/ein Studieren-*

different therapy strategies in English and in German

de(r)). In German, this is the predominant tendency, but due to the use of forms ending in *-ende(r)* gender-neutral expressions exist now, too, at least in the plural (*die Studierenden, die Lehrenden, Studierende wie Lehrende haben erkannt ...*). The main reason why English and German use different strategies is that German – as the majority of European languages – has grammatical gender, whereas English has natural gender (which is only important with pronouns). For languages like English it is much easier to find 'therapies' than for languages with grammatical gender. In the latter, women are invisible much more often, because masculine nouns (referring to animate referents) can also be used as gender-neutral (i.e. generic) expressions, while feminine nouns can have female referents only. Numerous psycholinguistic studies have shown that the invisibility of women in a language results in the absence of women in our thinking: generic masculine forms are often used to refer to male referents only. Try and test yourself: what referents do you think of when hearing the advice often given in pharmaceutical advertisements *For further information on benefits, risks and side effects, please consult your physician or pharmacist* or its counterpart in German *Zu Risiken und Nebenwirkungen fragen Sie Ihren Arzt oder Apotheker*?

Starting in the late 1980s, feminist linguistics, or more precisely feminist linguistic criticism, has become much less radical. The simple reason is that it is widely acknowledged in many western industrial countries that this criticism is fundamentally justified, and that, based on the strategies for planned language change proposed by feminist linguistics, measures have been taken in many places as an antidote to sexist language use. For the last 15-20 years, feminist linguistics has been more concerned with typical sociolinguistic and pragmatic issues. Its primary aim has been to investigate gender-specific language use, focussing on how variation interacts with gender, and finding answers to the question: Which linguistic features are characteristic of women and which are characteristic of men? Thanks to this line of research, it is clear now that (social) gender has an impact on language variation (besides other factors recognized by sociolinguistics such as geographical area, socio-economic status, and age), and the term "genderlect" has become widely accepted (analogous to "dialect" and "sociolect").

One of the main issues of feminist linguistics – which has also aroused great interest outside the academic community – is the behaviour of women and men amongst and towards each other in discourse and conversation. Various studies of communicative behav-

gender-specific language use

discourse behaviour of men and women

280

iour have shown that men are more conflict-oriented, more competitive and status-oriented and seek to initiate and control topics, whereas women are more consensus-oriented and more oriented towards cooperation, partnership, and creating an atmosphere of understanding and harmony. Here are some characteristic features of these two communicative styles – male report talk as opposed to female rapport talk:

Men
- frequently interrupt contributions of other speakers
- give no or very short answers, which may indicate lack of interest or attention, or discourage the other speaker from continuing talking (possible consequence: silence)
- frequently claim the right to speak
- talk more in public settings
- start topics and claim the conversational floor

Women
- are interrupted more frequently than men
- frequently use minimal responses which indicate attention and interest (I'm with you, go on) to encourage the other speaker to continue
- ask questions to elicit reactions
- claim the right to speak less frequently than men
- talk more in private settings
- are often hesitant and indirect (e. g. indirect speech acts used to make requests, frequent use of polite expressions, use of hedges such as *I think, I guess, perhaps, maybe,* and the use of tag questions for reassurance)
- 'collaborate' on topics with other speakers

As a matter of fact, communication between men and women is often regarded as a special instance of intercultural communication in feminist linguistics. The specifically male and female patterns of communicative behaviour are thought to result from cultural differences between the two sexes which start developing during the speakers' childhood and adolescence. How great these differences are may depend on the speakers' cultural backgrounds and the society they live in. Is it a female, 'horizontal' culture oriented towards consensus, cooperation and equality, or a 'vertical' male culture, oriented towards competition, power and social status? These cultural differences are responsible for many misunderstandings in the communication between the sexes, one example being that most women find sincere statements of sympathy and compassion agreeable while men sometimes find them patronizing or even face-threatening.

2 cultures approach

Those feminist linguists working within the sociolinguistic framework, i.e. those who use traditional sociolinguistic methods, are not satisfied with the theory of the two cultures. There is, for example, an interesting new interpretation of the observation that women's language is usually closer to the standard, the prestigious norm, than the language used by men, who tend to use more non-standard forms. This observation is supported by a multitude of studies on language use by both men and women of the same social group in identical communicative situations. Why do women follow the prestigious norm? Does this behaviour really reflect a female culture formed by education (at home and at school) and stereotypical role behaviour passed on from earlier generations? Sociolinguistic investigations made in different urban working-class areas in the United States and Northern Ireland suggest a different, or at least more differentiated explanation: the fact that women orient themselves towards the prestigious standard norm may simply be the result of their being more mobile and having more contact with other people, also with those of a higher socio-economic standing, whereas the private and professional life of men most of the time takes place in the same social group in their residential area. Hence, from the viewpoint of the sociolinguistic approach pioneered by Labov and the Milroys, the concepts of social gender and different cultures should not be regarded as the only explanations for gender differences in language use. Given the examples mentioned above, we could hypothesize that, in societies with clearly distinguished gender roles, those speakers with the greater (social and geographical) mobility are more strongly oriented towards the language use and linguistic norm of their respective "contact groups".

In conclusion, let us briefly return to feminist language politics. Its ultimate goal is to change the way people think by changing their linguistic habits. In the English-speaking world and in Europe, people have made quite some progress concerning the latter goal by changing certain linguistic forms and conversational habits, or at least by becoming aware of the necessity of such changes (think of *Ms* or the use of *they/their* as generic, gender-neutral singular pronouns). This is already part of the historical dimension of sociolinguistics. Usually, however, sociolinguistics is not concerned with pre-planned language change but with the normal, rather unconscious changes in language use and the social circumstances in which they occur.

The historical dimension of sociolinguistics, although of utmost importance, was mentioned in chapter I.3.2 and can be touched on only briefly here. The main branches of historical sociolinguistics are dialectology, variationist (or: Labovian) sociolinguistics, language contact research (think of the important role of language contact in the history of English) and creole studies (a sub-discipline of language contact research which studies the emergence of new varieties and languages, notably pidgins and creoles, due to language contact). Given the overall focus of the present chapter, only the importance of dialectology and variationist sociolinguistics for the study of language change will be addressed below.

Language varieties always represent a state of tension; they are torn between preservation and renewal, being at the same time conservative and innovative. Inevitably, they have therefore always been the object of investigation in historical language studies (in dialectology right from the beginning). It is a well-known comparison according to which anyone taking a journey through the different dialect regions of a language can be compared to a time-traveller visiting the past, sometimes even the future. Many linguistic features known from older stages of a language are still found in dialects, especially rural dialects. In English, these include (as we have seen above) multiple negation, zero relative clauses in subject position or different personal pronouns used for the 2nd person singular and plural. Thus, by observing present-day variation in (dialectal) language systems, we can in fact learn something about the history of a language.

Note, though, that this is a purely language-internal approach focussing on the comparison and reconstruction of language systems. This is not what is done in Labovian sociolinguistics and subsequent sociolinguistic approaches (network studies in particular); language-internal patterns (let alone presumed language-internal pressures) are not marshalled to explain why a specific language change has taken place or why it might even have been expected to take place. Instead, in his variationist approach to language change, which has had a lasting effect on historical linguistics for the last four decades, Labov is concerned with the language-external factors triggering language change and seeks to explain language change in connection with changes in social reality. Languages, to be sure, are changed by the people who use them, but which are the social factors that can actually cause linguistic norms to change or prevent them from changing? In trying to answer this question, sociolinguists stress the importance of

dialectology

variation and change

group identities, along the lines of socio-economic status, age or sex, but also in terms of social networks.

group identity on Martha's Vineyard

Among many other things, Labov studied two phonological variables (pronunciation of the diphthongs /aɪ/ and /aʊ/) in the speech of the people of Martha's Vineyard, a small island off the New England coast. He discovered that the innovative, centring realizations of these diphthongs (/ɐɪ/ and /əɪ/ and /ɐʊ/ and /əʊ/) were used much more frequently by those inhabitants who were especially attached to the island and its traditions. They were people of all different ages who, at the same time, showed a negative attitude towards the great number of mainland tourists who came to visit the island during their summer holidays. The Standard American English realizations of /aɪ/ und /aʊ/, on the other hand, were typically used by those inhabitants who were more open to tourists and did not feel that their presence presented a threat to the island community and its traditions. Obviously, the speakers of Martha's Vineyard unconsciously used one specific phonological feature – the centralization of two diphthongs – as an in-group marker to distinguish themselves from others. Labov's findings show that there is a direct connection between variation and change: change starts out as variation.

actuation

transition

Besides studying the original causes, i. e. the possible trigger(s) of language change (the so-called "actuation problem"), the primary concern of Labovian sociolinguistics is to determine which factors influence its spread (the so-called "transition problem") and to study the transitional stages of a language which result from (usually gradual) language change. These transitional stages are characterized by the coexistence of different linguistic alternatives, i. e. variation (the

embedding

so-called "embedding problem"). Therefore, the basic tenets of the approach are (a) that sociolinguistics is primarily concerned with studying language variation and language change, and that it studies these aspects simultaneously, (b) that by studying synchronic variation, a lot can be learned about the history of a language, and (c) that, ultimately, the strict distinction between synchrony and diachrony is impossible to maintain.

Checklist Sociolinguistics – key terms and concepts

actuation
African-American (Vernacular)
  English
adaptation
deficit ↔ difference
  hypothesis
dialect ↔ accent
dialect atlas
dialect continuum
dialect levelling
dialect universals
embedding
(New) Englishes
feminist linguistics
gender diffusion
genderlect

General American
gender (biological,
  sociocultural, grammatical)
isogloss
jargon
linguistic variable ↔
  linguistic variant
network (density; integration)
pluricentricity
pronoun exchange
rapport talk ↔ report talk
Received Pronunciation
register
rhoticity
slang
social stratification

sociolect
sociolinguistics ↔ sociology
  of language
language convergence
standard (accent)
style
traditional ↔ modern
  dialectology
transition
variety / lect (regional /
  diatopic; social / diastratic;
  functional / diasituative;
  diaphasic)
variationist/Laborian
  linguistics

Exercises

1 a. Explain the differences between the members of the following semantic field: dialect, genderlect, jargon, lect, register, slang, sociolect, standard, variety, vernacular

b. The term *dialect* can be used both in broader and in narrower ways compared with the definition adopted in this chapter. Comment on the following uses:

(A) Dialects can be distinguished along a horizontal and a vertical axis. The first gives us regional, the second social dialects.

(B) This person can't even speak proper English. All he's able to is produce some dialect which is unintelligible even to the most well-meaning ears.

(C) In my dialect you would have to say [paθ] rather than [pɑ:θ].

(D) We speak the same dialect but different accents.

2 Which of the following examples are candidates for true regionalisms? Try to identify the relevant regional dialects or dialect areas:

a. I'm needing a cup of tea.
b. It pull the mole up and he was dead in minutes.
c. We also had a girl worked in the house.
d. You were only after asking me.
e. You never seen nobody.
f. They make a wee hole for theirself.

3 Which of the following sentences are more representative of American English, which of British English?

a. The orchestra is divided.
b. Did you already see *Armageddon*?
c. I've had a bath just a minute ago.
d. She's gotten interested.
e. I insist that she leaves.
f. Where can I get some petrol?

4 Illustrate the correlation between social class and regional variation. Include in your discussion the pronunciation of words like *bar, card, singing* and *walking* as it is frequently found in England.

5 Explain the sociolinguistic approach known as "social network analysis".

6 a. What is striking about the following sentences in African-American English:

   (a) They real fine.
   (b) I gonna do it.
   (c) John be happy.
   (d) Sometime they be walking round here.

   b. Identify grammatical parallels between African-American English and regional varieties in the British Isles.

7 a. Discuss the following examples from the point of view of feminist linguistics.

   (A) Mr Brown and his wife arrived at ten o'clock.
   (B) Miss Elizabeth Prickett was elected chairman of the Waddington Private School Board last night.
   (C) Anyone talking with Chinese government officials has to choose their words cautiously.
   (D) I didn't feel well and went to the lady doctor round the corner.
   (E) All flight attendants fell ill during the flight.

   b. Identify some major differences between the communicative behaviour of women and men.

8 Which of the following statements are true, which are false?

   a. Traditional dialectology is concerned with the study of traditional dialects, modern dialectology with the study of modern dialects.
   b. Social variation correlates with regional variation.
   c. RP is a social accent.
   d. Multiple negation is the rule rather than the exception in many varieties of English.
   e. Accommodation is the term in sociolinguistics for the influence that housing has on the choice of a certain functional variety.
   f. There is far more regional variation in the British Isles than there is in the United States.
   g. You cannot speak a standard dialect with a regional accent.
   h. Most of the grammatical differences between British and American English can be observed in the verb phrase.
   i. Field, tenor and mode all relate to functionally motivated variation in language use.
   j. More as well as more complex subordination patterns are typical of written in contrast to spoken language.

9 Sketch the major differences between traditional and modern dialectology.

10 Recall the Sapir-Whorf hypothesis. To what extent could one argue that feminist linguists are Neo-Whorfians?

11 a. What is the relationship between Leech's socio-pragmatic approach and accommodation theory?
    b. Which role do face considerations à la Brown and Levinson play in feminist discourse analysis?

12 Give an account of the significance of sociolinguistics for the study of language change. Focus in particular on the work by William Labov.

Sources and further reading

Algeo, John, ed. 2001. *The Cambridge History of the English Language, vol. 6: English in North America.* Cambridge: Cambridge University Press.

Ammon, Ulrich/Norbert Dittmar, eds. 1987-1988. *Sociolinguistics: An international handbook of the science of language and society.* Berlin: de Gruyter.

Bex, Tony/Richard J. Watts, eds. 1999. *Standard English: The widening debate.* London/New York: Routledge.

Burchfield, Robert, ed. 1994. *English in Britain and overseas. Origins and development. (The Cambridge History of the English Language, vol. 5.)* Cambridge: Cambridge University Press.

Cameron, Deborah, ed. 1998². *The feminist critique of language: A reader.* London/New York: Routledge.

Chambers, J.K. 2003². *Sociolinguistic theory.* Oxford: Blackwell.

Chambers, J.K./Peter Trudgill. 1998². *Dialectology.* Cambridge: Cambridge University Press.

Chambers, J.K./Peter Trudgill/Natalie Schilling-Estes, eds. 2002. *Handbook of language variation and change.* Oxford: Blackwell.

Cheshire, Jenny, ed. 1991. *English around the world. Sociolinguistic perspectives.* Cambridge: Cambridge University Press.

Coates, Jennifer. 2004³. *Women, men and language. A sociolinguistic account of gender differences in language.* London: Longman.

Coulmas, Florian, ed. 1997. *The handbook of sociolinguistics.* Oxford: Blackwell.

Coupland, Nikolas/Adam Jaworski, eds. 1997. *Sociolinguistics. A reader and coursebook.* London: Macmillan.

Downes, William. 1998. *Language and society.* Cambridge: Cambridge University Press.

Green, Lisa J. 2002. *African American English: A linguistic introduction.* Cambridge: Cambridge University Press.

Hellinger, Marlis. 1990. *Kontrastive feministische Linguistik: Mechanismen sprachlicher Diskriminierung im Englischen und Deutschen.* München: Hueber.

Holm, John A. 1988-89. *Pidgins and creoles.* 2 vols. Cambridge: Cambridge University Press.

Kortmann, Bernd/Edgar Schneider with Kate Burridge/Rajend Mesthrie/Clive Upton, eds. 2004. *A handbook of varieties of English.* 2 vols . Berlin/New York: Mouton de Gruyter.

Kortmann, Bernd/Tanja Herrmann/Lukas Pietsch/Susanne Wagner. 2005. *A comparative grammar of British English dialects: Agreement, gender, relative clauses*. Berlin/New York: Mouton de Gruyter.

Labov, William. 1994. *Principles of linguistic change: Internal factors*. vol. 1. Oxford: Blackwell.

Labov, William. 2001. *Principles of linguistic change: Social factors*. vol. 2. Oxford: Blackwell.

Labov, William/Sharon Ash/Charles Boberg. forthcoming. *Atlas of North American English: Phonetics, phonology and sound change*. Berlin/New York: Mouton de Gruyter.

McArthur, Tom. 1998. *The English languages*. Cambridge: Cambridge University Press.

Milroy, James/Lesley Milroy, eds. 1993. *Real English: The grammar of English dialects in the British Isles*. London: Longman.

Mufwene, Salikoko S./John R. Rickford/John Baugh/Guy Bailey, eds. 1998. *African-American English. Structure, history and use*. London/New York: Routledge.

Romaine, Suzanne. 2000[2]. *Language in society: An introduction to sociolinguistics*. Oxford: Oxford University Press.

Samel, Ingrid. 1995. *Einführung in die feministische Sprachwissenschaft*. Berlin: Schmidt.

Strevens, Peter. 1972. *British and American English*. London: Collier-Macmillan.

Tannen, Deborah. 1992. *You just don't understand. Women and men in conversation*. London: Virago Press.

Trudgill, Peter. 1999[2]. *The dialects of England*. Cambridge, Mass.: Blackwell.

Trudgill, Peter/J.K. Chambers, eds. 1991. *Dialects of English. Studies in grammatical variation*. London: Longman.

Trudgill, Peter/Jean Hannah. 1994[3]. *International English: A guide to varieties of standard English*. London: Arnold.

Wells, John C. 1982 [1995]. *Accents of English*. 3 vols. Cambridge: Cambridge University Press.

Wolfram, Walt/Natalie Schilling-Estes. 1998. *American English: Dialects and variation*. Oxford: Blackwell.

The following general reference works will prove to be useful in addition to the chapters in the present volume. University students preparing for their exams may proceed as follows. In a first step, they should consult one or two more state-of-the-art survey articles on individual branches or topics in linguistics. Extremely useful in this respect are handbooks (for English linguistics, especially Aarts/McMahon 2006; for general linguistics, Aronoff/Miller 2001 or Newmeyer 1988) and encyclopaedias (for English linguistics, especially Crystal 1995 and McArthur 1992; for general linguistics, Bright 2003 and Brown 2005). In the relevant articles and chapters, the readers are referred to more specific literature, which leads up to step 2. For each exam topic, at least one textbook should be worked through in detail, complemented by selected chapters in relevant handbooks and readers. Especially since the 1990s, students can choose between a range of very good series of textbooks and handbooks. The classic among the textbook series still is the 'red' paperback series "Cambridge Textbooks in Linguistics", which offers the widest range of topics of all relevant series. Another highly recommendable textbook series is the "Understanding Language" series by Edward Arnold. The two best handbook series are those published by Blackwells and Mouton de Gruyter ("Handbooks of Linguistics and Communication Science"). Readers are collections of classic articles in a given field of linguistics; a good selection of readers has, for example, been published by Routledge. Anyone who wants to dig even more deeply into a given branch or topic in (English) linguistics may consult specialized journals or book series. Top journals include *Language*, *Linguistics*, and *English Language and Linguistics*. A highly respected series in English linguistics (both for Present-Day English and older periods) is "Topics in English Linguistics" (TiEL). Those who wish to adopt a more systematic way of finding relevant literature for individual topics in (English) linguistics should consult bibliographies like the *MLA Bibliography* or, especially informative, the *Annotated Bibliography of English Studies* (ABES). Finally, in order to come to grips with the rich professional jargon in linguistics, university students will find it immensely reassuring to know where to look up brief definitions and illustrations of all or at least the most widely used terms. For this purpose, the most important dictionaries in linguistics have been listed below.

General reference works

step 1

step 2

step 3

Bibliographies

Annotated bibliography of English Studies. Lisse: Swets & Zeitlinger. (every six months on CD-ROM or online)
Bibliographie linguistischer Literatur = Bibliography of linguistic literature. Frankfurt/M.: Klostermann. (annually or online)
Linguistic bibliography = Bibliographie linguistique. The Hague. (annually)
MLA International Bibliography of Books and Articles on the Modern Languages and Literatures. Ed. by Modern Language Association. New York. (annually or online)

Dictionaries

Bußmann, Hadumod. 2002³. *Lexikon der Sprachwissenschaft.* Stuttgart: Kröner.
Bußmann, Hadumod. 1999². *Routledge dictionary of language and linguistics.* London: Routledge.
Crystal, David. 1992. *An encyclopedic dictionary of language and languages.* Oxford: Blackwell.
Crystal, David. 2003⁵. *A dictionary of linguistics and phonetics.* Oxford: Blackwell.
Trask, Robert L. 1993. *A dictionary of grammatical terms in linguistics.* London: Routledge.

Encyclopaedias

Asher, R.E., ed. 1994. *The encyclopedia of language and linguistics.* 10 vols. Oxford: Pergamon Press. (see Brown, Keith for second edition)
Bright, William, ed. 2003². *An international encyclopedia of linguistics.* 4 vols. Oxford/New York: Oxford University Press.
Brown, Keith, ed. 2005². *Encyclopedia of language and linguistics.* 14 vols. Amsterdam: Elsevier.
Collinge, Neville E. 1990. *An encyclopaedia of language.* London: Routledge.
Crystal, David. 1997². *The Cambridge encyclopedia of language.* Cambridge: Cambridge University Press.
Malmkjaer, Kirsten. 2001². *The linguistics encyclopedia.* London: Routledge.
Smelser, Neil J./Paul B. Baltes, eds. 2001. *International encyclopedia of the social and behavioral sciences.* Amsterdam: Elsevier. www.iesbs.com

Aarts, Bas/April McMahon, eds. 2006. *Handbook of English linguistics.* Oxford: Blackwell.

Ahrens, Rüdiger/Wolf-Dietrich Bald/Werner Hüllen, eds. 1995. *Handbuch Englisch als Fremdsprache.* Berlin: Schmidt.

Bolton, W.F./David Crystal, eds. 1987. *The English language.* London: Sphere.

Crystal, David. 2002². *The English language.* London: Penguin.

Crystal, David. 2003². *The Cambridge encyclopedia of the English language.* Cambridge: CUP.

Lass, Roger. 1987. *The shape of English.* London: Dent & Sons.

McArthur, Tom, ed. 1992. *The Oxford companion to the English language.* Oxford: Oxford University Press.

Viereck, Wolfgang/Karin Viereck/Heinrich Ramisch. 2002. *Dtv-Atlas englische Sprache.* München: DTV.

English language and linguistics

Akmajian, Adrian/Richard A. Demers/Ann K. Farmer/Robert M. Harnish. 2001⁵. *Linguistics: An introduction to language and communication.* Cambridge, Mass.: MIT Press.

Aronoff, Mark/Janie Rees-Miller. 2001. *The Handbook of linguistics.* Oxford: Blackwell.

Fromkin, Victoria/Robert Rodman. 2002⁷. *An introduction to language.* Fort Worth: Harcourt Brace College.

Newmeyer, Frederick, ed. 1988. *Linguistics: The Cambridge survey.* 4 vols. Cambridge: Cambridge University Press.

O'Grady, William/Michael Dobrovolsky/Mark Aronoff, eds. 2001⁴. *Contemporary linguistics: An introduction.* New York: St. Martin's Press.

Introductions and surveys

Solutions Chapter I (Linguistics: An overview)

1 b, c, e

2 appellative – expressive
   arbitrary – conventional
   empirical – introspective
   icon – symbol
   nature – nurture
   paradigmatic – syntagmatic

3 a. competence – performance
       formalism – functionalism
       parole – langue
       prescriptive – descriptive
       signifier – signified
       synchronic – diachronic
    b. Ferdinand de Saussure: arbitrary – conventional, diachronic –
                               synchronic, langue – parole, signifier –
                               signified, syntagmatic – paradigmatic
       Noam Chomsky: competence – performance,
                               formalism, introspective, nature
       Charles S. Peirce: symbol – icon
       Karl Bühler and
       Roman Jakobson: expressive – appellative

4 a.

communicative dimension	function
world	referential
addresser	expressive
addressee	appellative
contact	phatic
message	poetic
code	metalingual

   b. • weather forecast – referential
       • speech by politician – appellative
       • small talk – phatic
       • Comment by another guest – poetic
       • "Oh, damn!" – expressive
       • Autumn is British English ... – metalingual

5 a. corpus linguistics   d. grammaticalization
    b. historical pragmatics   e. historical semantics
    c. historical sociolinguistics

6 c, d

7 a. CSAE (as the only non-BrE corpus)
  b. Brown (as the only non-historical corpus)
  c. Frown (as the only spoken corpus)
  d. BNC (as the only mega-corpus and mixed spoken-written corpus)
  e. Brown (as the only pre-1990s corpus)

8 a. false, b. true, c. false, d. true, e. false, f. true, g. false, h. false, i. true, j. true.

Solutions Chapter II (Phonetics and Phonology)

1 a.+b. Figure a: (inter)dental /θ ð/;
     Figure b: alveolar /t d s z l/;
     Figure c: palato-alveolar /ʃ ʒ tʃ ʤ/;
     Figure d: velar /k g/

2 a. [lɪŋ'gwɪstɪks]
   /l/ vocal folds vibrating (→ voiced sound), velum raised (→ oral sound), alveolar lateral
   /ŋ/ vocal folds vibrating, velum lowered (→ nasal sound), velar nasal
   /g/ vocal folds vibrating, velum raised, velar plosive
   /w/ vocal folds vibrating, velum raised, bilabial approximant
   /s/ vocal folds not vibrating (→ voiceless sound), velum raised, alveolar fricative
   /t/ vocal folds not vibrating, velum raised, alveolar plosive
   /k/ vocal folds not vibrating, velum raised, velar plosive
  b. homorganic: /l/ /s/ /t/ are alveolar; /ŋ/ /g/ /k/ are velar
  c. obstruents: /g/ /s/ /t/ /k/; sonorants: /l/ /i/ /ŋ/ /w/

3 a. toad /əʊ/; tour /ʊə/; toy /ɔɪ/; tea /iː/; toe /əʊ/; tear /ɪə/ or /ɛə/; tray /eɪ/; tire /aɪə/; Teddy /e/ /i/; Timmy /ɪ/ /i/; Tammy /æ/ /i/; Tommy /ɒ/ /i/; tummy /ʌ/ /i/
  b. /əʊ/ closing diphthong in /ʊ/; /ɔɪ/ and /eɪ/ closing diphthongs in /i/; /aɪə/ triphthong (=closing diphthong + schwa); /ʊə/ /ɪə/ /ɜə/ centring diphthongs

4 a.+b. a. voiced bilabial plosive /b/; b. voiceless velar dental -- (nonsensical); c. lax high back vowel /ʊ/; d. voiced dental

fricative /ð/; e. voiced velar nasal /ŋ/; f. rounded high vowel
--; g. voiced bilabial semi-vowel /w/; h. voiceless lateral
fricative --

5 a. 1. leave /liːv/; 2. bingo /ˈbɪŋgəʊ/; 3. question /ˈkwestʃn/;
4. flash /flæʃ/; 5. unique /juˈniːk/; 6. emergency /ɪˈmɜːdʒənsɪ/;
7. start /staːt/; 8. other /ˈʌðə/; 9. path /paːθ/
b. 1, 3, 4, 6.

6 ten – tin; ten – hen; tin – pin; hippo – hippie; live – love; leaf – thief

7 a. /m/ is neither an obstruent nor an oral sound; b. /uː/ is not a short
vowel; c. /g/ is not a fricative; d. /ɪə/ is not a closing diphthong;
e. /p/ is not voiced; f. /ʒ/ is neither an approximant not a sonorant;
g. /ʃ/ is not alveolar; h. /ŋ/ is not an approximant; i. /v/ is not a stop;
j. /ɒ/ is not a long vowel.

8 a. false, b. true, c. true, d. false, e. true, f. false, g. true, h. true,
i. true, j. false.

Solutions Chapter III (Morphology)

1 A morpheme is defined as the smallest **meaning**-bearing unit of
language. **Inflectional** morphemes, for instance, add only grammatical meaning to the stem they are attached to. They create a new
word-**form** (or: token). Lexical information, on the other hand,
is added by **derivational** morphemes. The result of this kind of
affixation is a new lexeme (or: type). Analogous to phonemes,
which may be realized by a set of **phones**, called **allophones**, there
may be more than one **morph** which instantiates a given morpheme. These are called the **allomorphs** of the relevant morpheme
and are normally **phonologically** conditioned.

2 a. {form}{al}{itie}{s}; *formality*=stem, {s} = inflectional suffix
(PLURAL); *form*=root; =base of *formal*; {al}=derivational suffix
(turning N into A); *formal*=base of *formality*; {ity}=derivational
suffix (turning A into N)
{in}{conclus}{ive}{ness}; {conclude}=root; =base of *conclusive*;
{ive}=derivational suffix (turning V into A); *conclusive*=base of
inconclusive; {in}=derivational prefix (negation); *inconclusive*=base of *inconclusiveness*; {ness}=derivational suffix (turning A into N)

b. /əˈprɪə(r)/ /əˈpæ(r)/ /ˈæpə(r)/ cf. *appear, apparent, apparition*
/lɒŋ/ /leŋ/ /lɒndʒ/ /lɒŋg/ cf. *long, length, longevity, longitude*

/ˈfɪzɪk/ /ˈfɪzɪs/ /fɪˈzɪʃ/ /fɪˈziːk/ cf. *physics, physicist, physician, physique*

/juːz/ /juːʒ/ /juːs/ cf. *to use, usual, the use*

/θiːf/ /θef/ /θiːv/ cf. *thief, theft, thieving*

/ˈfəʊtə.grɑːf/ /fəˈtɒgrəf/ /.fəʊtəˈgræf/ cf. *photograph, photography, photographic*

3 {en} 1. derivational morpheme, turning a noun into an adjective, meaning "made out of N": *earthen, wooden, silken*
    2. derivational morpheme, turning an adjective into a verb, meaning "making more A": *widen, sweeten, deafen*
    3. inflectional allomorph of {PLURAL}, lexically conditioned: *oxen*

4 *to netsurf: to surf the net, net + surfing* compounding; *to netsurf* backformation

rockumentary: document + ary derivation; *rock + documentary* blend

neocolonialism: colony + al derivation; *colonial + ism* derivation; *neo + colonialism* derivation

to enthuse: enthusiasm ˃ to enthuse backformation

campaigner: campaign ˃ to campaign conversion; *campaign + er*: derivation

laptop: compute + er derivation; *lap + top* compounding; *laptop computer* compounding; *laptop* elision

modem: modulation + demodulation: blend

sexist: sex + ist derivation

exec: execut + ive (adj) derivation; *executive* (n.) conversion; *exec* clipping

judgmental: judge + ment derivation; *judgment + al* derivation

sitcomy: situation comedy compounding; *sitcom* clipping; *sitcom + y* derivation

weatherwise: weather + wise derivation

to breathalyse: to analyse breath; breathalyse blend

language lab: language + laboratory compounding; *language lab* clipping

infotainment: inform + ation derivation; *entertain + ment* derivation; *information + entertainment* compounding; *infotainment*: blend

5 a. *classroom* the compound is a noun
   b. *doormat* the compound consists of two nouns

c. *flower-pot* endocentric compound

d. *motor-car* modifier + head structure

6 a. Usually, prefixes do not change the word class. The following forms are therefore exceptions: *be + witch* (N > V); *empower* (N > V); *encode* (N > V); *discourage* (N > V)

b. {ISH} 1. derivational morpheme, N > A, meaning "like N": *childish, feverish, eightish, foolish*

2. derivational morpheme on adjectives, no change of word class, meaning 'like A': *greenish*

3. *punish* is monomorphemic

7 I. d; II. g; III. a; IV. b; V. f; VI. c; VII. e

8 a. true; b. false; c. false; d. true; e. false; f. true; g. false; h. true; i. false; j. true

Solutions Chapter IV (Syntax)

1 Nouns: Number (plural), Case (possessive; object case only for pronouns)

Verbs: Progressive; Past; Passive; 3rd person singular; Person and Number (3rd person singular, present tense indicative); Tense (past tense), Aspect (progressive), Perfect, Voice, Mood (subjunctive: only *were*)

2 a. *Then* [Adverb] *the* [definite article] *boy* [noun] *rubbed* [verb] *the* [definite article] *magic* [adjective] *lamp* [noun] *and* [coordinating conjunction] *a* [indefinite article] *genie* [noun] *appeared* [verb] *beside* [preposition] *him* [personal pronoun].

b. Adjective: *the round table*, Preposition: *He walked round the table*, Noun: *He looked at the expectant round*, Verb: *He rounded the figures*, Adverb: *We went round to Alvin's house.*

3 a. *below the window:* prepositional phrase PP, no head
rather slowly: adverb phrase AdvP, *slowly*=head
Tom and Jerry: noun phrase NP, *Tom, Jerry*=heads
has been saying: verb phrase VP, *saying*=head
fast and expensive car: noun phrase, *car*=head

b. Compounding (chapter III.3.2); in English, heads follow their modifiers

4 a. [He]$_{NP}$ [spends]$_{VP}$ [all his money]$_{NP}$ [on horses]$_{PP}$ SVOO

b. [John]$_{NP}$ [called]$_{VP}$ [me]$_{NP}$ [an idiot]$_{NP}$ SVOC

c. [Mary]$_{NP}$ [left]$_{VP}$ [the next day]$_{NP}$ SVA

d. [They]$_{NP}$ [may be staying]$_{VP}$ [until next June]$_{PP}$ SVA

e. [His face]$_{NP}$ [turned]$_{VP}$ [pale]$_{AP}$ when [he]$_{NP}$ [saw]$_{VP}$ [me]$_{NP}$ SVCA

5 a. *honestly; briefly; yesterday; in the park; when he was feeding the ducks*

b. Adverbials are usually optional and can occupy various positions. In the example, however, [*a mere thirty seconds*] is obligatory.

6 a. [That cities will attract more and more criminals]$_{subject\ clause}$ is a safe prediction.

b. This shows [how difficult the question must have been] $_{object\ clause}$

c. [Being a farmer]$_{adverbial\ participle\ clause}$, he is suspicious of all governmental interference.

d. We knew [that he was a lousy driver]$_{object\ clause}$

e. I am very eager [to meet her]$_{complement\ clause\ (adjective\ complementation)}$

f. The problem is [who will water my plants]$_{complement\ clause}$ [when I am away]$_{Adverbial\ clause\ of\ Time}$

g. [No further discussion arising]$_{adverbial\ participle\ clause}$, the meeting was brought to a close.

h. I'll show you [what you can open the bottle with]$_{object\ clause}$

7 Non-restrictive relative clauses form a separate intonational unit; cannot be substituted by the present participle; require a relative pronoun; cannot be introduced by *that*.
Restrictive relative clauses: b, c, d, f.

8 a. false; b. true; c. true; d. false; e. true; f. false; g. true; h. true; i. true; j. false

Solutions Chapter V (Contrastive Linguistics)

1 a. /tel/ with a clear /l/ instead of a dark /ɫ/; /vɒt/: /v/ instead of /w/; /ɪs/: instead of /ɪz/; /zə/ instead of /ðə/; /prɒbləm/ instead of /prɔbləm/; /vɪs/: /v/ instead of /w/, /s, z/ instead of /θ, ð/; /sɛt/ instead of /ðæt/

b. Because of substitution of a German phoneme for a phoneme that occurs in English only.
pat – pet: no vowel contrast /æ/ /e/, cf. *bad – bed; lag – leg.*
thin -sin: /θ/ is substituted by /s/, cf. *mouth – mouse; think – sink*
wine – vine: /w/ is substituted by /v/, cf. *wet – vet, wow – vow*
cherry – sherry: /ʧ/ is substituted by /ʃ/, cf. *chin – shin*

lag – lack: /g/ in word-final position is substituted by /k/
(final devoicing), cf. *bag – back; dog – dock*
plays – place: /z/ in word-final position is substituted by /s/
(final devoicing), cf. *his – hiss; lose – loose*
jazz -chess: /ʤ/ is substituted by /ʧ/, underdifferentiation of
vowels (no /æ/ - /e/ contrast)

2 a. /ɛ/ is substituted for /æ/, cf. *bat, cat*
/oː/ is substituted for /əʊ/, cf. *so, low*
/ø/ is substituted for /ɜː/, cf. *bird, hurt*
/a/ is substituted for /ʌ/, cf. *up, but*

b. *output, got:* no aspiration of /t/ in non-initial position
obtain: substitution of aspirated /p/ for /b/ in syllable-final
position
bedtime: substitution of /t/ for /d/ in syllable-final position
rag: final devoicing (/k/ for /g/)
she lives: final devoicing (/fs/ for /vz/)
and: final devoicing (/t/ for /d/)
finger: /ŋ/ substituted for /ŋg/ in analogy with German
so: word-initial /z/ for /s/ (phonotactic rule of German)

3 English permits zero relatives (e.g. *The man I met yesterday*) and
shortened relative clauses (participial clauses, e.g. *The man walking down the street was whistling*). English has an invariant relative pronoun (*that*); the choice of a *wh*-pronoun depends on
semantic criteria (human vs. non-human referent).

4 In the domain of non-finite adverbial clauses English has more
structural possibilities than German (for example German does not
have the option in 4b). In general, English makes much more
frequent use of adverbial participles than German both in written
and spoken language. German prefers finite adverbial clauses.

5 a. Sie strich mit ihren langen Fingern über den neuen Mantel.
b. Er wischte das Geschirr mit dem feuchten Tuch ab.
c. Er durchschwamm den Kanal in einem Tag.
d. Sie flohen aus der Hauptstadt.
e. Der Albatros segelte auf dem Wind.
f. Er drohte mit Gewalt.
g. Auf der Demonstration wurde gegen die Invasion von Haikutu
protestiert.
h. Dieses Buch wurde zwei Millionen mal verkauft/verkaufte sich
zwei Millionen mal.

6 a. relatively free (pragmatic) word order in German
   b. middle voice in English
   c. subjectless sentence in German, impossible in English
   d. obligatory *do*-support in English
   e. SOV order in subordinate clauses in German
   f. preposition stranding in English
   g. deletion of relative pronoun in English
   h. non-agentive subject in English
   i. raising construction: more options in English than in German

7 a. German uses the present perfect as a narrative tense
   b. German uses the present tense for the English experiential perfect
   c. German uses the present perfect for future perfect reference (English: future perfect)
   d. English has a progressive aspect
   e. German regularly uses the simple present for future reference (English: future)
   f. Only in restricted contexts can the simple present have future meaning in English.

8 a. false; b. false; c. true; d. false; e. true; f. true; g. true; h. true; i. false;

Solutions Chapter VI (Semantics)

1 b, e, f.

2

	sense	reference	intension	extension	denotation	connotation
a		+		+	+	
b	+		+	+	+	+
c				+	+	
d	+		+			(+)
e			+			

3 a. heteronymy: three verbs of perception; *see* (primary meaning) versus *hear, feel*
   hyponymy: three verbs of visual perception; *see* superordinate of *look at, watch*
   synonymy; *see* via metaphorical extension 'understand'
   synonymy; *see* via metonymical extension 'imagine'

synonymy; *see* via metonymical extension 'visit', 'meet'
homonymy (→ homophony): *sea*
  b. meaning extension through metaphor or metonymy, homonymy

4 *frame – window:* meronymy
expand – contract: directional oppositeness (reversives)
mole – spy: synonymy
fill – empty: directional oppositeness (reversives)
in – out: directional oppositeness (reversives)
fail – succeed: antonymy
hyponym – hypernym: converseness (relational opposites)
picture – painting: synonymy
zero – love: synonymy
semantics – linguistics: meronymy
freedom – liberty: synonymy
after – before: converseness (relational opposites)
book – index: meronymy

5 a. two senses of *party*: 'political group' versus 'social event'
  b. syntactic ambiguity: *eats shoots and leaves* has the structure

VO+O; the panda reinterprets it as V, V+V. Different intonation
contours resolve the ambiguity.

6 a. Semantics deals with meaning out of context, pragmatics with
meaning in context.
  b. Ambiguity is resolved (disambiguated) in a context, vagueness
not necessarily (meaning can be modulated by the context).
  c. Total synonyms are synonymous in all contexts, cognitive
synonyms are not.

7 a. Language is a network (system, structure) of interrelated units;
the meaning of a part can only be specified with reference to the
whole. The structure thus determines the meaning of a word,
e.g. through syntagmatic and paradigmatic sense relations
(both through what a word has in common with other words,
and by what it is different).
  b. Cognitive semantics investigates meaning through categorisa-
tion; meaning is directly related to human cognition; language
reflects conceptual categories. Relation *signifié – signifiant* is
motivated; allows language comparison.
Structural semantics: the relation *signifié – signifiant* is completely arbitrary; meaning is always language-specific; the

meaning of a word is determined by its position in the network of the language, no direct link to cognitive structures.

8 a. false; b. false; c. false; d. false; e. true; f. true; g. false; h. false; i. true; j. false

Solutions Chapter VII (Pragmatics)

1 Pragmatics can be defined as the study of **meaning** in **context,** with the speaker and their **intentions** at the centre. Its two most important theories operate on the **utterance** level. Speech act theory was developed by **Austin** and his pupil **Searle,** and the theory of **conversational** implicatures by **Grice.** All of them belong to the movement of **ordinary** language **philosophy.** Grice's theory helps us account for the frequently observable fact that we read more into an utterance than what is **literally** said. In this respect it links up with the study of **illocutionary acts** within speech act theory. Different from Grice's theory, the **relevance** theory developed by Sperber and Wilson is not a pragmatic, but rather a **cognitive** theory. What stands at the heart of this theory is the calculation of contextual **effects** against **processing effort.**

2 a. <u>There</u>[Place:anaphoric] <u>she</u>[Person: deictic] was, sitting right next to <u>my</u>[Person: deictic] mother.
   b. Listen, mate, there is only one solution to <u>your</u>[Person: anaphoric] problem: <u>you</u>[Person: anaphoric] finish <u>your</u>[Person: anaphoric] essay and submit <u>it</u>[anaphoric] <u>next Monday</u>[Time: deictic].
   c. There <u>you</u>[Person: deictic] go.
   d. The hotel was just terrible. So <u>the next Monday</u>[Time: anaphoric] <u>we</u>[Person: deictic] left <u>this hotel</u>[Place: anaphoric] for good.
   e. <u>Two days ago</u>[Time: deictic] <u>I</u>[Person: deictic] met Mary. <u>She</u>[Person: anaphoric] looked tired and said <u>she</u>[Person: anaphoric] wasn't looking forward to <u>her</u>[Person: anaphoric] sister's birthday party <u>a week from today</u> [Time: deictic].

3 a. *today:* (a) symbolic meaning: the 24 hour interval (from midnight to midnight) around coding time (i.e. the time of utterance); (b) indexical meaning: the 24 hour interval around the coding time (the now) of the respective speaker.
   this morning: (a) symbolic meaning: the 12 hour interval (from midnight to midday) on the day of the utterance; (b) indexical meaning: the 12 hour interval of the day of the respective utterance

b. *Deictic projection* means a shift of the deictic centre. As speakers switch, so does the deictic centre. Fred's right is Mary's left; "right" and "left" (of speaker) shifts with the speaker. Fred and Mary face each other.

4 b. = promise.

5

	direct	indirect		direct	indirect
a.	question	request	d.	question	invitation
b.	statement	request	e.	statement	question
c.	statement	warning	f.	question	reproach

6 a. shared background: You cannot see a pram and a bag full of nappies. If the baby is there, you can see a pram and a bag full of nappies.
conversational implicature: B did not bring the baby.
Maxim: Relevance.

b. shared background: B was supposed to clean the kitchen and do the shopping. If of a conjoined statement A + B only A is the case, then B is not the case.
conversational implicature: B has not cleaned the kitchen.
Maxim: $Quantity_1$, $Quality_1$.

c. shared background: A and B know George; "last spring" is not the same as "recently".
conversational implicature: B did not see George recently.
Maxim: $Quantity_1$.

d. shared background: All cats chase mice (obvious truth)
conversational implicature: A's question was also an obvious truth.
All dogs like bones.
A's dog likes bones.
Maxim: Relevance, $Quantity_1$, Manner.

e. shared background: If you have an essay to finish, you cannot watch TV at the same time.
conversational implicature: B will not watch the film on BBC2.
Maxim: Relevance.

7 a. cancellability, calculability, non-conventionality

b. The use of a particular scalar expression implies that the use of a stronger expression was not possible. If the speaker has said as much as he can, nothing stronger can be read into the utterance (negative inference).

8 a. true; b. false; c. true; d. true; e. true; f. false; g. false; h. true; i. true; j. true

Solutions Chapter VIII (Sociolinguistics)

1 a. *dialect:* regional variety
  genderlect: gender variety (special type of sociolect)
  jargon: professional (technical) variety (special type of sociolect and register)
  register: functional variety
  slang: informal variety (special type of register)
  sociolect: social variety
  standard: non-regional prestige variety
  variety: superordinate term (= *lect*)
  vernacular = non-standard variety

  b. A=broader: 'social dialects' = sociolects
  B=narrower: dialect = 'incorrect standard', 'substandard variety'
  C=narrower: dialect=accent
  D=narrower: dialect relates only to lexical and grammatical variation

2 widespread: regionalisms:
  a. extended use of the progressive
  b. gender diffusion: *he* refers back to *mole* (Southwest)
  c. zero relatives in subject position
  d. *be after*-perfect: (Irish English)
  e. multiple negation, *seen* = past tense
  f. *wee*= 'small', *theirself* = reflexive (Scottish English)

3 a. AmE; b.AmE; c.BrE; d.AmE; e.BrE; f.BrE.

4 The lower the social class, the more likely it is that a regional variety will be spoken and that speakers will use regional variants such as preconsonantal /r/ or the pronunciation of -*ing* as /ɪn/; the highest number of occurrences of such regionalisms is found in the lower working class.

5 Social network analysis is concerned with social interaction on a microsociological level. Virtually everybody is part of a social network. The sizes of these networks may differ, though, and the degree to which you are integrated into them. A high degree of integration correlates with group-specific systems of values, norms, shared knowledge, attitudes, etc. which are also reflected in language use (i.e. group identity manifests itself in language). Such close social networks tend to be linguistically conservative. Language change can rather be observed in open social networks.

6 a. (a) deletion of copula (in those environments where Standard English permits cliticisation, e.g. *I'm, you're*; (b) deletion of copula; grammaticalization of *gonna* to future marker; (c) habitual *be*, no third person *-s*; (d) habitual *be*, no plural marking
   b. habitual *be* (Southwest, Irish English); multiple negation; no third person *-s* (East Anglia); dummy *it* instead of dummy *there*

7 a. A. order should be reversed: *Mrs and Mr Brown, Mrs Brown and her husband*
      B. *Miss* should be *Ms*; *chairman* should be *chairperson*
      C. generic quantifier (*any*-form) is followed by 3rd person plural pronoun
      D. *lady doctor* is marked, should simply be *doctor*
      E. *flight attendant* instead of *steward/stewardess*
   b. Rapport talk: women interrupt less, make shorter contributions, encourage contributions by others, more indirect, work together on a topic

8 a. false; b. true; c. true; d. true; e. false; f. true; g. false; h. true; i. true; j. true

Author index

Subject index

rapport talk 281
RECEIVED PRONUNCIATION 58-65,
    72, 77f., 260-65
reciprocity 16, 78
reduction 73f., 77, 94, 174, 185,
    267, 274
reductionist 30, 242, 246
redundant 57f., 72, 180
reference 21, 196f.
reflexivity 140, 148, 266, 270
register 33-38, 201, 255-57, 277
relative clause 26, 75, 129, 132f.,
    157, 160, 173, 180, 267, 283
report talk 281
representativeness (degrees of)
    210
restriction 42, 71, 132, 167, 177,
    192f., 213, 233f., 266
rheme 166
rhoticity 261f., 271-75
rhythm 72-75, 185
robustness (of maxims) 238
roll 61, 65f.
root 15, 73, 87-92, 108, 124, 126
R-Principle 243
rule 12, 19-21, 25, 72, 91, 93, 96,
    98, 108, 116f., 124, 182, 206,
    234, 238, 270, 273

Sapir-Whorf hypothesis 217, 255
schwa 68f., 73
segmental phonology 69-72
selection restrictions 193, 212
semantic feature 102, 197, 200-2,
    207
semantic field 199
semantic implication 235
semantic role 133f., 138, 148,
    169f., 175-77, 194
semantics 13-17, 30, 39-44, 46,
    137, 139, 175, 191-217, 224-26,
    230f., 239f., 245-47
semi-auxiliary 137
semiotics 17, 44, 223
semi-vowel 65f., 72, 181f.
sense 196f.
sense relations 201-, 212, 235

sentence meaning 191, 194, 207,
    235
sentence semantics 193
sentence stress 73, 76f.
shortening 95, 106-9
sign 14-18, 192
signe différentiel 198
signifiant/signifier 16, 192, 217,
    226
signifié/signified 16, 192, 217,
    226
slang 257, 277
social gender 277, 282
social meaning 195f.
social network 254, 275f., 284
social stratification 272, 275
sociolect 255, 257, 273, 280
sociolinguistics 13, 18f., 31, 45,
    48, 253-84
sociology of language 254
sonorant 64f.
source domain 212
speech act 23, 44, 230-35, 241,
    246
    see also indirect speech act
speech act theory 226, 230-32,
    235
speech act verb 43, 232-34
standard accent 59f., 65, 257-61,
    275
standardization 45, 235
stem 87-90, 95, 118, 120, 137,
    142, 162, 167
stop 66, 185, 274, 279
    see also plosive
stress 72-77, 94, 96, 102, 141,
    184f., 261f.
stress-timing 74
strong form 73, 87
structural semantics 197-208,
    212, 217
structuralism 14-18, 31f., 224
style 37, 254-57, 272, 276, 281
subject 21, 39, 76, 121-25,
    129-35, 138-40, 148, 160,
    164-66, 169-78, 264, 267, 269,
    283

subjectification 42f.
subordinator/subordinating
    conjunction 27, 40, 129, 133,
    157, 195
substitution 70, 157f.
sufficient condition 209
suffix 38, 87-93, 96-99, 102, 104,
    108, 120f., 124, 126, 142, 271,
    279
suffixation 94-96, 123
suppletion 92
suprasegmental phonology 184
syllable 39, 66, 67-78, 86, 94,
    118, 127, 182, 185, 261
symbol 16f., 191, 226, 230
synchrony 11, 13f., 18, 30, 46f.,
    284
synonymy 201, 204
synsemantic terms 87, 127, 194
syntagmatic 15, 131, 192, 198,
    200, 212
syntagmatic differentiation 131
syntagmatic semantics 192, 212
syntax 15-19, 28, 30, 46, 89, 104,
    116, 120f., 125, 127, 137, 175,
    223-55, 268
synthetic 118-23, 126

target domain 212f.
telic verb 145
tenor 212, 256
tense 14, 21, 40, 86, 88, 116, 119,
    121, 129, 137, 141-47, 157f.,
    162f., 178f., 194, 227, 233, 267,
    270
tense (vowel) 69f.
tense system 14
thematic 133
thematic role 169
    see also semantic role
theme 166
tight-fit language 174
topic-comment 166, 169f.
traditional dialectology 264-69
transcription 59-61, 67, 70, 73
transfer 156, 159
transition 284